Kyle Rote, Jr.'s Complete Book of SOCCER

with Basil Kane

Simon and Schuster
New York

Published by Simon and Schuster
A Division of Gulf & Western Corporation
Simon & Schuster Building
Rockefeller Center
1230 Avenue of the Americas
New York, New York 10020

Designed by Irving Perkins
Manufactured in the United States of America
1   2   3   4   5   6   7   8   9   10

Library of Congress Cataloging in Publication Data
Rote, Kyle.
Kyle Rote, Jr.'s Complete book of soccer.
Bibliography: p.
Includes index.
1. Soccer—United States—History.   2. Soccer.
I. Kane, Basil G.   II. Title: Complete book of soccer.
GV944.U5R67   796.33′4′0973   77-16625
ISBN 0-671-22714-9

To Mary Lynne and Nancy

Contents

Introduction, *by Basil Kane*   9

Preface, *by Kyle Rote, Jr.*   11

PART ONE

CHAPTER ONE   In the Beginning   15

CHAPTER TWO   The British Are Coming   24

CHAPTER THREE   Modern Soccer   39

CHAPTER FOUR   The World Cup   49

CHAPTER FIVE   The North American Soccer League   86

CHAPTER SIX   The Stars of the First Ten Years   115

PART TWO

CHAPTER SEVEN   The Team in Action   127

CHAPTER EIGHT   The Lonely Breed   135

CHAPTER NINE   The Modern Defenders   142

CHAPTER TEN   The Fluent Technicians   148

CHAPTER ELEVEN   The Priceless Gems   154

CHAPTER TWELVE   Team Tactics   160

PART THREE

CHAPTER THIRTEEN   The Future of American Soccer   179

APPENDIX A   Who's Who in the NASL   187

APPENDIX B   NASL Facts and Figures   201

APPENDIX C   Other U.S. Tournaments and Leagues   208

APPENDIX D   International Soccer   212

APPENDIX E   Advice to Young Players   232

APPENDIX F   Glossary   237

APPENDIX G   Laws of the Game   241

Signals by Referee and Linesmen   281

Bibliography   291

Index   293

Introduction
by Basil Kane

A young man of great talent and even greater character, Kyle Rote, Jr., would have fitted in perfectly with the British gentlemen of the 19th century who started soccer on the path to success as the world's number one sport.

Like those students at Harrow, Eton, Oxford and Cambridge and all the top amateur players of that period, Kyle is a firm believer in the "Corinthian" spirit of 19th-century sport which stressed sportsmanship ahead of winning. And just like those brave, honorable gentleman athletes of a century ago, he accepts the punishing body contact of soccer—both the fair and the illegal—without flinching and without retaliating.

In five years of professional soccer he has never been ejected from a game or even cautioned. (A referee cautions a player in soccer by waving a yellow card for all to see; if the player persists in his illegal or ungentlemanly conduct, he is shown a red card and ejected from the game.) If all professionals played Kyle's style of soccer, there would be no need for the yellow-card and red-card signaling devices. But then, this 27-year-old soccer star is not the average professional athlete.

Some might say he is an anachronism in this modern age of professional sports. He seldom drinks alcoholic beverages, never smokes, sees no need to use profanity to express himself, spends most of his free time working with children or performing ministerial work at his church in Dallas, donates much of what he earns to charities; and wonder of wonders, he does not consider his sport—or any, for that matter—to be a matter of life and death.

He is one professional who would like to see the chauvinistic, and at times hysterical, aspects of sports deemphasized so that they can once again mean physical exercise and entertainment rather than contests of brute force or miniwars. This is not to imply that Kyle attempts anything in life without a dedicated commitment, be it a soccer game or running a kids' summer camp. Far from it. Nothing less than a 100-percent effort satisfies him. Indeed, he has had a reputation as a fierce competitor ever

9

since he gave up a promising football career at Oklahoma State in 1968 and surprised the sports world by transferring to the tiny University of the South at Sewanee, Tennessee—to play soccer.

Not happy being a part of the athletic-scholarship syndrome, Kyle sought a quieter campus where amateur sport really meant playing for the love of the game. At Sewanee he found exactly the campus life he desired —a quiet pastoral world of serious scholarship and good fellowship; and it was here that he met his charming wife, Mary Lynne.

Above all Kyle was a serious student at Sewanee, but upon his graduation in 1972 he was drafted by the Dallas Tornado. In 1973 he became a first-team starter, and in fairy-tale fashion he led the league in goal scoring and earned the Rookie of the Year title. In 1974 he won his first *ABC's Superstars* competition, a triumph he repeated in 1976 and 1977.

Despite his successes, Kyle is still the same low-key, unassuming person he has always been and remains convinced that the real measure of success on the athletic field is whether or not the athletes perform to the best of their abilities, and not whether or not the team wins.

In today's commercialization of professional sports, in which many stars have no concept of the meaning of "sportsmanship" and in which it is sometimes difficult to decide whether some of them are athletes or business tycoons, the emergence of Kyle Rote, Jr., as a superstar has been a refreshing tonic.

Preface

by Kyle Rote, Jr.

On Christmas Day, 1914, during the first year of World War I, British and German soldiers opposing each other in France climbed from their static trenches into no-man's-land—not to shoot at each other, but to play an impromptu game of soccer.

Such is the powerful urge of this game, a paradoxical phenomenon of the 20th century that can incite the most uncontrollable passion and intense parochialism on one hand and yet can bridge nationalistic, political and religious differences on the other.

What other sport could halt a war, albeit temporarily (until Pelé had passed through the war zone), as in Nigeria in 1968; or start one, in 1969 (El Salvador vs. Honduras); or incite bloody riots, as in Peru in 1964, when 301 spectators died; while at the same time providing euphoric delight to over a billion viewers who watched the marvelous 1974 World Cup Final on television?

Soccer offers fluidity of action unmatched by any other team sport—an unbroken chain of constant and generally spontaneous movements from one end of the field to the other. Add the fierce body contact, the collisions of feet, legs, chests (and at times, even heads), plus the tactical deployments in attack and counterattack, and you have the ingredients for bringing the emotions to a boil.

In the rest of the world they call it "football fever." In the United States, where we are just learning all about it, we call it "soccer fever," and the sports scene will never be the same in San Jose, Minneapolis, Seattle, Portland, Tampa, Dallas and other cities where the quickly spreading virus has infected sports fans.

I do hope this book will help you to discover for yourself the wonderful world of soccer—a game perhaps not for the fainthearted, for it will so manipulate your emotions that you will experience ecstatic joy as well as the deepest of depressions once you get to know it. But above all, I wish to give you a chance to agree with me that as a game it is without a doubt the most exciting in the world.

PART ONE

Chapter One

In the Beginning

*"Football is a devilistic pastime with brawling, mur-
ther, homicide and a great effusion of blood, as experience daily teacheth."*

Phillip Stubbes, *Anatomie of Abuses* (1583)

Researching the early history of association football (the word "soccer" was not coined until the 1880s) is at once fascinating, intriguing and more than a little confusing. Since nearly every country has laid a claim to being its originator, modern historians have enjoyed themselves immensely seeing who could go furthest back in antiquity in search of football's elusive origins.

In 1802 Joseph Strutt, in his edifying book *The Sports and Pastimes of the People of England,* claimed there was no evidence of the game's "appearing among the popular exercises before the reign of Edward III" and, most becoming for a historian, refused to hazard a guess as to when the game was first played, even though he was probably well aware of the annual Shrovetide game at Chester—a commemoration of a legendary 10th-century victory over an unfortunate Danish raiding party whose chieftain's head was later used for a celebration kick-around.

This innovative use of the Dane's skull by the uncouth 10th-century Britons was soon discovered to be antedated by an earlier group of British sportsmen who had played a similar game with the skulls of the defeated Romans at Derby in A.D. 217. Legend or no legend, the news about Derby prompted further professorial studies, and before long a rapid sequence of dissertations and tomes rolled off the university presses alleging that it was the patricians of Rome with their *harpastum* and the philosophical Greeks indulging in their unpronounceable *episkyros* who had in fact played the game long before the barbaric Britons.

Some historians, still not satisfied with the lengthening longevity of the sport, now turned their eyes eastward and began to circulate evidence that it was none other than Chinese athletes of the Han Dynasty who had started the ball rolling. Archaeologists did their share of digging too, exposing Thai vases, Inca scrolls, Persian artifacts and even an Egyptian pharaoh's tomb to prove soccer's ancient provenance. Few discoveries were as convincing as the tomb, which conveniently contained among its

15

treasured contents a round object that strangely resembled the ball used at the 1977 NASL Soccer Bowl. And so it goes on, ad infinitum: one expects momentarily to read that Adam and Eve found the sport a splendid body conditioner and a stimulus to the appetite.

And yet, no matter how suspect and exaggerated the stories are, I for one like to think they all have merit, for it seems clear that some kind of soccer has been played for thousands of years. Kicking, after all, is a natural reflex, and be the object a stone on an ancient Roman road, a dried-out bladder of a Han Dynasty pig or even the posterior of a good-natured friend, it is an urge that is compelling.

Certainly there is good authority for believing that the early Chinese did play a kicking game as far back as the fourth century B.C. Professor Giles, a Cambridge scholar, suggested that *tsu chu* (kickball) resembled soccer, whereas Professor Gardiner, an Oxford scholar, in his *Athletics of the Ancient World* disagrees, describing *tsu chu* as having little in common with soccer other than that a ball was kicked. Apparently the players took turns at kicking the round ball (leather strips filled with hair) either over 30-foot-high posts or through a hole in a silk curtain. It does not, from all accounts, seem to have been a very active game, but nevertheless it was considered a vital part of physical training for the emperor's warriors. Most of the more athletically inclined emperors took part; but none could claim to be a fair-minded or reasonable sportsman, for as often as not, losing teams were flogged, and for those foolish enough to beat the emperor's own team there was literal rolling of heads.

What exactly the ancient Greeks' *episkyros* was all about still confounds historians. We do know that it was very rough, but whether it was a kicking or a carrying game still has not been decided. Whatever it was, it must have been a revealing experience for players and spectators alike, since the Greek athletes of that time played completely naked.

The Romans, far less exuberant but equally violent, played their *harpastum* fully clothed, but here again little evidence is forthcoming, for all the efforts of our learned researchers, to suggest that it was a kicking game. Professor Gardiner maintains that it was not even a team sport, since the players could leave the game whenever they felt tired or depressed, or decided they were not playing well—a custom many frustrated sports spectators of today might wish to see reintroduced.

With the expansion of the Roman Empire the game spread in all directions, but it was in Britain that *harpastum* found a permanent home. It was the Britons who polished and shaped the game through the next nineteen centuries. Not that it was all garlands and roses on the way to the formal birth of modern soccer at the historic 1863 meeting in London of the Football Association; broken skulls, riots and royal prohibitions were just some of the obstacles encountered on the long, arduous journey. As far back as 1314, King Edward II, weary from his losing battles with the Scots and probably having trouble sleeping, issued a proclamation: "Forasmuch as there is great noise in the city caused by hustling over large balls from which many evils might arise which GOD forbid; we command and forbid on behalf of the King, on pain of imprisonment, such game to be used in the city in future." This edict (one of the few things for which Edward II is remembered) startled the populace, who had been merrily playing football for hundreds of years without interference from the establishment. In villages, towns and cities the rowdy and at times ferocious rush for the ball had been made by peasants, students, gentlemen and the clergy alike. After all, chasing the ball through fields or along city streets was not only fun but also cheaper than fox hunting or cockfighting. Unfortunately, at the turn of the 14th century the game was evolving into a series of miniwars with village against village, town against town and sections of cities opposing each other in intense rivalries, and one can sympathize with the monarchs who tried to ban the game over the next three hundred years.

Edward III tried to stop it in 1349. Infuriated by the amount of time spent on "footballe" and not on archery practice, he banned it completely from England. At least, he thought he had. Forty years later, Richard II issued a similar ban and again stressed the need for archery practice. Henry IV in 1401 tried his best to subdue the game, as did the Scottish kings of that era, but it was of no use. Football simply would not go away. Elizabeth also tried to do away with it, but the sport was soon back in vogue. During the reign of James I it was again played by the "respectable segment of society"—which, one must assume, was the educated class. However, not all gentlemen were ready to give approval. Phillip Stubbes in his *Anatomie of Abuses* clearly stated his abhorrence of the sport. Describing it as fighting more than a sport, he goes on to complain about the violence, particularly of the broken necks, backs and legs and eyes popping out. And no wonder, for ". . . they dash him against the hart with their elbows, butt him under the short ribs with gripped fists and a hundred such murthering devices." (Any resemblance to the NFL is purely coincidental.)

The end of football's official illegality came when Charles II openly encouraged the game. Even that somber Puritan, Oliver Cromwell, took time out from brooding to play. In a letter written by the Reverend Cotton Mather to a friend in 1700, Mather mentions how Cromwell had been reluctant to play against a certain Reverend Wheelwright, for Cromwell

". . . had been more afraid of meeting this gentleman at football than of anything else since in the field; as he was infallibly sure of being tripped up by him."

While all this frenetic activity was taking place in England, news about foreign football was trickling in. The Japanese, it seemed, had watched the Chinese at play and had adapted *tsu chu* into a rougher game called *kemari*. The Normans were playing *soule,* and the overdressed Florentines had their *calcio,* a game that was elaborately decorative. In spectacular costumes they played in such delightful surroundings as the Piazza della Signoria, the Piazza della Croce and other Florentine landmarks. And it should not come as any surprise to learn that *calcio* is still performed for hordes of delighted American tourists on festival days.

There was news from the New World too. One of the big surprises awaiting the early American colonists was that the Indians had their own form of football—a game that served as a ceremonial fertility rite. The part fertility rites played in the early days of football should not be overlooked. Many groups believed that the ball represented the sun, and a serious game of football on and around a plot of land was thought to do wonders for crop yield. Others, convinced that the ball was an image of the moon, played the game to encourage rain. The game was also performed at all the better sacrifices, where an animal's head was kicked over soil that needed replenishing, then buried underneath the revitalized plot of land. An animal's head was also used during the mating season (when fertility was presumably at a premium), with innocent young maidens playing against married women and young bachelors taking on married men. All in all, a busy yet interesting stage in the development of the world sport.

By the end of the 17th century, football had become the most popular sport in England. The game could last for many hours, sometimes all day. It remained a simple one: kicking and catching a ball from one designated goal to another, usually half a mile or more away.

In the 18th century wise heads decided that smaller dimensions were needed, and by the end of the century the football field had been reduced to about the size now used in modern soccer. In *The Sports and Pastimes of the People of England,* Joseph Strutt conveniently describes just such a field in 1802: "When a match at football is made, two parties, each containing an equal number of competitors, take the field, and stand between two goals, placed at the distance of eighty or an hundred yards the one from the other. The goal is usually made with two sticks driven into the ground, about two or three feet apart. The ball, which is commonly made of a blown bladder, and cased with leather, is delivered in the midst of the ground, and the object of each party is to drive it through the goal of their antagonists, which being achieved the game is won. The abilities of the performers are best displayed in attacking and defending the goals; and hence the pastime is more frequently called a goal at football than a game of football. When the exercise becomes exceeding violent, the players kick each other's shins with the least ceremony, and some of them are overthrown at the hazard of their limbs."

In the 19th century the field could still be as long as 200 yards, depending upon whose set of rules was used, for it was about this time that the sport was embraced with a passion by the British public schools, each one devising its own code. It was in these bastions of upper-class communal life that football found the necessary enthusiasm and leadership for sustained growth. Harrow, Eton, Cheltenham, Rugby, Charterhouse, Shrewsbury—they all played it, in different forms but each one basically a kicking game, with a fair amount of handling and catching but no running with the ball permitted.

William Webb Ellis, an audacious young student at Rugby, almost single-handedly altered the evolution of football by his anarchistic disregard for the rules during a game at Rugby when he picked up the ball and ran down the length of the field. Although reprimanded and shunned by his fellow students, Ellis is now considered the father of rugby and American football, and many grateful fans of these two sports journey to the playing field of Rugby to read the historic marker erected there:

This Stone
Commemorates the Exploit of
WILLIAM WEBB ELLIS,
Who with a fine disregard for the rules of
Football,
As played in his time,
First took the ball in his arms and ran with it,
Thus originating the distinctive feature of
The Rugby game
A.D. 1823

As impressive as that tablet may appear today, there were many in the mid-19th century who blamed Ellis for the return of mayhem to football. Once again the pleasant green fields of England were filled with cries of anguish as young men smashed into each other.

The controversy over carrying the ball spotlighted the problems mid-19th century football was having with the rules. Some schools permitted handling, others did not; offsides, throw-ins and hacking (kicking at the legs below the knees) and even the number of players were all variables depending upon which school was the opponent.

In 1848 a few of the former students of the public schools (graduates of these private prep schools are affectionately known in England as "Old Boys") agreed that some effort had to be made to produce a common set of rules if the game was to prosper. These Old Boys, at the time students at Cambridge, drew up the "Cambridge Rules," under which there was to be no tripping, pushing or holding, and handling was permitted solely for catching the ball or knocking it down so that it could then be kicked. This was obviously an antirugby code, and the increasing number of adherents to the rugby branch of football were not very happy when in 1862 J. C. Thring, brother of Edward Thring, the headmaster at Uppingham School, published the rules for what he called "The Simplest Game."

Simple and straight to the point, the rules were obviously written so that the schoolboys at Uppingham could understand them. Thring also hoped his rules would enable football to become a safer game than that being practiced by many of the rougher schools. The ten rules were as follows:

1. A goal is scored whenever the ball is forced through the goal and under the bar, except it be thrown by the hand.

2. Hands may be used only to stop a ball and place it on the ground before the feet.

3. Kicks must be aimed only at the ball.

4. A player may not kick the ball whilst it is in the air.

5. No tripping up or heel kicking is allowed.

6. Whenever the ball is kicked beyond the side flags, it must be returned by the player who kicked it, from the spot where it passed the flag line, in a straight line towards the middle of the ground.

7. When a ball is kicked behind the line of goal, it shall be kicked off from that line by one of the side whose goal it is.

8. No player may stand within six paces of the kicker when he is kicking off.

9. A player is "out of play" immediately he is in front of the ball, and he must return behind the ball as soon as possible. If the ball be kicked by his own side past a player, he may not touch it, kick it nor advance until one of the other side has first kicked it or one of his own side, having followed it up, has been able, when in front of him, to kick it.

10. No charging is allowed when a player is out of play—i.e., immediately the ball is behind him.

There were others, too, busy devising rules. The powerful and influential Sheffield Football Club, comprising many Old Boys from Harrow, had its own code, as did the two important rugby-oriented clubs Richmond and Blackheath, both keenly advocating hacking and carrying. The overriding question for football players in those days, whether a uniform set of rules could be established, was finally met head on in 1863 when a group of London clubs sent representatives to the Freemasons Tavern in Great Queen Street.

The gentlemen who attended the first of the series of meetings on October 26 to straighten out the little unpleasantness over the questions of running with the ball and hacking were mostly Old Boys and university men. All of them were aware that devising a set of rules acceptable to both the ball carriers (as the rugby men were called) and the dribblers would be difficult, and few were surprised when the meeting resulted in a stalemate.

Suggested rules 9 and 10 were the villains. These two proposals embodied the fundamental differences between the two groups. The carriers were all for Rule 9, which stated that a player could run with the ball if he so desired provided he made a fair catch or caught the ball on the first bounce. They also endorsed Rule 10 with enthusiasm, since it allowed hacking as well as tripping and holding.

The dribblers refused to adopt either rule, insisting that it was precisely these actions that were making the game of football brutal. The carriers replied that without running with the ball and a liberal amount of hacking, tripping and holding, the game would be suitable only for schoolboys and sissies. And so inevitably both groups went their own ways: those withdrawing from the new body off to form the Rugby Union and those remaining printing up a set of rules and naming themselves the Football Association.

The rules they produced look suspiciously like a combination of soccer and rugby when one reviews them today, and some of them—those specifically included as a concession to the carriers—were soon discarded as the Football Association expanded. The field dimensions were back to a 200-yard maximum, double that mentioned by Strutt in his 1803 observations. Rule 3 made it mandatory for sides to change goals after each goal scored, no doubt making it difficult for a Victorian imbiber to know which team to cheer for. Goals could be scored if the ball passed between or above the space between the posts, and Rule 8 allowed for a free kick for any player catching the ball. Rules 9 and 10 were, of course, revised; running with the ball was outlawed in Rule 9, and Rule 10 prohibited hacking. Ironically, one of the first things the organizers of the Rugby Union did upon its foundation was to outlaw hacking.

Absent from the rules was any reference to referees or umpires—an error, we modern sports fans would think, accustomed as we are to the world of professional gamesmanship. Surprisingly, the game prospered without a neutral third party. It was up to the captains of the opposing teams to make decisions on rules infractions, and generally their authority was seldom questioned.

The Football Association rules were as follows:

1. The maximum length of the ground shall be 200 yards; the maximum breadth shall be 100 yards; the length and breadth shall be marked off with flags; and the goals shall be defined by two upright posts, 8 yards apart, without any tape or bar across them.

2. The winners of the toss shall have the choice of goals. The game shall be commenced by a place-kick from the centre of the ground by the side losing the toss. The other side shall not approach within 10 yards of the ball until it is kicked off.

3. After a goal is won, the losing side shall kick off, and goals shall be changed.

4. A goal shall be won when the ball passes between the posts or over the space between the posts (at whatever height), not being thrown, knocked on, or carried.

5. When the ball is in touch, the first player who touches it shall throw it from the point on the boundary-line where it left the ground in a direction at right angles with the boundary-line, and it shall not be in play until it has touched the ground.

6. When a player has kicked the ball, any one of the same side who is nearer the opponents' goal-line is out of play, and may not touch the ball himself nor in any way whatever prevent any other player from doing so until the ball has been played; but no player is out of play when the ball is kicked from behind the goal-line.

7. In case the ball goes behind the goal-line, if a player on the same side to whom the goal belongs first touches the ball, one of his side shall be entitled to a free-kick from the goal-line at the point opposite the place where the ball shall be touched. If a player of the opposite side first touches the ball, one of his side shall be entitled to a free-kick (but at the goal only) from a point 15 yards from the goal-line opposite the place where the ball is touched; the opposing side shall stand behind the goal-line until he has had his kick.

8. If a player makes a fair catch, he shall be entitled to a free-kick, provided he claims it by making a mark with his heel at once; and in order to take such a kick he may go as far back as he pleases, and no player on the opposite side shall advance beyond his mark until he has kicked.

9. No player shall carry the ball.

10. Neither tripping nor hacking shall be allowed, and no player shall use his hands to hold or push an adversary.

11. A player shall not throw the ball or pass it to another with his hands.

12. No player shall take the ball from the ground with his hands while it is in play under any pretence whatever.

13. A player shall be allowed to throw the ball or pass it to another if he made a fair catch or catches the ball on the first bounce.

14. No player shall be allowed to wear projecting nails, iron plates or gutta percha on the soles or heels of his boots.

While association football enthusiasts rushed to their dictionaries to discover what exactly gutta percha was, across the sea in the United States, William Webb Ellis' influence on the game had yet to be felt. Up to 1870, football played in American towns was of the soccer variety. As far back as 1820, Princeton undergraduates were playing a kicking game called ballown, and by 1827 Harvard was also the scene of a crude brand of soccer. The famous annual "Bloody Monday" was nothing more than the meeting each fall of the freshman and sophomore classes at Harvard, a contest so rough and vicious that for the rest of the century the phrase "American football" unjustly connoted brutality. The "Bloody Monday" series was finally banned by the Harvard authorities, and a similar game between Yale lowerclassmen was stopped not by the school, but by the concerned city fathers of New Haven.

The high schools in Boston, playing a gentler form of soccer, received better treatment from the local authorities and by 1860 were playing organized soccer on Boston Common. The roster of teams included Boston English, Boston Latin, Dixswell School, Dorchester High and Roxbury High. It was in Boston too that the first official football club in the United States was formed: the Oneida Football Club of Boston, which in its early days was a formidable team, remaining unbeaten from the year of its founding, 1862, all the way through 1865. But like all the early pioneers of football in the United States, Oneida would fall victim to the seductive charms of the carrying game in the 1870s once the split between the association and rugby adherents became permanent. The rugby followers, headed by Harvard, were to dominate American football completely, and over a hundred years were to pass before the kicking game would once again be as common a sight in Boston as the carrying game.

No matter what form of football an Englishman or an American favored in the 1870s, the game had come a long way from the days of the Han Dynasty and the stuffed leather ball. Both rugby and its offspring, American football, were ready to emerge as major sports, and Mr. Thring's "simplest sport," soccer, was poised to sweep across every longitude and latitude like no other social phenomenon before it.

Chapter Two

The British Are Coming

"The new Yale Stadium going up will be needed to eventually hold the huge crowds that will flood to see the Yale soccer team just as they do the English cup finals."

Member of the Stadium Committee at Yale,
March 17, 1912

"Soccer is making great progress and in the not too distant future will rank only second to baseball as the leading pro game."

Thomas Cahill, Secretary of the United States
Football Association,
January 13, 1924

I've always enjoyed the company of optimists, and I wish it were possible for both Mr. Cahill and the unnamed Yale official to travel with me around the country to see the strength and growth of American soccer today. They may have been half a century off in their predictions but I have a feeling that upon seeing the soccer fields that now dot the landscape around American cities and suburbs they would nonchalantly say, "We told you so." Certainly the pioneers of American soccer had to possess a single-mindedness bordering on the fanatical to believe in the future of such a minor sport—so minor, in fact, that the majority of Americans between 1900 and 1967 had never seen it played.

The reason for soccer's remaining America's most concealed sport is undoubtedly traceable to the unsociable Harvard football players of the 1870s. About that time an attempt was made by football clubs to draw up a set of rules that would unify the game, just as had been done in England in 1863. What could have been America's equivalent of the historic Football Association meeting took place at the Fifth Avenue Hotel in New York on October 19, 1873. There Yale, Princeton, Columbia and Rutgers met to form the Intercollegiate Football Association. Harvard refused to attend, declaring it could not compromise its "Boston Game"—a carrying game—by joining in any agreement with the dribbling teams of the four other clubs. The Harvard players, like the rugby men attending the 1863 London meeting before them, took a separate path and after testing the pure rugby rules in a series of games with McGill University of Montreal began to encourage other prestigious colleges, of the type that now form the Ivy League, to join them.

Unlike their rugby counterparts in England, who were never able to compete for the hearts and passions of the football-playing masses, the Harvard players' lone stand against association football practically killed the sport and no doubt would have extinguished it completely from the American sporting scene but for the likes of Thomas Cahill. So rugby football, adapted by Walter Camp, became America's fall spectacular, while association football, or soccer, was relegated to minor leagues, ignored by the majority of sports fans and benignly neglected by the press, leaving the soccer proselytizers to concentrate on small pockets of interest in a few Eastern prep schools and colleges and in the ethnic neighborhoods of the larger cities.

The first of the official soccer games was the historic Rutgers–Princeton match of 1869. Now considered the first collegiate football game, it was nonetheless played under the then-existing rules of soccer, and it was not until 1876, the year the Intercollegiate Football Association decided to adopt the rugby code and throw out the round ball, that college games switched to rugby rules. The 1877 game between Harvard and Princeton was cause for much glee among soccer disciples. Not only was Harvard, the developer of American rugby, beaten at its own game, but its players committed the unpardonable error of making a touchdown at the wrong end of the field.

Meanwhile, in England soccer developed at a much faster pace than rugby. Between 1863 and 1876 the Football Association—or the FA, as it came to be called—took complete control of English soccer. Sheffield and the other centers of active rival soccer associations came under its wise authority, particularly after the FA inaugurated the first open soccer competition, the FA Cup, in the 1871–72 season.

An immediate success, the FA Cup within ten years was attracting crowds of 10,000. Another spur to the success of the English soccer movement was the formation in 1888 of an organized league. The brainchild of William McGregor, a Scotsman who had moved to Birmingham in England, the Football League was welcomed if for no other reason than to ensure that the teams could play on a regular basis. The successful 'National League of American Baseball was the model, and 12 clubs agreed to try it. Nearly a hundred years later, of the 12 teams—Accrington, Aston Villa, Blackburn Rovers, Bolton Wanderers, Burnley, Derby County, Everton, Notts County, Preston North End, Stoke, West Bromwich Albion and Wolverhampton Wanderers—only one club, Accrington, has left the soccer scene, a victim of bankruptcy in 1962.

The league awarded 2 points for a win, 1 for a draw (tie) and none for a loss—a method for computing points still in effect everywhere in the world except for the North American Soccer League.

Today the Football League comprises 92 professional teams organized into four divisions, but in the 1800s the term "professional" was derogatory. Even though it was clear that some teams were paying their players illegally, the Football Association tried to ignore the matter until it came to a head in 1885 when payment was finally legalized. The split between the carriers and the dribblers was nothing compared with the dichotomy between the "gentlemen" (as the amateurs called themselves) and the "players" (professionals). It was many years before "gentlemen" would associate themselves socially with the "hired mercenaries" or even change in the same dressing room with them.

At first the amateurs were able to compete successfully against the pros. Teams like the Wanderers, the Old Etonians and the Corinthians were as good as or better than the pros, as were players like C. B. Fry (who represented England at soccer, rugby and cricket, and found the time and strength to break the world's long-jump record); G. O. Smith, an elegant center forward and one of the true greats of soccer's history; W. N. Cobbold, the Pelé of his time with his elusive dribbling; Vivian Woodward, the high-scoring inside forward of English soccer, and two Walter brothers, A. M. and P. M., who naturally were called "morning" and "afternoon." Two other amateurs should be mentioned here: the Reverend R. W. Vidal, probably the only player ever to score 3 successive goals without an opposing player's touching the ball, and the Corinthians' splendid center half, Charles Wreford-Brown, the man who gave the world the name "soccer" by telling a friend at Oxford University that instead of playing "rugger" (rugby) he was going to play "soccer" (association)—a word he derived by manipulating the letters "assoc." Even though fans in most countries a century later still prefer to call the game "football," the name "soccer" has become a useful tool (especially in the United States) for distinguishing association football from all other forms of football—American, rugby, Gaelic, Australian and so on.

By 1900 the amateurs had been eclipsed by the pros—the only exception being the Corinthians, who were still a match for any team and were providing the majority of "internationals" (soccer players selected to play for their country) for the English national team.

The rise of professionalism lifted the game to new heights, with pro teams springing up in the smallest of towns. Tactics and training sessions were introduced into soccer, and under the influence of the Scots (most professionals in the early days were Scots) soccer became more skillful.

Until the Scottish pros "invaded" English soccer, there was little teamwork to be seen. A goalkeeper and two defenders were left behind to guard the goal while the rest of the team moved up en masse to race after the man in possession. To get through this congestion of teammates and opponents, English players had developed the art of dribbling to a fine degree. The Scots, on the other hand, made the ball do the work and became masters of the passing game. The Scottish style was eagerly accepted after a string of victories by the Scottish national team over England in the late 1870s and early 1880s.

Preston North End was one of the first clubs to employ the Scottish passing style; having added its own tactical refinement of two fullbacks, three halfbacks and only five forwards, it was able to win "the double" (both the Football League Championship and the FA Cup) in 1889.

Professionalization of the sport also saw attendances climb rapidly. The 1885 Cup Final drew 12,500 fans. In 1895 the Cup Final gate had increased to 45,000, and in 1901 over 110,000 soccer fans filled the famous Crystal Palace stadium.

Another attendant feature of pro soccer's growth in Britain was the introduction of a new breed of journalist—the sports reporter. The object of the sports reporter's attention was the glamorous new heroes: Steve Bloomer, the cannonball artist of the Derby County team, a forward who scored 352 goals in his twenty-two-year career; Billy Meredith, the legendary winger from Manchester who played for the Welsh national team forty-eight times, the final occasion when he was 46 years old; Bob Crompton, the ferocious fullback and captain of both the Blackburn Rovers and the England teams for so many years, and "Fatty" Foulke, the fiery goalkeeper of Sheffield United and Chelsea, who often weighed in at 300 pounds.

The history of English soccer abounds in curious characters, but none other quite so immense or eccentric as Foulke. Forever in trouble with opposing players and referees, Foulke would make the present-day angry young men of sports look like debutantes. He thought nothing of picking up terrified opponents and throwing them into the back of the net or chasing them all over the field if he thought they had made a disparaging remark about his oval shape. In one of his more infamous fits of anger he ran through the dressing-room corridors completely naked, searching for the referee, who had seen Foulke's colossal figure approaching (proving that not all referees are blind) and moved with alacrity to a good hiding place.

Players have changed somewhat since Fatty Foulkes, and so have the rules. By 1907 they were nearly what they are today, except for the change in the offside law that was to come in 1925. Gone was the one-handed throw when the ball went over the touchlines (sidelines). Also discarded was the rule that permitted whoever reached the ball first to throw it back in. Crossbars replaced tapes over the goalposts, teams no longer had to make the long trek from one end to the other after each goal was scored and referees had taken over the captains' positions as the sole arbiters in soccer.

Soccer was now ready for export, and it was with exuberance that it was carried around the world by British sailors, soldiers, miners, engineers and, of course, the Old Boys, who were now businessmen, academicians and diplomats. The simple game, as easily played on the sunbaked terrain of Brazil or the frozen tundra of Russia as on the damp British fields, found favor wherever it was transplanted. In the Broadway vernacular it was a smash hit, sweeping through Europe and encoring with equal success in South America. Between 1876 and 1900, football associations were formed in 16 countries, as wave after wave of British enthusiasts organized the "natives."

In Denmark a group of businessmen from Britain formed the English Football Club as early as 1876. Russia discovered the game when the two Charnock brothers from Lancashire introduced it to the workers at their family-owned cotton mill. Spain and Rumania saw it demonstrated by British miners; Sweden, by the British Embassy staff; Brazil, by sailors and Argentina and Uruguay, by visiting school and university professors.

Soccer was introduced into Austria by English gardeners working for the Baron de Rothschild in Vienna. In Italy it was the English again, this time the members of the Genoa Cricket and Football Club, and in Germany, the English Football Club of Dresden.

This expanding world of soccer needed a governing body to coordinate and control the game, and at first it was assumed with some logic that since soccer was a British game, the Football Association, the mother of all football associations, would step in. But the FA was an insular and a smug organization; for illustration one need look no further than its name, which even now has no identifying prefix, despite the presence of 141 other national football associations in the world today. It had no particular interest in involving itself with the developing soccer associations, and in 1904 FIFA (Fédération Internationale de Football Association) was founded. England waited two years before joining reluctantly in 1906. The FA seemed convinced that there was little the novices of the game could offer to the well-organized milieu of English soccer. After all, the English had dominated the worldwide game for the first forty years, and the FA was confident it would continue to do so for another forty. Nevertheless, the FA kept a wary eye out for any muddling around with the laws of the game and insisted that the International Board formed in 1882 (comprising the four "Home Associations"—the FA plus the Scottish,

Irish and Welsh Football Associations) should continue to control the laws. FIFA happily consented, and even now, seventy years later, the four British associations still control the International Board, which now consists of twenty members, sixteen of whom are appointed by the British and four appointed by FIFA.

Never really happy in FIFA, the four British associations left twice—in 1919 over FIFA's permitting Germany and the other former Central Powers to play FIFA members in international matches and again in 1928 in a dispute over FIFA's definition of "broken time" expenses for amateurs. Their second departure resulted in a twenty-year absence and meant that no British teams played in the World Cup tournaments of the 1930s.

Today the majority of FIFA's 142 members have adopted professionalism, and apart from the dubious amateurs of the East European block, amateur soccer has practically ceased to interest the avid soccer fan. The big exception, of course, is the Olympic soccer tournament, in which viewers can be assured of first-class soccer from the four perennial contenders, Poland, East Germany, Russia and Hungary. The "amateur" players from these four countries, masquerading as students, policemen, soldiers and so on, often are the very same players who compete in the World Cup.

In the early days of the Olympics, however, soccer players entering the tournament were all amateurs, pure and keen, and none more so than those representing the United States. In the 1904 Olympics the Americans, the host country, held the soccer matches in St. Louis, which by that time had already emerged as the soccer city of America; it was to produce, in the next seventy years, more homegrown American soccer stars than any other part of the country. Only the United States and Canada, however, bothered to send soccer teams, so there was little glory in getting into the record books. It would be many decades before the United States, the beaten contestant in this unofficial Olympic final, would again draw international attention in soccer.

On the East Coast, the American Football Association, founded in 1885, was trying its best to recruit players for soccer, but generally it was the new wave of British immigrants, arriving with their own soccer balls, that welcomed the chance to play. Little headway was made until the 1905 visit to America of the splendid English amateur team, the Pilgrims, among whose players was the great Vivian Woodward. They played 23 games, winning 21 and losing 2. It was an extremely successful tour, and the high standard of soccer displayed gave American soccer a needed jolt. In the same year the Intercollegiate Association Football League was formed, with Columbia, Cornell, Harvard, Haverford and Pennsylvania prepared to accept the challenge of furthering U.S. collegiate soccer—unlike the original Intercollegiate Football Association, which had switched in 1876 to rugby.

In 1906 the Corinthians visited the United States, and interest in soccer increased considerably. Both the Pilgrims and the Corinthians returned for additional tours in the next few years, and by 1912 the growth of American soccer was such that two rival organizations went to the 1912 FIFA Congress in Stockholm vying for FIFA's recognition as the official U.S. national body. Both the American Football Association, representing the professionals in the New England states, and the American Amateur Football Association, whose power base was centered in New York, were politely told by FIFA to go home and work out a merger.

The amateur group, with the help of other leagues in Philadelphia and Chicago, overrode the objections of the pros and formed the United States Football Association on June 21, 1913. Thomas Cahill, who had been instrumental in the success of the old American Amateur Football Association, was named secretary, and Dr. Randolph Manning, president. On August 15, FIFA gave the USFA temporary membership and on June 27, 1914, permanent membership. Dr. Manning (yet another optimist) addressed the FIFA Congress and spoke of great advances in the spread of soccer in the United States that were going to make the sport a "major one in the near future."

Charles M. Schwab, the president of Bethlehem Steel, also thought U.S. soccer was heading for the big time prior to World War I. He spent over $125,000 (the equivalent of at least a million today) on a soccer field and facilities for his pet project, a soccer team for the steel company. On the same day war broke out in Europe, August 1, 1914, Schwab announced he had raided the best clubs in the country in order to put together the best team the United States had ever seen. Among the recruits were three forwards from Brooklyn: inside forward, Robert Millar, considered to be the top soccer player in the United States; the lanky center forward, Neil Clarke, and a tricky winger, James Ford. The mighty James Campbell, the crack center half of the Tacony Club of Philadelphia, was another formidable addition.

The majority of the Bethlehem players were former Scottish pros, and it was not surprising that the team won the U.S. championship (the National Challenge Cup) in both the 1914–15 and the 1915–16 seasons. The National Challenge Cup, or Dewar Cup, was presented to the American Amateur Football Association in 1912 by Sir Thomas Dewar, the British sportsman, who wrote to Thomas Cahill to express his hope that one day, "football will be found a formidable rival of that great national game, baseball." The National Challenge Cup was an amateur competition at first, but once the USFA was organized it became an open tournament for pros and amateurs alike. By 1923 the teams competing for the cup were so numerous that another tournament was organized for amateurs only, the National Amateur Cup.

In the 1915–16 season Bethlehem also won the American Challenge Cup, thus completing for the first and only time "the double" in American soccer. The American Challenge Cup, which was retired since it was duplicating the USFA's new Challenge Cup, had first been offered by the American Football Association in 1884. The first winners were the O.N.T. team of Newark, New Jersey, and then for the next four years it was to be won by a Massachusetts club, Fall River, a team that would remain great for seventy years. Even in the 1914–32 period, when Bethlehem was at its zenith, Fall River was able to win the National Challenge Cup five times.

When Bethlehem won "the double" in 1916, its opponent in the National Challenge Cup Final was none other than Fall River. Bethlehem won 1–0 before a crowd of 10,000 at Pawtucket. At the end of the game there was a miniriot as players and spectators fought each other—a distasteful scene that would be only too familiar in American soccer in the next fifty years. The fighting was sparked by a questionable decision of the referee, but the real reason for the mayhem was the intense rivalry growing between these two top American teams. This rivalry was to be a prominent feature of American soccer in the 1920s, when both teams, brimming with imported stars, would join the powerful new American Soccer League.

The teams for the 1916 Cup Final were as follows:

Bethlehem

Duncan (goalkeeper)

Fletcher (right back)   Ferguson (left back)

Murray (right half)   Campbell (center half)   Morrison (left half)

Pepper (inside right)   Butler (inside left)

McDonald (outside right) Clarke (center forward) Fleming (outside left)

Garant (outside left)   Dalton (center forward)   Morgan (outside right)

Swoords (inside left)   Sullivan (inside right)

Stone (left half)   Bouchard (center half)   F. Burns (right half)

C. Burns (left back)   Booth (right back)

Albis (goalkeeper)

Fall River

This is the way teams lined up throughout the world prior to the change in the offside law in the mid-1920s. It was an offensive-orientated formation with only two fullbacks and a center half who was in reality a sixth forward. This "attacking" center half was expected to go up with his forwards while the two flanking halfbacks stayed behind to help the fullbacks. The center half position was a showcase for talented and creative players, but tactical changes brought about by the alteration of the offside law doomed it to extinction.

Up to the early 1920s, the offside law was nothing more than a useful device to ensure that no team gained an unfair advantage by placing men ahead of the ball. To be onside in the opponent's half of the field, the attacking player had to have three opponents between himself and the defending team's goal whenever the ball was played to him. This in effect meant a goalkeeper and two other opponents, usually the two fullbacks. For over fifty years this rule existed without causing any serious problems, but once the fullbacks started to move upfield, forwards found they were often being caught offside. The frequency increased alarmingly when fullbacks Bill McCracken and Frank Hudspeth of England's Newcastle United put their minds together and introduced the dreaded "offside trap." These two prime exponents of the offside trap stayed close to the halfway line, one slightly ahead of the other, and every time an opponent prepared to pass the ball forward, either McCracken or Hudspeth would move upfield, past the other opponents, thereby putting one or more in an offside position. They were so successful with this ploy that a popular story circulated that when an opposing team arrived at the Newcastle train station, a member heard the train guard blow his whistle and quickly remarked, "Blimey, offside already!"

This constant use of the trap by the Newcastle backs and others who imitated them was beginning to destroy soccer as a spectator sport. Action, or what was left of it, was restricted to the halfway line and around it—the monotony of all this broken only by a series of blasts from the referee's whistle declaring yet another case of offside. The four British football associations, which at that time still commanded all four seats on the International Board, experimented before concluding that the best thing for the game would be to change the offside law so that it would require only two instead of three opponents to be between the attacker and the opposing goal when the ball was played to him.

In 1925 after the new law came into effect, an avalanche of goals went past beleaguered English goalkeepers. Over 6,373 were scored in the 1925–26 Football League season, compared with only 4,700 the previous year. Defenses, confused and shaky, seemed unable to devise methods to stop the flood of goals, and soccer officials became convinced that the International Board had acted too hastily. One imaginative manager, however, Herbert Chapman, found a solution to the goal glut. By withdrawing the attacking center half into the back line, between the right and left backs, Chapman stopped the goal rush and introduced the "stopper," or "third back," to world soccer. The days of the attacking center half were numbered.

Chapman had been the manager of the top club in England, Huddersfield Town, but by 1925 was the manager of Arsenal. His first big accomplishment was to acquire the services of Charlie Buchan, an English international who was approaching the end of his career but was still one of the best inside forwards in the country. Buchan, a thoughtful tactician, worked with Chapman on countering the surfeit of goals, and between them they concocted not only the "third back" but also the W–M system, in which both of the inside forwards dropped back to help in the midfield. This new formation was made even more effective by the acquisition of Alex James, the most brilliant inside forward of his time. James's long accurate passes made constructive long-range counterattacks possible for the first time.

Arsenal, which had been a rather average London club, would under Chapman's leadership begin a long reign as the top club side, not only in England but also in the world, and the W–M system would be adopted by almost all professional teams. Some Latin American teams, particularly Brazilian and Uruguayan, clung to the attacking center half, but generally by World War II W–M, based on the Arsenal model, was the fashion.

This is how Arsenal lined up in the late twenties:

Preedy (goalkeeper)

Parker (right back)   Roberts (center half)   Hapgood (left back)

Seddon (right half)   John (left half)

Jack (inside right)   James (inside left)

Hulme (outside right)   Lambert (center forward)   Bastin (outside left)

While all the clamor over the offside rule was being raised in England, American soccer was enjoying its "golden decade," and at last it seemed that the optimists were going to be proved right. Led by the professionals of the newly formed American Soccer League, soccer was big-time on the Eastern seaboard and comfortably entrenched in St. Louis, Chicago and Los Angeles. The American Soccer League (the ASL), like the North American Soccer League forty-five years later, attracted many influential backers when it was formed in 1921. Edgar Lewis of Bethlehem Steel was the power behind the league, and he wasted no time in importing some of the better players from Scotland, including Young, of Hibernians; McFarlane and McNivin, of Partick Thistle; Terris, of Falkirk; Raeside, of Dumbarton; Rattray, of Raith, and Goldie, of Clydebank.

As the league's size and attendance increased (8,000 to 10,000 was an average gate for the top clubs), so did the quality of player enticed to America. Paying a $50–70 weekly salary to soccer stars accustomed to earning less than $25 in Britain enabled Bethlehem to sign up both Wattie Jackson and his brother Alex. The latter was destined to become one of the finest wingers in British history when he returned to England to play for Huddersfield Town and the Scottish national team. Others coaxed to the States by the free-spending ASL owners included outside right Sam Chedgzoy, of Everton, a six-time member of the English national team; Jimmy Howieson, an inside right from Hull City, and Tom Blair, a splendid goalkeeper from England's famed Manchester City club. All three played for New Bedford. In the late 1920s, Boston was fielding such notable Scottish internationals as Alex McNab, a powerhouse in American soccer for so many years; Barney Battles, the brilliant left winger, and Bill Harper, the former Arsenal goalkeeper.

Not all the stars of the booming soccer scene of the 1920s and early '30s were transplanted Britishers. Probably the best player of the period was Billy Gonsalves. Born in the right place for any future soccer player, Fall River, Gonsalves strode through the various professional leagues of American soccer like a colossus. A big man for soccer—he was over 6 feet 1 and weighed 190—Gonsalves, an inside forward, could hit the ball with such power that he often scored goals from 35 yards out. He was a member of both the 1930 and 1934 U.S. World Cup teams, attracting many foreign scouts and receiving offers to play overseas, including one from the top Brazilian team, Botafogo, but he preferred to remain in U.S. soccer. So did another American-born star, Buff Donelli, who is perhaps better remembered for his coaching of the other kind of football at Duquesne, Boston University and Columbia. Donelli was so impressive in the 1934 World Cup games that he received an offer from an Italian club, Lazio.

Two other American products on view at that time, capable of playing with the best, were Francis "Hun" Ryan, the fine winger from Philadelphia who captained the 1934 World Cup team, and Archie Stark, the phenomenal center forward who scored 67 goals in 44 games for Bethlehem in the 1924–25 season—an American record that will probably never be beaten. In the same year Stark set another record that also remains unchallenged to this date when he scored 5 goals for the U.S. national team against Canada. Probably the highlight of his long career came when he scored a hat trick (3 goals) in the 1926 final of the National Challenge Cup. Bethlehem won that game 7–2, defeating the Ben Millar team of St. Louis before a crowd of 18,000 at Ebbets Field.

Some idea of the strength of American soccer of this period can be gauged by what happened to visiting foreign teams. In the spring of 1927 the Uruguayan national team—the 1924 Olympic champions and destined to win the Olympics again in 1928 and the World Cup in 1930 with practically the same makeup—toured the United States and was beaten for the first time in three years by the Newark All-Stars. A year earlier the famous Sparta Club of Prague and the star-studded Hakoah team from Vienna, both playing in the delicate style of mid-European soccer, were surprised by the high standard of American soccer, and both teams suffered defeats.

Hakoah drew the largest crowds ever to watch soccer in America up to that time: three successive games drew 25,000, 30,000 and 36,000 spectators. Yet the tour was still a financial failure; the club reported that it had lost over $30,000, and as a result the club's president resigned upon his return to Vienna.

The great Depression of the early '30s hit American professional soccer harder than any other sport. There was a general retrenchment; the pros were replaced by the semipros, and all hopes of establishing soccer as a national sport appeared doomed forever. But the optimists stuck it out in such places as St. Louis, Chicago, Los Angeles, New York, Philadelphia and other cities with large foreign neighborhoods. Soccer became known as the "immigrant sport," a game for the un-American and the nonconformist, and such, as we shall see later, it was to remain until the 1970s, when the grandchildren of those who had shunned it would accept soccer as freely as baseball, football and any other American institution.

In the rest of the world, soccer—or football, as most non-Americans continued to call it—had developed into an obsession with the sports fans. Under its spell, reasonable men could turn into savages. The slightest mistake by a referee could cause a riot, especially in Latin America and Southern Europe, where soccer games drew enormous crowds. Moats, barbed-wire fences and tommy-gun-toting police become common sights, and international matches became tests of national prestige and honor. The World Cup, instituted in 1930, although it produced breathtaking soccer, hardly mollified international soccer passions, which were even further exacerbated by German and Italian claims of fascist superiority during the 1934 and 1938 World Cups, as well as the 1936 Olympics.

The Italian national team, under the guiding hand of the greatest of all

Italian managers, Vittorio Pozzo, won both the 1934 and '38 World Cups, but was closely challenged by the "Wunderteam" of Austria, coached by the adroit Jimmy Hogan. A firm believer in the short-passing Scottish style of soccer, Hogan, an Englishman, was coaching in Vienna as early as 1912. He and Hugo Meisl, the wealthy organizer of Austrian soccer, produced players and teams that were the envy of the rest of Europe in the 1920s and '30s.

Other formidable rivals of the Italians during the '30s were the Uruguayans, the World Cup winners of 1930; the Hungarians; the Czechs; the Germans; the Argentinians and the Brazilians, whose emerging black stars were displaying unparalleled soccer magic before the decade was over.

Despite the rising standards throughout the world, the English continued to consider themselves the dominating force in world soccer. Their refusal to play in the three World Cups of the 1930s made it difficult to determine just who really was the world champion, but there was no doubt that the most famous and feared club team in the world was Arsenal, a team that epitomized the power of English soccer.

In 1934 the selectors of the English national team filled seven of the eleven places on the team that was to meet the Italian World Cup team with Arsenal players—Moss (goalie), Male (right back), Hapgood (left back), Copping (left half), Bowden (inside right), Drake (center forward) and Bastin (outside left). The Italians, fresh from their World Cup triumph, were beaten 3–2 in one of the roughest internationals ever staged.

The seven Arsenal men on the 1934 England team, along with four other regular members of the London club side—Crayston (right half), Roberts (center half), Hulme (outside right), all three also English internationals, and Scottish international Alex James (inside left)—formed the nucleus of a brilliant team that won the first-division championship five times during the 1930s.

Probably the most famous player in the world at this time was Stanley Matthews. The king of dribblers, Matthews was the scourge of left backs. It was claimed he had never met a defender he couldn't run rings around. He first played for England in the 1934 game against Italy. He was only 19 at the time and was unable to withstand the physical punishment and fouls so prevalent in this violent match; few thought he would get another chance to play for England after his mediocre performance. But he did, and he was still playing for England as late as 1957 at the age of 42. It was not until five days after his fiftieth birthday that he finally retired from first-division soccer.

There are many today who, with some justification, state that against modern soccer's speedier and better-coached defenders, Matthews would seldom have had a chance to display his wizardry; but this is difficult for anyone who saw him in his younger days to accept. My coauthor, Basil Kane, remembers the time during World War II when Matthews, appearing for Blackpool against the mighty Arsenal, put on one of the greatest displays of dribbling ever seen in top-class soccer. He completely demoralized the Arsenal defense, gliding past three or four opponents at a time with his marvelous ball control, body swerve and acceleration. Leslie Compton, a massive defender, bore the brunt of Matthews' magic and spent most of the 1943 game in a state of bewilderment. Like so many other left backs whose unhappy task it was to shadow the "Prince of Dribblers," he was a sad, forlorn figure at the end of the match.

Another great star of the '30s was the legendary Dixie Dean of Everton, whose record of 60 goals in 39 matches still stands in the English first division. Although he had a tremendous shot in either foot, Dean was most feared for his ability in the air. Considered the finest header (hitting the ball with the head) in soccer's history, he could score goals from outside the penalty area with a quick flick of his head and a tightening of his large neck muscles. Dean's prowess in the air prompted many stories, of which the most popular concerned Elisha Scott, the Irish international goalkeeper of Liverpool, a club only a few miles across town from Everton. Whenever Dean encountered Scott on the street, so the story went, he would nod his head and Scott would automatically go diving across the sidewalk.

There were many other excellent players and teams in the British Isles, but none that captured the imagination as did the Scottish national team of 1928. Producing a brand of attacking soccer seldom seen since, the Scots defeated England 5–1 at London's Wembley Stadium. Dubbed the "Wembley Wizards," the Scots fielded a forward line in which only one man was over 5 feet 7—outside right Alex Jackson, the former Bethlehem Steel import, who scored 3 goals in the rout. On the other wing was the 5-foot-5 Alan Morton of Glasgow Rangers, considered by many the greatest winger of all time. Five-foot-6 Alex James, the Arsenal star, was also playing, as was Hughie Gallagher, unquestionably the finest small center forward in British soccer history.

The Wembley Wizards demonstrated just how Scottish soccer had been played in the earlier days of professional soccer. Unfortunately, this rich inheritance of short passing, unmatchable ball control and individualistic brilliance was, for the most part, relinquished in the rush to adopt the W–M system—a system that would be prevalent not only in Scotland but throughout the world. It would not be until the 1950s, when the Hungarians and the Brazilians produced equally fascinating and exciting soccer, that the 1928 exhibition of soccer skill would be duplicated.

By the end of the 1930s it was clear to soccer pundits that quality soccer was no longer an English or even a British monopoly. Both the English and the Scots were losing the occasional international away from home, and England was indeed fortunate to maintain its unbeaten home record against the Wunderteam of Austria in 1932 by a score of 4–3. Yet just as its days of soccer mastery of the world were about to end, England assembled one of the best teams in its history. In addition to Stanley Matthews, there were the classical fullback and captain, Eddie Hapgood; his club colleague Wilf Copping, the hardest-tackling halfback of prewar soccer; Stan Cullis, the dominating center half from Wolverhampton; inside forward Willie Hall, of Tottenham Hotspur, who scored 5 goals in one international, including 3 in 3½ minutes, and the man who gave the team a definite edge—center forward Tommy Lawton. The "boy wonder" from Dixie Dean's old club, Everton, Lawton was fast, agile and often thought a better header than his predecessor on the Everton and England teams.

There were many other exceptional players in the English squad, a team that seemed destined to embark on a long undefeated sequence of victories. In 1938 it had gone to Berlin to defeat Germany by the score of 6–3 in a game heralded by Goebbels as a test of Germany's new superman invincibility. In 1939 England drew 2–2 in Rome against the 1938 World Cup champions, Italy, and were indeed unlucky not to come away with a victory. There was much talk about England's rejoining FIFA in time for the 1942 World Cup, and there was little doubt that it would have been the favorite to win it. But Hitler had other ideas, and the next World Cup would not be held until 1950, by which time soccer—and indeed the world—would be greatly changed.

Chapter Three

Modern Soccer

"This is all we need to make the game go over in the States."

Bill Jeffrey, Coach of the United States World
Cup team which defeated England 1–0 in 1950

After the cataclysm of World War II, the "immigrant sport" of the American urban areas gained a new lease on life as a steady stream of European immigrants and displaced persons arrived in the harbors of the Eastern seaports. Numbering in the millions, this new group encompassed multitudes of dedicated soccer players eagerly willing to join one of the many new clubs sprouting up in ethnic neighborhoods.

The ethnic clubs' gain was soccer's loss as the foreign image of the sport was reinforced. The United States Soccer Football Association had made diligent efforts to Americanize soccer (even going so far as to finally admit that "football" in America would never mean "soccer" and thus adding the word soccer to its title in 1945). Most of its work was undone as the new ethnic clubs, with names like Teutonia, Liederkranz, Sons of Italy, Philadelphia Ukrainians, Azzuri Pozzalesi, Polonia and Hungaria, did not bother to recruit players of any other nationality. Worse yet, English was rarely spoken on or off the field.

Even the old established clubs succumbed to the tempting prospect of taking full-fledged players right off the boat rather than persevere with local talent. Now the USSFA's main hope lay with the city of St. Louis. There, a splendidly organized league of youth and adult clubs continued to produce thousands of young American-born players to fill the ranks of the many colleges and universities turning to soccer in the late 1950s and '60s. Both the St. Louis Simpkins, winner of the National Challenge Cup in 1948 and 1950, and the powerful Kutis club filled their rosters with local players, and when the 1950 World Cup approached, six St. Louis players were chosen to go to Brazil with the U.S. national team.

Across the ocean in the birthplace of soccer, the game continued to be played in the same style in which it had been played in 1939. Coaching was still considered something only foreigners needed, and with familiar British insularity there was complete disregard for the innovations and

39

developments in European and South American soccer. It was the Russians who were the first to show the British just how far soccer had advanced outside the tight little island. They came to London in October of 1945 while the euphoria of victory still lingered and in front of 80,000 paying spectators (and 25,000 more who simply broke or jumped over fences) tied 3–3 with a strong Chelsea team led by Tommy Lawton. In a fascinating and exciting game the Russians put on an exhibition of one-touch soccer not seen since the glorious Scots had set the Wembley turf alight in 1928.

This fluid display should have awakened the British administrators, but their general consensus was that the Russians' success was just a fluke. Foreigners might know how to do all the fancy stuff but they did not know how to shoot was their familiar dismissal of the Russians and other subsequent entertaining teams visiting Britain.

And perhaps the British critics were right, for the postwar English team proved nearly unbeatable, winning 14, tying 3 and losing just 1 game out of 18 played between 1946 and the beginning of 1950. English part-time soccer during the war had produced some fine new talent, including right half Billy Wright, soon to be England's captain; Neil Franklin, the elegant center half; Stanley Mortensen, the extraordinary opportunistic center forward; Wilf Mannion, small, creative and a marvelously effective inside forward, and winger Tom Finney, the best all-around player in Britain.

Northern Ireland was the first country after the war to feel the sting of this fine team, losing 7–2 in Belfast. Other European teams stunned by big scores were Holland, 8–2; Switzerland, 6–0, and Portugal, 10–0. England's most significant victory, however, was its superb 4–0 win over Italy in Turin in 1948, which marred the Italians' celebration of the fiftieth anniversary of the founding of the Italian national soccer body.

The unhappy Italians were to suffer a more severe blow the following year, when many of their national side would die in the Superga air disaster. The plane carrying Torino, champions of Italy for the last four years, crashed into a hill near the city of Superga. All seventeen Torino players aboard were killed.

The loss of so many of the great stars of Italian soccer coupled with the loss of prestige resulting from the defeat by England set Italian soccer on the road to *catenaccio*, a defensive system employing far too many defenders. *Catenaccio* would, unfortunately, take the joy out of Italian soccer for the next twenty years.

Down in South America, soccer was still the freewheeling open attacking game of the pre–third-back era. Not for the South Americans the defensive center half or the W–M formation; attack was their métier, and it was to remain so until the mid-'50s, when a series of defeats effected wholesale tactical changes. Each of the top three teams in South America —Brazil, Uruguay and Argentina—stood poised to assume England's mantle as the world's number one team, and in 1950 the World Cup, held in Brazil, promised to bring England face to face with the South American teams for the first time.

Unfortunately, the long-awaited contests between the top three Latin teams and England never materialized. The unknown U.S. team ruined it all by, unbelievably, defeating England in the opening round of the cup. This defeat of the favorites by a bunch of amateurs and semiprofessionals was the biggest upset in the fifty years internationals had been played among nations. Most European wire services asked for verification when the 1–0 score came over the news wires, but it was no practical joke: the mighty England had been beaten by a splendid header of Joe Gaetjens, the Haitian-born center forward from the New York Brookhattans Club.

Apart from the United States' moment of glory, the 1950 World Cup was significant in that it gave the Brazilians and the Uruguayans a chance to demonstrate to the Europeans the extent of Latin America's devotion to attacking soccer. The eventual winner of the cup was Uruguay, better organized than but nowhere near as skillful as the brilliant rhythmic Brazilians. There was no doubt the Brazilians were unlucky not to have won the trophy when they possessed such remarkable forwards as Zizinho, Ademir, Jair and Chico, all of whom scored goals at will until the final game. A world-record crowd of 199,850 saw the home team, Brazil, lose that game to Uruguay by a score of 2–1 in the newly constructed Maracana Stadium. In the Uruguayan team was Juan Schiaffino, probably the finest inside forward playing in South America, who, like so many talented Uruguayans, Argentinians and other South Americans of the '50s and early '60s, would be lured by the lire to play in Italian soccer.

The breathtaking performance of the Brazilians and Uruguayans went unnoticed by the English; they had left for home after being eliminated in the preliminary round. The defeat by the U.S. team, once the shock of it had subsided, was also considered insignificant by the English. They regarded it as just another of those occasional inexplicable freak occurrences in sport. It was not until 1953, when the Hungarian national team, arguably the most brilliant group of men ever to pool their talents on a soccer field, came to Wembley Stadium, that the English finally concluded that something was seriously wrong with English and, since it was so interconnected, British soccer.

On the sacred turf of Wembley, the Hungarians, by a score of 6–3, pulverized the English team, which included such notables as Stanley

Matthews, Billy Wright, Stan Mortensen and Alf Ramsey, an elegant back, who was destined to become England's manager a decade later.

Using a withdrawn center forward, Nandor Hidegkuti, the Hungarians destroyed the confused English defense by sending their inside forwards into the space left open by Hidegkuti. Johnson, the English center half, was faced with an unexpected dilemma: should he follow Hidegkuti and thereby leave a hole in the center of the defense, or stay put and deal with the two Hungarian inside forwards? To further complicate Johnson's decision, the Hungarian wingers also played behind the two inside forwards, and with them went the two English backs, leaving Johnson without cover. It was an unenviable choice, and the Hungarians had a field day as Johnson vacillated.

This was the Hungarian team of that November afternoon:

Grosics (goalkeeper)

Buzansky (right back)   Lorant (center half)   Lantos (left back)

Bozik (right half)   Zakariás (left half)

Budai (outside right)   Hidegkuti (center forward)   Czibor (outside left)

Kocsis (inside right)   Puskás (inside left)

The greatness of Hungary during the early and middle 1950s was not due simply to its innovative use of tactics. Teamwork and amazing skill were the essential keys to its success. It was also fortunate to have four world-class players: Josef Bozsik, a creative attacking halfback; Sandor Kocsis and Nandor Hidegkuti, two exceptional goal-scoring forwards, and the overall star and inspiration of the team, Ferenc Puskás, nicknamed the "Galloping Major," whose army life as a major was restricted to the pursuit of soccer. Short and tubby, Puskás may not have looked like a professional soccer player, but his greatness was never in doubt; he ranks as one of the top ten soccer stars of all time. He is best remembered for his devastating left foot, with which he scored nearly all of his hundreds of goals.

Any doubt that this Hungarian national team was truly the best team in the world was resolved in 1954 when the Hungarians overwhelmed the English in a return match by a score of 7–1.

The era of Hungary's invincibility came to a sudden end with the 1956 Hungarian revolution as many top players fled the country. Never again would Hungarian soccer reach the sublime heights of the 1950–56 period. During those six glorious years the Hungarian team played 48 games with only 1 defeat. Ironically enough, the sole defeat was in the World Cup final of 1954, when West Germany surprised the Hungarians and the rest of the world by winning the World Cup.

Gracefully gliding into Hungary's vacated position as the leader of world soccer was Spain—more specifically, the incomparable club Real Madrid. Led by Alfredo di Stéfano, the Argentinian forward, considered by many critics to be a better all-around player than Pelé, Real won the newly inaugurated European Cup for Champions (known simply as the European Cup) five times in its first five years of competition.

Owner Santiago Bernabeu spared no expense in bringing the very best talent to his new 130,000-seat Bernabeu Stadium. In addition to Di Stéfano he signed up a host of international stars: the defecting Puskás from Hungary; Francisco Gento, the fastest winger in Europe; Hector Rial, the clever inside forward from Uruguay; Raymond Kopa, the legendary French outside right; José Santamaria, a tough but effective center half; Luis Del Sol, another world-class forward, and Didi, the phenomenal midfield star of the Brazilian national team of the '50s and early '60s.

During the 1955–61 period, Real was probably the finest club side ever fielded; even Pelé's dazzling club, Santos, did not have the same irresistibility as Real in top gear. Critics still consider Real's display in the 1960 final of the European Cup for Champions the finest ever seen in club soccer. Bewitching and bewildering their Eintracht Frankfurt opponents with inventive, fluid soccer, the Spaniards won by a score of 7–3 before 127,000 ecstatic fans in Glasgow's huge Hampden Stadium.

Another great team of this period was Manchester United of England, a young team, dubbed the "Busby Babes" after its manager, Matt Busby. United promised to be the team of the '60s, but in 1958 eight of its members were killed when the plane carrying the team from a European Cup semifinal match in Belgrade crashed on takeoff at the Munich airport. Among the eight were four members of the English national team: Roger Byrne, the left back; Tommy Taylor, center forward; David Pegg, left winger, and Duncan Edwards, possibly the best English halfback in twenty-five years and a member of the English national team when he was only 18.

Survivors of the crash included Bobby Charlton, who would go on to become the best forward in Europe, and two other English internationals associated with American soccer: Bill Foulkes, team manager of the Chicago Sting until his resignation in 1977, and Dennis Viollet, former head coach of the Washington Diplomats. Charlton and Foulkes shared in the 1968 European Cup triumph of a rebuilt United team. Scoring one of the goals in the 4–1 defeat of the Portuguese team Benfica was Georgie Best, the gifted winger and one of the world's top players in the 1960s. (Best is now plying his magic with the Los Angeles Aztecs in the NASL.)

Just as Real Madrid was the finest club of the late '50s, so Brazil was the finest national side. Didi and Pelé were the guiding geniuses around which the Brazilian team revolved. Didi, a master of the midfield, was a creative dynamo who could slow up a game with coolness approaching arrogance one moment, then run through the defense to unleash an amazingly accurate shot the next. Pelé, the most exciting player the world had ever seen, was the goal scorer par excellence. A diamond in the rough when he played his first game for Santos at the age of 15, a world star at 17 and a superstar by the time he reached the age of consent, Pelé had incredible ball control, a tremendous shot and the ability to outjump the tallest of defenders to reach high balls for spectacular headers.

Winner of the 1958 and '62 World Cups, Brazil failed miserably in 1966, but came back again in full glory to take the cup for the third time in 1970 and thereby win the treasured Jules Rimet Trophy outright. (In 1974 a new cup, called simply the World Cup, replaced the retired Rimet Trophy.)

In 1958 the Brazilians overwhelmed all opposition with their sheer artistic brilliance allied to a tactical formation that was to change modern soccer, the 4–2–4 formation. By adding another player to the backline so that there were two center halves (now called center backs), the 4–2–4 solved once and for all the problems caused by the withdrawn, or roaming, center forward.

In the 1958 World Cup final against Sweden, the victorious Brazilians lined up like this (notice the new names for some of the positions):

Gylmar (goalkeeper)

D. Santos	Bellini	Orlando	N.Santos
(right back)	(center back)	(center back)	(left back)

Zito (midfielder)   Didi (midfielder)

Garrincha (winger)   Vavá (striker)   Pelé (striker)   Zagalo (winger)

With two center backs permanently stationed in the middle of the defense, this was a far cry from the attacking-center-half system Brazil and other South American teams had employed earlier. With one man removed from the forward line, it would seem that attacking soccer had been dealt a knockout punch; but the Brazilians were able to adapt this new formation to produce sparkling attacking movements whose like had seldom been seen before.

Unfortunately, the 4–2–4 formation prompted many teams to counter it with more defensive formations. The Italians, not satisfied with two center backs, introduced the "sweeper," a player who stationed himself behind the two center backs as a safety man. Helenio Herrera, the ultra-defensive-minded manager of Inter Milan, won the European Cup twice in the early 1960s using the *catenaccio* system, in which most players are assigned a defensive role, leaving two and sometimes only one striker upfield.

This defensive trend continued throughout the '60s, and England's first conquest of the World Cup in 1966 only intensified the glorification of all things defensive. Dispensing with wingers and employing a 4–3–3 formation based upon hard tackling, hard running and dedicated team-work, the English style was not as aesthetically pleasing as the Brazilians' of 1958 or '62, but it was very effective, and England beat West Germany 4–2 in the final.

Three members of the team played in the NASL in the mid-1970s: Gordon Banks, probably the greatest goalie of his time (with the Fort Lauderdale Strikers); Bobby Moore, the supreme center back of the '60s (with San Antonio); and the scorer of a hat trick in the 1966 final, Geoff Hurst (with the Seattle Sounders). The complete English team in the 1966 final lined up like this—a 4–3–3 or 4–4–2 depending on whether Ball played in the midfield or in the attack:

Banks (goalkeeper)

Cohen (right back)	J. Charlton (center back)	Moore (center back)	Wilson (left back)

Stiles (midfielder)   R. Charlton (midfielder)   Peters (midfielder)

Ball (striker)   Hunt (striker)   Hurst (striker)

In spite of worldwide concern over the trend toward defensive soccer and dropping attendances, a group of American business tycoons decided the time was ripe to sell professional soccer to a new nationwide market. Chapter Five explores the early disasters of the NASL in greater detail, but it is sufficient to state here that although the NASL was beset with all manner of difficulties—among them erratic performances by overage imported players and an uninterested press—its underlying problem was its adoption of the defensive systems in vogue elsewhere. Instead of the bright, entertaining soccer necessary to entice new fans, Americans were offered a heavy dose of seven-man defenses and sweepers. Even the more riot-prone soccer fans found it difficult at times to stay awake.

And yet the fascination of soccer is such that despite the uninspiring bill of fare offered by NASL teams, Americans—particularly the young exposed to it for the first time—took to it in such numbers that by the end of the 1960s it was the fastest-growing sport in the country.

The first to be converted were residents of the cities and suburbs where the 17 NASL clubs were located. Some of these metropolitan areas—like

Dallas, Atlanta and Baltimore—were unlikely places for soccer to gain a following. Not so surprising were soccer's gains in the urban North where ethnic soccer was still strong. The new interest in soccer gained momentum and swept across the nation, no doubt helped by the Saturday-afternoon CBS television coverage of the NASL's first two years.

That truly great players can destroy even the best of defenses was emphatically proved by the Brazilians in the 1970 World Cup. Their opponents in the final match, Italy, still relying on *catenaccio,* were turned inside out. Brazil's one-sided 4–1 victory was badly needed to jolt the defensive-minded teams of the day. Even the reigning champion, England, was content with only two forwards as it tried to retain the cup with a 4–4–2 formation.

Brazil, with five of the top players in the world on its squad—Pelé, Tostão, Gerson, Jairzinho and Rivelino—played a 4–3–3 formation, but its interpretation of the system, commonly held to be defensive, turned out to be a joyful brand of offensive soccer. Gerson and Rivelino sparked the midfield play with incisive passes, while Jairzinho, on the wing, and Pelé and Tostão, striking, created havoc with their precise interpassing and deadly shooting. Vintage soccer had returned once more to the international scene.

The example set by the Brazilians was followed by the Dutch and German teams of the 1970s, who have gone even further in their attempts to revive attacking soccer by playing what is now called "total soccer."

The Dutch club Ajax, with the masterful Johan Cruyff leading the way, won the European Cup in 1971, '72 and '73 with this brand of nonstop soccer, in which positions are rotated constantly by defenders and attackers alike. When Cruyff was sold to Barcelona for approximately $2,500,000 in 1973 along with a brilliant teammate, midfielder Johan Neeskens, Ajax was no longer the same force, and the German club Bayern Munich became the number one club in Europe, winning the European Cup in 1974, '75 and '76. Bayern relied heavily upon stocky, muscular Gerhard Müller, its key striker, and the classical center back Franz Beckenbauer. They and teammates Sepp Maier (goalie), George Schwarzenbeck and Paul Breitner (defenders) and Uli Hoeness (midfielder) formed the nucleus of a splendid German national team during the early and mid-1970s.

The attacking soccer of West Germany, Holland and Poland dominated the 1974 World Cup, won by West Germany, which beat Holland 2–1 in a close final. The total-soccer concept of these three teams has prompted others to adjust their approach to soccer strategy. Wingers are back in favor again, enabling attacking formations to sweep along the touchlines as in the pre—4-3-3 days; midfielders are being pushed up into the attack more often and wonder of wonders, Franz Beckenbauer and other daring center backs are scoring goals too.

Where the total-soccer system often fails, of course, is in teams with mediocre talent. Far too many teams lack skillful players and are forced to mitigate this deficiency by concentrating on "stopping"—which, as in most sports, is always easier than "creating."

Many soccer enthusiasts are still concerned over the dominant defensive philosophy of top professional teams. In the United States, however, the NASL has discouraged safety-first soccer by awarding additional points for goals scored. Although FIFA only reluctantly gave permission for this experiment with the rules, and foreign critics blast it as a typical American gimmick, the bonus-points-for-goals idea has proved most successful, for it has increased goal scoring in remarkable fashion as well as generating an open style of attacking soccer. While most of the soccer world ponders the correlation between defensive soccer and falling attendances, the "new boys" in America have doubled their attendances since 1973.

Soccer has come a long way since the emergence of the Football Association in 1863. On the professional level it has become big business, with enormous fortunes to be made by both top players and clubs. Winning is more important than ever for the pro teams if they want to compete in the lucrative arena of international club tournaments. In Europe, besides the European Champions Cup (for national league champions), there are also the less prestigious European Cup Winners Cup (for national cup holders) and the UEFA (Union of European Football Associations) Cup (for top clubs that come close to winning either their national championship or their national cup). In South America there is the Liberators Cup (Copa de los Libertadores), a competition started in 1960 for all national league champions. The winner of the Liberators Cup qualifies to meet the winner of the European Champions Cup for the World Club Championship.

From 1960, when Real Madrid beat Peñarol, the Uruguayan champions, until 1966, when Peñarol turned the tables on Real Madrid, the World Club Championship was a great success. For the next five years, however, violence on the field of play nearly destroyed this tournament. In 1967 a bloody contest between Glasgow Celtic and the Racing Club of Buenos Aires was one of the ugliest international matches ever seen. The following year the Manchester United–Estudiantes of Argentina game was also a bitter, brutal affair, as were the 1969 Estudiantes–Milan and the 1970 Estudiantes–Feyenoord of Holland matches.

Ajax, in 1971 and '73, and Bayern Munich, in 1974, both refused to play in the tournament—their places taken by the beaten finalists in the European Champions Cup. In 1975 neither the European nor the South American champions wanted to play, but in 1976 moderation and common sense returned to the World Club Championship, with Bayern and Cruzeiro of Brazil both behaving themselves. It remains to be seen if this tournament will ever become as popular as the European Champions Cup, which is consistently the most successful of all the club contests. (A complete listing of all international tournaments can be found in Appendix D.)

This emphasis on international soccer, with its huge attendances and gate receipts (sometimes as high as $400,000 a game), has set the top teams on a never-ending pursuit of commercial success. Just as in American pro sports, coaches have been forced to adopt the "winning is the only thing" philosophy. Teams that once had the same manager for twenty years now have a new one every two years. Insecurity is the result and the main reason teams replace attractive attacking soccer with dull safety-first defensive styles. The manager's anxieties have been intensified by the promotion-and-relegation system—a system used throughout the world except in the United States. In this punish-or-reward system, the bottom clubs at the end of the season are demoted to lower divisions and the top ones promoted to higher. A team may one year play before 40,000 fans in first-division soccer and three years later before one-tenth as many in the fourth division. Indeed, this happened to the once-famous Huddersfield Town of England in the early 1970s.

With such a depressing prospect looming, it is not surprising that teams near the bottom of the standings use a seven- or eight-man defense when playing away from home. Home advantage is so important in soccer that even a winning team vying for a league championship will often risk attacking soccer only when playing before its own friendly home crowds. If a team can earn 1 point from its away matches and 2 every time it plays at home, it can be reasonably certain of winning a league title: hence the dismal proposition that at any given professional match the visiting team will be trying its best to play for a 0–0 tie.

One wonders what the original founders of the Football Association 115 years ago would have thought about these different tactics for home and away games. I suspect they would be far happier with our NASL's bonus points—points that motivate American teams to go all out for goals no matter where the games are played.

Chapter Four

The World Cup

"Victory or death!"

A chant by Argentinian fans at the
1930 World Cup Final

The shining jewel of modern soccer is the World Cup, a quadrennial tournament open to all of FIFA's 142 members. The number of participants is reduced to 16 for the finals by elimination through regional qualifying rounds. (The United States participates in the CONCAF section—Confederation of North and Central American and Caribbean Association Football.)

A showcase for the very best worldwide soccer has to offer, the World Cup has in recent years even overshadowed the Olympics as sport's superspectacular. Over a billion viewers worldwide saw the 1974 final televised from Germany; this figure is expected to be surpassed at the 1978 final to be held in Argentina this year.

But it was not always so popular. When the first World Cup was held in Uruguay in 1930, only 4 European countries—Belgium, France, Rumania and Yugoslavia—agreed to send teams. Four other European countries that had been hoping to stage the tournament—Holland, Italy, Spain and Sweden—boycotted it when Uruguay was given the honor of being the host. Uruguay was celebrating the one-hundredth anniversary of its independence, and it seemed to FIFA only fitting that the small South American country, winner of the 1924 and 1928 Olympics, should be chosen.

The other powerful European soccer countries—Austria, Czechoslovakia, Germany, Hungary and Switzerland—after contemplating the four-week round trip on the high seas and the cost of providing salaries for the players for nearly two months, also decided not to send teams. In addition, the 4 British associations, out of FIFA since 1928, were not eligible to go even if they had wanted to.

The 4 countries that finally agreed to send teams on the lengthy sea voyage did not make up their minds until a few months before the tournament was due to start. The French Football Federation was under great pressure to send a team from the two Frenchmen who more than anyone else had shaped FIFA's progress: Henri Delaunay, secretary of FIFA since 1919, and Jules Rimet, president since 1921 and for whom the World Cup (The Jules Rimet Trophy) was named. The pressure on the Rumanian Football Federation came from a different and unlikely source: King Carol, an ardent soccer fan, who telephoned reluctant employers for leaves of absence for members of the team—a team that he is said to have personally picked for the trip.

The 4 European teams were joined in Montevideo by 7 Latin American entries, Argentina, Bolivia, Brazil, Chile, Mexico, Paraguay and Peru, besides the host nation, Uruguay. One other entry, a formidable collection of stern-faced strapping athletes, traveled down from the north—the United States team.

Drawing upon many of the former British pros of the American Soccer League who were now citizens, the American team played surprisingly well in its first two games. Against Belgium in the first match the Americans, biceps and thighs bulging in their tight-fitting white uniforms, swept past their opponents with their typically British style: strong running, powerful tackling defense and swift breakaways. Former Scottish star James Brown of New York and Bill Gonsalves, playing for Fall River at that time, were outstanding. Another who performed well was the 21-year-old Bert Patenaude, also from the Fall River club, who had recently scored 5 of the 6 goals Fall River had netted in its 1930 National Challenge Cup Final victory.

In the second game it was Paraguay's turn to try to withstand the American whirlwind—but to no avail, as the Americans were still in devastating form. Florie and Gonsalves scored in the first half and Patenaude in the second half. The team that day was as follows:

Douglas (N.Y. Nationals)

Wood (Detroit Holly Carburetors)   Moorhouse (N.Y. Giants)

Gallagher   Tracy   Auld

(N.Y. Nationals)   (St. Louis Ben Millers)   (Providence)

Gonsalves (Fall River)   Florie (New Bedford)

Brown (N.Y. Giants)   Patenaude (Fall River)   McGhee (Philadelphia)

So well did this team play that the United States was now the favorite to win the first World Cup. In the semifinal against Argentina, the team that had started the tournament as the favorite, the United States finally met its match. Although trailing only 0–1 at the end of the first half, the Americans were thoroughly outplayed in the second and were badly beaten 1–6.

It might have been different if Ralph Tracy had not been seriously injured in the first half with a broken leg. There being no substitutes in soccer at the time (they would not come until the 1970 finals), the United States was forced to play with only ten men, with star forward Bill Gonsalves dropping back to the center-half position. Two other players were injured in addition to Tracy: goalie Jimmy Douglas was kicked in the head, and left half Andy Auld in the mouth, as the Argentinians gave the world a preview of the 1960s and '70s, when they would become known as the hatchet men of international soccer.

In the final the Argentinians played the Uruguayans, who had been their opponents in the 1928 Olympic final and to whom they had lost 1–2. The Argentinians confidently expected to exact revenge on the Uruguayans; but before a home crowd of 100,000 in the magnificent new Centenary Stadium, the Uruguayans, with Andrade and Cea outstanding, beat the Argentinians 4–2.

Overall the tournament was a success, especially for the Uruguayans, who now had completed a hat trick of world tournaments—two consecutive Olympic championships plus the World Cup—and were extremely proud of their new stadium, the most modern in the world. (Incidentally, it was built for a paltry $800,000, a sum that would not even build a restaurant in one of our new dome stadiums.)

The major discouraging aspect was the virulent nationalistic fervor of some of the fans; the Argentinian–Chilean game had the dubious honor of providing the first World Cup riot. There was also a great deal of poor refereeing, the worst example being the Brazilian referee's stoppage of the Argentinian–French game six minutes before the end, just when the French looked as if they were going to score. (He did, however, permit the remaining six minutes to be played after a linesman had verified that there was indeed six minutes left in the game.) As for the goodwill generated by the tournament, it would be many years before the Argentinians and the Uruguayans would consent to play each other again.

1930 WORLD CUP RESULTS:

Pool 1

France 4, Mexico 1		Final Standings			
Argentina 1, France 0		Won	Lost	Tied	Points
Chile 3, Mexico 0	Argentina	3	0	0	6
Chile 1, France 0	Chile	2	1	0	4
Argentina 6, Mexico 3	France	1	2	0	2
Argentina 3, Chile 1	Mexico	0	3	0	0

Pool 2

| Yugoslavia 2, Brazil 1 | | Final Standings | | | |
Yugoslavia 4, Bolivia 0		Won	Lost	Tied	Points
Brazil 4, Bolivia 0	Yugoslavia	2	0	0	4
	Brazil	1	1	0	2
	Bolivia	0	2	0	0

Pool 3

| Rumania 3, Peru 1 | | Final Standings | | | |
Uruguay 1, Peru 0		Won	Lost	Tied	Points
Uruguay 4, Rumania 0	Uruguay	2	0	0	4
	Rumania	1	1	0	2
	Peru	0	2	0	0

Pool 4

| United States 3, Belgium 0 | | Final Standings | | | |
United States 3, Paraguay 0		Won	Lost	Tied	Points
Paraguay 1, Belgium 0	United States	2	0	0	4
	Paraguay	1	1	0	2
	Belgium	0	2	0	0

Semifinals

Argentina 6, United States 1
Uruguay 6, Yugoslavia 1

Final

Uruguay 4, Argentina 2

Chauvinism dominated the 1934 World Cup when the Italian Federation, with Mussolini's prompting, staged the tournament with typical fascist fanfare and military precision. This was the opportunity for Mussolini to prove beyond a shadow of a doubt that Italia was Numero Uno notwithstanding England's absence and Uruguay's refusal to participate.

To ensure success, the Italians were sent away six weeks before the tournament to the country, where in semi-incarceration they trained under the expert guidance of Vittorio Pozzo, one of the game's most extraordinary coaches. Pozzo was to remain Italy's coach and manager until England inflicted that crushing 4–0 defeat in 1948. His team included Monti, the very same center half who had played for Argentina against the United States in the 1930 semifinal, and two other Argentinians, Guaita and Orsi. FIFA permitted the bending of the eligibility rules after the Italians had insisted that all three players had Italian ancestry. Thirty years would pass before FIFA would insist that national teams be made up only of citizens and players who had not previously appeared for any other country.

Pozzo ensured the correct mental attitude of his team, Italians and Argentinian-Italians alike, by promising enormous cash bonuses if they won the cup. He trained them hard, and by the time the tournament opened they were in prime condition. In Monti, Meazza and Ferrari, Pozzo had three of the top players in the world, and the only group of men he feared was the Wunderteam of Austria. If Italy had three world-class individuals, the Austrians could counter with four of their own: Seszta, Smistik, Zischek and the most skillful player of his day, Mathias Sindelar, a forward of great elegance and agility.

With Mussolini and American Ambassador Long watching, the U.S. team played a preliminary match against Mexico. Bill Gonsalves, George Moorhouse and Tom Florie were the only members of the 1930 World Cup team present as the Americans beat Mexico 4–2. The Mexicans were technically superior but smaller than the more vigorous Americans and were unable to contain the fast-moving Yankee attack. Florie scored for the United States shortly after the beginning of the first half. Mexico equalized within minutes, and Florie scored again just before halftime. In the second half, Mexican defender Camarena was ejected for fouling left-winger MacLean. Shortly afterward, Nilsen scored, making it 3–1. Meija replied for Mexico once again, but the United States continued to attack, and a few minutes before the final whistle, Florie got his hat trick with yet another goal.

The United States team that day was as follows:

Julian (Chicago)

Czerkiewiz (Pawtucket)   Moorhouse (New York)
Lehman (St. Louis)   Gonsalves (St. Louis)   Pietras (Philadelphia)
        Nilsen (St. Louis)   Donelli (Curry, Pennsylvania)
Gallagher (Cleveland)   Florie (Pawtucket)   MacLean (St. Louis)

A crowd of 30,000, including Mussolini, was on hand when the United States took on Italy in the opening game of the first round. The Italians were in an explosive mood, having just escaped the spartan conditions of their training camp, and they tore into the Americans, ripping their defense apart in a 7–1 massacre. It was 3–0 at halftime and would have been more but for the outstanding performance of goalie Julius Julian of Chicago. Buff Donelli made it 3–1 in the second half, but the Italians continued to score almost at will, and the match ended with a score of 7–1. Schiavio completed a hat trick, Orsi scored 2 goals and Meazza and Ferrari scored 1 apiece. The expression on Mussolini's face was one of great satisfaction.

In the second round, Italy faced Spain and its world-famous goalkeeper, Ricardo Zamora, who at 33 was still capable of performing miracles between the posts. Although Spain was thoroughly outplayed, Zemora kept his goal intact except for one shot by Ferrari, and the game ended in a 1–1 tie after overtime was played. Without the injured Zamora, Spain lost the replay 0–1.

The Austrians, meanwhile, won two closely contested games against France and Hungary to reach the semifinal. They were unfortunate to meet Italy on a day when the heavy rain had left the field muddy and slippery, the worst possible kind of field for a team that relied on delicate, precise ball control. Yet it was a close game, won by a solitary goal by the Italian-Argentinian Guaita.

The Czechoslovakians, winners of their semifinal match with the German team, met the Italians in the final. The Czechs, who had beaten England in Prague shortly before the tournament, had played well throughout the '34 series, utilizing to great advantage the Central European style of short passing. It was the Czechs who dominated the first half of the final, with Planicka, the goalie; Cambal, the center half, and two forwards, Nejedly and Puc, all outstanding. In the second half Puc scored, and the Czechs held the lead until eight minutes from the end, when Orsi scored with a splendid swerving shot that fooled Planicka. Overtime was necessary. It was obvious the Italians had benefited from their lengthy training period when they outlasted the Czechs. And so a tired and unlucky Czechoslovakian team conceded a goal and the World Cup when Schiavio hit a hard shot past Planicka in the seventh minute of overtime.

A jubilant Italian team looked on as Mussolini presented the Jules Rimet Trophy to its captain, Combi, but many in Rome's Centenary Stadium felt the best team in the tournament was Czechoslovakia.

1934 WORLD CUP RESULTS:

First Round	Second Round
Italy 7, United States 1	Germany 2, Sweden 1
Czechoslovakia 2, Rumania 1	Austria 2, Hungary 1
Germany 5, Belgium 2	Italy 1, Spain 1 (after overtime)

Austria 3, France 2   Italy 1, Spain 0 (replay)
Spain 3, Brazil 1   Czechoslovakia 3, Switzerland 2
Switzerland 3, Holland 2
Sweden 3, Argentina 2
Hungary 4, Egypt 2

SEMIFINALS

Czechoslovakia 3, Germany 1
Italy 1, Austria 0

THIRD-PLACE GAME

Germany 3, Austria 2

FINAL

Italy 2, Czechoslovakia 1 (after overtime)

There were no Austrian, Spanish or American teams present when FIFA held its third World Cup in France during the tense summer of 1938. Austria—incorporated into Hitler's Third Reich—had temporarily vanished from the map, Spain was in the midst of a tragic civil war and the United States was unable to qualify.

Argentina and Uruguay were also absent, the former upset at not having staged the 1938 tournament and the latter still fuming over the refusal of the European countries to go to the 1930 tournament. England, still at odds with FIFA, stayed out of the tournament as well, despite being offered Austria's vacant berth.

The Italians and Germans were cofavorites to win the Cup. The German team, as strong as it was, had become even more potent by the addition of the better players on the Austrian team—or rather, those individuals of the team who could pass the Aryan test. The Italians were considered even better than they had been in 1934, having been strengthened by the arrival of Andreolo, the Uruguayan center half—another one of the foreign-born "Italians"—and the powerful new scoring sensation, center forward Silvio Piola.

Another possible contender for Italy's title was Brazil. Its secret weapon was Leonidas, the first of the many great black Brazilians. The "Black Diamond," as he was called, was a small man for a center forward, nimble, elusive, a prolific goal scorer and credited with being the first player to use the overhead scissors kick.

The Germans had a new manager for the tournament, Sepp Herberger.

After their shock defeat by Switzerland in the first round, it seemed they would be looking for another. It was bad enough that the Swiss had held the fancied Germans to a 1–1 tie, but to lose 2–4 in the replay against a team that played with only ten men for much of the second half was enough to send any manager packing. Surprisingly, Herberger survived to lead the Germans for the next two decades and to a World Cup title.

The Italians also encountered a shock in the first round, being held to a 1–1 tie by the amateurs of Norway at the end of the regulation ninety minutes. The plucky Norwegians, who had one goal disallowed for offside and hit the crossbar twice with Olivieri, the Italian goalie, beaten, were eliminated in the overtime period by a Piola goal. Against France in the second round, the Italians fared better, thanks largely to the fine form of Piola, who scored two goals in the 3–1 win.

Brazil found the route to the semifinal an uphill battle. Overtime was needed before Poland was overcome by the startling score of 6–5, and a replay before Czechoslovakia was defeated 2–1. Nevertheless, Leonidas was in top form, scoring four goals against Poland and one in each of the Czechoslovakian meetings. He would be the one the Italians would have to neutralize when the two teams met in the semifinal; but much to Italy's amazement and joy, Leonidas, along with the dazzling inside left, Tim, were benched so that both of them, as Pimenta, the confident Brazilian coach, confided, "would be in prime shape for the final." Even without the two star opponents, Italy was hard pressed to beat the Brazilians; the 2–1 victory included a goal scored from the penalty spot.

The other semifinalists were Hungary and Sweden. Hungary strolled through its game against an unknown Dutch East Indies team, winning 6–0, then beat the strong Swiss squad 2–0. The Swedes, receiving a bye in the first round because of Austria's absence, played only one match. They had no trouble in disposing of the Cubans 8–0, but were overwhelmed by the nonstop attack of the Hungarians in the semifinal. Szengeller of Hungary scored a hat trick in Hungary's 5–1 victory.

In the final, the fluid artistry of the Hungarians found its match in the faster and more powerful style of the Italians. Piola and left winger Colaussi each scored two goals in the sweeping Italian offense. It was a well-earned victory for the Italians and their astute coach, Pozzo. This time they achieved victory without the immeasurable advantage of playing in front of their own passionate partisan Italians, as they had done in 1934. The Italians were to remain the official world champions until 1950—World War II causing the twelve-year hiatus. Only England could claim an equal right to the world title, on the strength of a 2–2 tie with the Italians in Milan in 1939 and the postwar 4–0 win in 1948. But when the next World Cup was staged in Brazil, neither Italy nor England would be crowned with the victor's garland.

1938 WORLD CUP RESULTS:

First Round

Switzerland 1, Germany 1
 (after overtime)
Switzerland 4, Germany 2 (replay)
Cuba 3, Rumania 3 (after overtime)
Cuba 2, Rumania 1 (replay)
Hungary 6, Dutch East Indies 0
France 3, Belgium 1
Czechoslovakia 3, Holland 0
Brazil 6, Poland 5 (after overtime)
Italy 2, Norway 1 (after overtime)

Second Round

Sweden 8, Cuba 0
Hungary 2, Switzerland 0
Italy 3, France 1
Brazil 1, Czechoslovakia 1
 (after overtime)
Brazil 2, Czechoslovakia 1 (replay)

Semifinals

Italy 2, Brazil 1
Hungary 5, Sweden 1

Third-place Match

Brazil 4, Sweden 2

Final

Italy 4, Hungary 2

The 1950 World Cup in Brazil was the scene of England's first appearance in the tournament. Back in FIFA since 1946, England arrived in Brazil as cofavorite with the Brazilians and was determined to show the rest of the world that previous World Cups were meaningless as far as determining the true world champions went. The English were willing to concede that without center forward Lawton and center half Franklin the team was not as strong as the 1946–49 scoring machine; but with the world's top two wingers, Matthews and Finney, on the team, as well as the fiery, goal-hungry Mortensen, they felt they had every reason to exude confidence.

The one team causing them concern was the Brazilian, whose reputation for dazzling unorthodox soccer had trickled through the nearly impenetrable barrier of English apathy toward foreign soccer. But it was not Brazil that stopped England in 1950, nor was it the defending champs, Italy (which had yet to recover from the disastrous Superga airplane crash of 1949). No, it was another team that dealt England a crippling blow—a team of part-time professionals from the most unlikely place, the United States. These players, whose names meant nothing to world soccer experts and who outside their own small clubs were unknown even in their own country, treated the English greats with scant deference in their second match of the tournament. They had lost to Spain in a marvelous game by a score of 1–3, after leading 1–0 from a goal by John Souza until nine minutes from the end. This surprisingly strong showing should have prompted the English to take a closer look at the U.S. contingent. If they had, they would have seen that this time, unlike 1930 or '34, the Yanks were nearly all American-born, most of them being products of amateur and semiprofessional neighborhood clubs. There were, of course, a large number from St. Louis, still the miracle city of American soccer, where native-born youngsters learned to play soccer while still in their preteens. Only three members of the team—Joe Maca, Joe Gaetjens and Ed McIlvenny (a former Scottish professional from England's third division side, Wrexham)—were foreign.

On June 28 the two teams met on a rough field at Belo Horizonte before a crowd of 20,000, including a sizable and jovial group of British miners from a nearby British-owned gold mine. England did not play Matthews against the United States—not that it would have made much difference, for Frank Borghi, the American goalie, was playing the game of his life. The English forwards, Finney, Mortensen, Bentley, Mannion and Mullen, saw their best efforts either go over the bar, hit the bar or be blocked by Borghi.

But the game was not, by any means, totally one-sided. The Americans were extremely fit and, much to the surprise of their distinguished opponents, very fast. The speed of the two Souza brothers, Ed and John, from Fall River caused Billy Wright and Alf Ramsey problems all afternoon, and big Joe Gaetjens, the acrobatic center forward, was a constant source of trouble for English center half Laurie Hughes. Gaetjens' name is still recalled more frequently than any other when soccer fans reminisce about the 1950 cup, for it was he who caused shock waves to flash around the world when he headed a hard shot from Walter Bahr past Bert Williams, the English goalie, for the only goal of the game. Some say it was a lucky deflection, others that it was deliberately angled—the type of deflection the great Dixie Dean would have been proud of. Whichever it was, it won Gaetjens and his American teammates a permanent place in soccer's history.

At the end of the game, thousands of spectators rushed onto the field. The American players froze momentarily, wondering if this was a violent mob. But there were smiles on the Brazilian faces, and each American was hugged, kissed and carried off the field in tribute—a fitting end for one of the most remarkable days in recorded sports history.

Unfortunately, after their euphoric triumph the Americans were brought back to earth by Chile as they were thoroughly beaten 5–2. Pariani and John Souza scored goals, but this time the American defense was found wanting. Cremaschi, the Chilean inside right, scored three magnificent goals and was a danger every time he got the ball. So the 1950 World Cup was all over for the Americans, but they went home happy, having enjoyed every moment of it.

The 1950 tournament, unlike the previous ones, was not a single-elimination competition, but rather a four-divisional setup with the winning four teams meeting each other in the final pool—all rather complicated and never again to be used in a World Cup. Sweden, Spain, Uruguay and Brazil were the eventual final four, and by the time the latter two countries met, Brazil needed only a tie to take the cup, whereas Uruguay had to win.

The Brazilians, who had failed to impress in the first few games in Pool 1, played brilliantly in the Final Pool. They defeated Sweden 7–1 and Spain 6–1—Ademir scoring four goals against the Swedes and Jair scoring two against the Spaniards. The ball control, agility and elasticity of the Brazilians, especially the three astonishing forwards, Zizinho, Ademir and Jair, left Europeans speechless. Nothing quite like them had been seen before; it was as if the Brazilians were playing an entirely new game. There was little doubt as to who the 1950 champions would be. Certainly, few outside the small country of Uruguay thought the Uruguayans had a chance. After all, the Uruguayans had nearly lost to Sweden in a lucky 3–2 victory and had scrambled through against Spain with another close call, tying 2–2, then winning the replay 2–1.

In the impressive new Maracaná Stadium—with the customary South American moat around the playing field—over 200,000 fans, mostly Brazilian, waited for the kick-off. The white-shirted Brazilians attacked from the opening whistle, while the determined Uruguayans in their blue shirts retreated into a defensive shell for most of the first half, coming out only for an occasional breakaway. For forty-five minutes, the Uruguayans withstood a terrific pounding; goalkeeper Maspoli seemed to be playing the Brazilians on his own. It was almost inevitable that the clever ball-juggling Brazilians would score, and in the second half when Friaca's hard shot went into the Uruguayan net, most Brazilians considered the game won.

Being a goal behind, however, forced the Uruguayans to change their tactics and go onto the offensive. Much to the dismay of the partisan crowd, the game began to swing away from Brazil as Uruguay, still using an attacking center half, Varela, took control of the midfield. Andrade at left half, nephew of the great Andrade who played in the 1930 World Cup side; Schiaffino, the supreme inside forward of his day, and Varela pressured the Brazilian defense with dangerous passes to Ghiggia and Morán, Uruguay's speedy wingers.

A justly deserved equalizer came twenty minutes into the second half when Schiaffino scored from a pass from Ghiggia. Brazil, instead of fighting harder as expected, seemed to slow up, and when Ghiggia ran in from the wing to score the second goal for Uruguay, the Brazilian defense was left standing. Uruguay maintained the pressure until the end of the game and thoroughly deserved to win its second World Cup.

As for the Brazilians, it was a case of individual riches squandered through a lack of wholehearted teamwork. Perhaps the European critics were right after all with their cynical observation that the Brazilians' temperament would always be a stumbling block to world success.

1950 WORLD CUP RESULTS:

Pool 1

Brazil 4, Mexico 0
Yugoslavia 3, Switzerland 0
Yugoslavia 4, Mexico 1
Brazil 2, Switzerland 2
Brazil 2, Yugoslavia 0
Switzerland 2, Mexico 1

Final Standings	Won	Lost	Tied	Points
Brazil	2	0	1	5
Yugoslavia	2	1	0	4
Switzerland	1	1	1	3
Mexico	0	3	0	0

Pool 2

Spain 3, United States 1
England 2, Chile 0
United States 1, England 0
Spain 2, Chile 0
Spain 1, England 0
Chile 5, United States 2

Final Standings	Won	Lost	Tied	Points
Spain	3	0	0	6
England	1	2	0	2
Chile	1	2	0	2
United States	1	2	0	2

POOL 3

Sweden 3, Italy 2		Final Standings			
Sweden 2, Paraguay 2		**Won**	**Lost**	**Tied**	**Points**
Italy 2, Paraguay 0	Sweden	1	0	1	3
	Italy	1	1	0	2
	Paraguay	0	1	1	1

POOL 4

Uruguay 8, Bolivia 0		Final Standings			
		Won	**Lost**	**Tied**	**Points**
	Uruguay	1	0	0	2
	Bolivia	0	1	0	0

FINAL POOL

Uruguay 2, Spain 2		Final Standings			
Brazil 7, Sweden 1		**Won**	**Lost**	**Tied**	**Points**
Uruguay 3, Sweden 2	Uruguay	2	0	1	5
Brazil 6, Spain 1	Brazil	2	1	0	4
Sweden 3, Spain 1	Sweden	1	2	0	2
Uruguay 2, Brazil 1	Spain	0	2	1	1

The Brazilians, talented as ever, came to Switzerland in 1954 eager to demonstrate how much better organized and disciplined they were under new coach Zeze Moreira. They brought with them some exciting new players: two splendid backs with the same surname, Djalma and Nilton Santos; the dynamic ball handler and playmaker Didi, and two marvelous wingers, Julinho and Maurinho. It was essentially a new team, only right half Bauer having played on the 1950 squad.

It was the Hungarians, however, who were the favorites this time. At the peak of their long undefeated run in international soccer, winners of the 1952 Olympics and victors over England by the scores of 6–3 and 7–1 in 1953 and 1954 respectively, the Hungarians were not only the favorites but also considered to be unbeatable.

Uruguay also came to Switzerland with a strong record in the early '50s; moreover, it could boast of never having lost a World Cup match, having won the tournament both times it had entered. Varela, Andrade and Schiaffino were still with the team, and they would be ably supported by two talented new wingers, Abbadie and Borges.

Of the other contestants, Austria, with its strong forward line, was a possible choice to win the cup, but neither England nor Italy was given much of a chance, since both teams were in the rebuilding stage. West Germany, recently readmitted into FIFA, had seen little international competition since 1939 and was considered far too inexperienced. As for the host nation, Switzerland, it was not expected to advance past the quarter-finals, even though it had an inventive *verrou* (bolt) defense (the precursor of *catenaccio*).

The Americans had not qualified this time, having been eliminated by Mexico in the preliminary round. A professionalized-soccer country, Mexico would block the way for the United States in all future World Cup qualifiers except in 1970, when Mexico as host country did not have to enter the preliminary rounds. (Not that the absence of Mexico helped any, since Haiti beat the Americans in the 1970 North and Central American qualifying round anyhow.)

The 1954 tournament was played according to another complicated arrangement in which the teams were divided into four sections. Two teams from each were seeded—that is, not scheduled to meet each other until the quarter-finals. The seeded teams played the two nonseeded teams, and if two teams finished level on points there would be a play-off game to see which team would move on to the quarter-finals, at which time the tournament would switch to single elimination games. Under this confusing system a nonseeded team could lose to a seeded team and still meet the same team in the final, provided it could beat the other seeded team in its group and then win the group play-off game, as indeed was to happen.

When the World Cup opened, all eyes were on Hungary—including those of the television cameras, seen at the World Cup for the first time. Every match the team played was a sellout, and each match offered something extraordinary. In the first, the South Koreans reeled before the Hungarians' fluid attack, losing 9–0. Then it was the West Germans' turn to be destroyed, this time to a score of 8–3, the biggest defeat for Germany since it had first begun to play international games in 1908. But it was a score that flattered the Hungarians, since the Germans fielded seven reserves in an obvious effort to deceive the Hungarians, whom they expected to meet again in a later round of the tournament. The Germans, having already demolished the Turkish team 4–1, knew that even if they lost to the Hungarians they would have no trouble disposing of the Turks again in a play-off game.

In the quarter-finals, high scoring was still the order of the day. Uruguay scored 4 goals against England's 2 in a splendid game with the two sides evenly matched; the vital difference in the result was attributable to Merrick's poor performance in the English goal. Austria and Switzerland shared 12 goals in a memorable game won by Austria 7–5. The Swiss were leading by 3–0 within the first twenty minutes of play. Then the Austrians hit 5 goals in seven minutes, so that by halftime the score was already a turnabout 5–4 in their favor. Wagner, the Austrian inside right, scored a hat trick.

West Germany managed only 2 goals in its 2–0 win over Yugoslavia, but the goals flowed in the fourth quarter-final game between Hungary and Brazil. In what was to become known as the "Battle of Berne," Hungary beat Brazil 4–2. It was less a soccer game than an unarmed-combat exercise as both teams tripped, hacked and punched each other in as violent an exhibition of nonsport as had ever been seen in international soccer. Three of the combatants—Nilton Santos and Humberto Tozzi of Brazil and Josef Bozsik of Hungary—were thrown out of the game by the referee. When the game was over some of the players fought on the field and then later in the dressing rooms, when the Brazilians in a group attacked the Hungarians. As is often the case when a game goes sour the referee was made the scapegoat, and Arthur Ellis, the Englishman who had officiated, was threatened with loss of his life if he ever decided to visit Brazil.

In the semifinal, the Hungarians settled down to play their usual exquisite soccer against an equally attractive Uruguayan eleven. This match, a direct opposite of the "Battle of Berne," was a glorious exhibition of soccer skills and is still considered by many the best World Cup match of all time. Both teams displayed fast and imaginative attacking patterns that left the fans hoarse and happy. The Hungarians dominated the first half but scored only once, on a tremendous shot by Czibor. In the second minute of the second half Hidegkuti headed in the second goal, and it seemed that the Hungarians were through to the final. Fifteen minutes from the end it was still 2–0; then Hohberg, running onto a pass from Schiaffino, scored for the Uruguayans. Suddenly Schiaffino was everywhere, cutting up the Hungarian defense with his deadly passes and his fierce shooting. With less than four minutes of time left, he broke through again and passed to Hohberg, who equalized, thus sending the game into overtime.

As the crowd roared, Hohberg tore through the Hungarian defense, but his hard shot hit the post, with Grosics, the Hungarian goalie, unable to get anywhere near it. This escape and Schiaffino's injury and subsequent ineffectiveness revitalized the Hungarians. Two splendid headers from Sandor Kocsis within five minutes settled the game for Hungary. Unlucky Uruguay had lost its first World Cup match, and Hungary was on its way to its first World Cup title—or at least, that was how it appeared to soccer aficionados.

After this marvelous game it seemed rather anticlimatic for the Hungarians to find themselves facing in the final West Germany, a team they had defeated 8–3 a week earlier. But the Germans were a strong, muscular side, improving in each of their games. Especially impressive was their 6–1 semifinal victory over Austria, a brilliant performance that made it quite clear to the Hungarians that the German team they were now to play was quite different from the one they had crushed earlier. There was no longer any doubt that Sepp Herberger had deliberately disguised the true potential of his side by playing so many reserves in their first meeting. The Hungarians sensed that the final would be a difficult one to win, but not, of course, impossible. One question still nagging the Hungarian manager, Gustav Sebes, however, was what to do about Puskás, who had been injured in the first Germany match and out of the team since. He was not fully fit, but whereas lesser stars would have been passed over, Puskás' authority and prestige were such that Sebes decided to play him. Sebes also dropped Budai, a player who had done so well against Uruguay. These were to prove to be costly errors.

It was raining heavily on the afternoon of the final at Berne. The Hungarians opened with their usual flowing attack and scored twice in the first eight minutes through Puskás and Czibor. It seemed that Sebes had made the right choices. But the Germans were an inspired and an extremely fit team that wet afternoon. Never giving up, they continued to field their wingers, Rahn and Schaefer, and before halftime had tied the score through goals by Morlock and Rahn. Hidegkuti and Kocsis revived the Hungarians in the second half, but goalkeeper Turek had to make one miraculous save after another to keep the score level. The quick-tackling German defense, particularly center half Leibrich and left back Eckel, played magnificently, and even though the Hungarians attacked constantly, they did not display the same decisiveness they had in their game with Uruguay—a game in which Puskás had not played.

But it would be unfair to blame Sebes' decision to play Puskás for what happened next. Bozsik, playing his customary stylish game, ran into trouble on the wet pitch and was robbed of the ball by Schaefer, who in turn quickly found Fritz Walter, the German captain. Walter sent a high ball across the goal mouth. It was headed out by a Hungarian defender, but only as far as the powerful Helmut Rahn, who smashed it straight into the net.

In the final moments of the game Puskás scored, but the referee disallowed the goal for offside. Then Turek leaped across his goal to make one more incredible save from a powerful shot by Czibor. The game was over, and West Germany had won its first World Cup. The Germans had thoroughly deserved their victory, for they had played better than their illustrious opponents, who had been undefeated since May 11, 1950. But when soccer buffs look back, it is the Hungarians, not the Germans, they remember as the greatest team of the 1954 World Cup and of the mid-'50s.

1954 WORLD CUP RESULTS:

GROUP 1

| Yugoslavia 1, France 0
Brazil 5, Mexico 0
France 3, Mexico 2
Brazil 1, Yugoslavia 1 (overtime) | | Final Standings | | | |

		Won	Lost	Tied	Points
Yugoslavia 1, France 0					
Brazil 5, Mexico 0					
France 3, Mexico 2	Brazil	1	0	1	3
Brazil 1, Yugoslavia 1 (overtime)	Yugoslavia	1	0	1	3
	France	1	1	0	2
	Mexico	0	2	0	0

GROUP 2

		Won	Lost	Tied	Points
Hungary 9, Korea 0		Final Standings			
West Germany 4, Turkey 1					
Hungary 8, West Germany 3	Hungary	2	0	0	4
Turkey 7, Korea 0	West Germany	1	1	0	2
	Turkey	1	1	0	2
	Korea	0	2	0	0

Group 2 Play-off: West Germany 7, Turkey 2

GROUP 3

		Won	Lost	Tied	Points
Austria 1, Scotland 0		Final Standings			
Uruguay 2, Czechoslovakia 0					
Austria 5, Czechoslovakia 0	Uruguay	2	0	0	4
Uruguay 7, Scotland 0	Austria	2	0	0	4
	Czechoslovakia	0	2	0	0
	Scotland	0	2	0	0

GROUP 4

		Won	Lost	Tied	Points
England 4, Belgium 4 (overtime)		Final Standings			
England 2, Switzerland 0					
Switzerland 2, Italy 1	England	1	0	1	3
Italy 4, Belgium 1	Italy	1	1	0	2
	Switzerland	1	1	0	2
	Belgium	0	1	1	1

Group 4 Play-off: Switzerland 4, Italy 1

QUARTER-FINALS

West Germany 2, Yugoslavia 0   Austria 7, Switzerland 5
Hungary 4, Brazil 2   Uruguay 4, England 2

SEMIFINALS

West Germany 6, Austria 1   Hungary 4, Uruguay 2 (overtime)

THIRD-PLACE GAME

Austria 3, Uruguay 1

FINAL

West Germany 3, Hungary 2

If the 1954 World Cup had been a goal feast, with 140 goals in all, then the 1958 tournament would run it a close second with 126 goals. The restraining "safety first" tactics of the 1960s had not yet been applied to the game, and the soccer displayed at the 1958 World Cup was generally bright, attacking soccer.

Brazil brought to Sweden not only a team bristling with astonishingly talented forwards but also a new tactical formation, the 4–2–4. The 4–2–4 formation enabled the Brazilians to tighten up their defense, thereby permitting the two midfielders, Didi and Zito, to move up to help the four forwards. And what marvelous forwards the four Brazilians were. Garrincha, the little bowlegged wizard on the right wing, was the star of the tournament; Vavá was a strong, hard-shooting striker; Pelé, a shy 17-year-old newcomer, would play an important role in the later games and Zagalo was a clever, hardworking winger.

Hungary, having lost so many of its finest players during the Hungarian uprising of 1956, came to Sweden with only four aging survivors of the legendary '54 squad: Grosics, Bozsik, Hidegkuti annd Budai.

Another diluted team was England's. Although it had enjoyed a most successful run of victories over Brazil, West Germany and Spain since the last World Cup, its chances for success seemed dim as a result of the Manchester United plane crash a few months before the World Cup. Not even the most optimistic British fan really thought there was a chance of replacing the late Duncan Edwards, Roger Byrne and Tommy Taylor with comparable talent. England did have its brilliant winger Tom Finny; a top inside forward in the person of Johnny Haynes and its splendid center half, Billy Wright, but the rest of the team were not of world-class status.

The West Germans arrived as current champions, but few thought them likely to retain their title, as they had been plagued by the loss of many of their 1954 players through either retirement or loss of form. Fritz Walter, the 1954 captain, was still with the team, but at 37 seemed a little long in the tooth for World Cup play. And yet it would have been a mistake to dismiss the Germans prematurely, since there had been an injection of young blood into the team—strong, aggressive players like Uwe Seeler at center forward and Horst Szymaniak at left half. (Szymaniak finished off his splendid career with the old Chicago Spurs in 1967, a pale shadow of his former self after a leg injury.)

The hosts, the Swedes, had an undistinguished team—or at least, so it appeared before the tournament began. But they did have the shrewd Englishman George Raynor back as coach, the very same Raynor who had coached Sweden when it won the 1948 Olympics and third place in the 1950 World Cup. And of course, they were playing on home territory, always an advantage in World Cup play.

Three countries were appearing in the final sixteen for the first time: the U.S.S.R., Wales and Northern Ireland. None was considered formidable, although Wales could field some fine talent, including John Charles, probably the best center forward of his time, who had been spending the latter part of his career scoring goals in the defensive milieu of Italian soccer. The Irish too had a world-class individual in Danny Blanchflower, a highly creative halfback and captain of Tottenham Hotspur, the team that was to win the "double" in England in 1960–61. When CBS televised NASL soccer in the late 1960s, it was the eloquent Blanchflower who provided the color.

In the opening game Brazil failed to impress the fans in the new Ullevi Stadium in Göteborg as it easily defeated Austria 3–0. The young Pelé did not play, nor was he to play against England, when the Brazilians were lucky to get away with a 0–0 tie in a game that could have gone either way. The critics began to reassess Brazil's chances. Had the Brazilians once again promised more than they could deliver? In each previous World Cup the team had failed to harness its individual brilliance. There was an inconsistency in its team effort, due more than anything else to the fiery Brazilian temperament. But this time the Brazilians were well prepared for temperamental displays: they had brought along a team psychologist.

Perhaps this precaution—extraordinary for this period in soccer's history—was worthwhile, for the Brazilians thrust all doubts aside in a superb performance against Russia, which they defeated 2–0. Pelé and

Garrincha, playing in their first World Cup match, were a delight to the spectators and a torment to the baffled Russians. Pelé, controlling fast-incoming balls with every part of his body—one moment his instep, the next his thigh, then his head—was a danger every time he came near the ball. Out on the right wing, Garrincha, moving like a greyhound despite his misshapen legs, streaked down the right flank like the Stanley Matthews of old, only much faster. Garrincha and Pelé both possessed the calm and confidence of seasoned performers. Like many popular players in Brazil, Garrincha had been given a nickname. His meant "Little Bird" in Portuguese; his real name was Manoel Francisco dos Santos. Pelé, whose nickname has no meaning, was born Edson Arantes do Nascimento.

Garrincha and Pelé played in the quarter-final against the stubborn, plucky Welsh team weakened by the absence of John Charles, the team's heart. In a hard-fought game, Pelé's single goal proved decisive. Brazil drew France as its opponent in the semifinal. The French had surprised everyone by scoring 15 goals in their first game. They relied heavily upon Raymond Kopa, the brilliant forward fresh from his triumphs at Real Madrid, and Juste Fontaine, the strong center forward who had scored 8 of the 15 goals.

Vavá scored quickly in the game's opening minutes. Fontaine equalized shortly after, and it was an even game until the French center half Jonquet was injured late in the first half. In the second half Brazil dazzled the weakened French defense and won 5–2, with Pelé—now thoroughly enjoying the World Cup—scoring a hat trick.

Meanwhile, the hosts, Sweden, were also playing before large, enthusiastic crowds—crowds who were getting more than they had dared to hope: an unbeaten home team. Among the Swedes' victims was the reigning World Cup holder, West Germany, which they beat 3–1 in a fascinating, fast-moving game. Wingers Sköglund and Hamrin were the trump cards for Sweden as they ripped the German defense apart at the seams. They, along with many other Swedish players, had left the amateur-soccer milieu of Sweden to play in the high-paying first division of Italy. George Raynor, one of the most knowledgeable coaches in World Cup history, built the team around the Italian exiles, all of whom had been permitted to play for the national team now that at long last professional soccer had begun in Sweden.

Brazil, having waited so long for a World Cup title, played a careful game in the early part of the final. The well-trained Latins refused to allow a goal by the Swedish inside forward Leidholm in the sixth minute to upset their rhythm or concentration, and by halftime they were in a commanding position. The two backs Djalmo and Nilton Santos nullified the twin threat of Sköglund and Hamrin; Didi and Zito, dominating the midfield, pushed the ball around with uncanny accuracy; and up front Pelé's and Garrincha's rapierlike thrusts cut through the Swedish defense with consummate ease. The first half ended with Brazil leading by 2 goals to 1; Vavá had scored twice from glorious passes from Garrincha.

In the second half, the Brazilians opened with their full arsenal of dazzling combinations, shots and headers and scored 3 more goals, including 1 by Pelé that is still talked about today. He brought down a high ball with his thigh, flipped it over his head, turned and volleyed it into the net, all in one continuous movement.

The Brazilians were swarming around the Swedish goal when the game ended amid much rejoicing and embracing. Pelé, overwhelmed by it all and in tears, was comforted by the father figure of Didi before he joined his teammates in running a lap of honor. The Brazilians, holding aloft the Brazilian and then the Swedish flag as they ran, were world champions, and highly popular ones at that, as the cheering and applause of the fans clearly indicated. Even the King of Sweden was caught up in the festive mood and willingly posed for a photograph with the smiling Brazilians while the rest of the stadium roared its approval.

1958 WORLD CUP RESULTS:

GROUP 1

West Germany 3, Argentina 1
Northern Ireland 1, Czechoslovakia 0
West Germany 2, Northern Ireland 2
West Germany 2, Czechoslovakia 2
Argentina 3, Northern Ireland 1
Czechoslovakia 6, Argentina 1

Group 1 Play-off: Northern Ireland 2, Czechoslovakia 1

Final Standings

	Won	Lost	Tied	Points
West Germany	1	0	2	4
Czechoslovakia	1	1	1	3
Northern Ireland	1	1	1	3
Argentina	1	2	0	2

GROUP 2

France 7, Paraguay 3
Yugoslavia 1, Scotland 1
Yugoslavia 3, France 2
Paraguay 3, Scotland 2
France 2, Scotland 1
Yugoslavia 3, Paraguay 3

Final Standings

	Won	Lost	Tied	Points
France	2	1	0	4
Yugoslavia	1	0	2	4
Paraguay	1	1	1	3
Scotland	0	2	1	1

GROUP 3

		Final Standings			
Sweden 3, Mexico 0			**Won**	**Lost**	**Tied**	**Points**

Sweden 3, Mexico 0
Hungary 1, Wales 1
Wales 1, Mexico 1
Sweden 2, Hungary 1
Sweden 0, Wales 0
Hungary 4, Mexico 0

Final Standings

	Won	Lost	Tied	Points
Sweden	2	0	1	5
Hungary	1	1	1	3
Wales	0	0	3	3
Mexico	0	2	1	1

Group 3 Play-off: Wales 2, Hungary 1

GROUP 4

England 2, Russia 2
Brazil 3, Austria 0
England 0, Brazil 0
Russia 2, Austria 0
Brazil 2, Russia 0
England 2, Austria 2

Final Standings

	Won	Lost	Tied	Points
Brazil	2	0	1	5
England	0	0	3	3
Russia	1	1	1	3
Austria	0	2	1	1

Group 4 Play-off: Russia 1, England 0

QUARTER-FINALS

France 4, Northern Ireland 0
Sweden 2, Russia 0
West Germany 1, Yugoslavia 0
Brazil 1, Wales 0

SEMIFINALS

Brazil 5, France 2
Sweden 3, West Germany 1

THIRD-PLACE GAME

France 6, West Germany 3

FINAL

Brazil 5, Sweden 2

When the 16 hopefuls arrived in Chile for the 1962 World Cup, Brazil stood out as the odds-on favorite to regain the cup. Didi, now 34, was back, as were Garrincha, Nilton Santos, Zagalo, Vavá and Pelé, now the world's most prolific goal-scoring machine. Much to everyone's disappointment, Pelé was injured in the second game and out of action for the rest of the tournament.

Without the "Black Pearl," Brazil was unable to dominate the tournament as it had in 1958; and for that matter, few teams enhanced their reputations in a World Cup that was sadly ultradefensive. The strategies employed by most teams were designed to stifle individual artistry, for there was no shortage of great players in Chile. The Italians had Gianni Rivera and Omar Sivori, two gifted inside forwards; England had Bobby Charlton and Bobby Moore, the two giants of English soccer in the 1960s; Hungary could call upon the elegant Florian Albert, worthy of comparison with any of the Magyars of the mid-'50s, and in the Spanish team were two of the most famous players ever, Argentinian-born Alfredo di Stéfano, who because of injury never did play in Chile, and Ferenc Puskás, the former Hungarian major (both now Spaniards as far as FIFA was concerned). But the moments of greatness were few and far between.

Violence, however, was all too visible. In the Chile–Italy game two Italians were sent off the field, and another Italian player, Maschio, had his nose broken by a terrific left hook thrown by Sánchez, the Chilean winger, which probably everyone viewing the game, both at the stadium and on television, saw, excluding the referee. The Russia–Yugoslavia match was little better, and the Yugoslavia–Uruguay was a horrendous affair with numerous brutal fouls.

One redeeming feature of the tournament was the remarkable performance of the unfancied Czechs. Strong in midfield, with Masopust and Pluskal outstanding, the Czechs beat Spain and then held Brazil to a 0–0 tie in the first of their group matches. They did lose to Mexico, but by then had already qualified for the quarter-finals. There they met the strong, skillfull Hungarians, who had disposed of Argentina and England in winning their group. The Hungarians had played entertaining, sophisticated soccer that bespoke a Hungarian revival to match that of the Puskás era.

The Czechs, although on the defensive for most of the game, managed to get the sole goal of the match and eliminate the unlucky Hungarians from further participation in the tournament. The Czechs were fortunate in the semifinal as well. Their Yugoslavian opponents missed many opportunities to score, whereas the Czechs took the few offered to win 3–1. Surprisingly, then, they reached the final, where they met the overwhelming favorites, the Brazilians, who had ambled through the tournament, never having really been tested—England and Chile having been dispatched 3–1 and 4–2 in the quarter- and semifinals respectively.

Brazil did have a fright when Garrincha, in fine form and playing the best soccer of his career, got himself ejected from the semifinal and was not expected to be permitted to play in the final. The FIFA officials, however, simply cautioned him; either they did not want to deny the fans another opportunity to see the star of the tournament or else they felt compelled to bow before the pressure being exerted by such high sources as the President of Brazil himself, who had sent a telegram requesting leniency. As it happened, Garrincha did not have a good game in the final. Novak, the Czech left back, stuck to him like a leech, and Garrincha, frustrated, faded out of sight as the game progressed.

The Czechs, playing very well, scored the first goal through Masopust, the towering midfield player. Brazil equalized two minutes later when Amarildo, a newcomer to the team, beat Schroiff in the Czechs' goal. But for the rest of the first half, the Czechs continued to surprise the Brazilians. At one time the Czechs' midfield and defense were so impenetrable the Brazilians were resorting to long shots outside of the penalty area.

At halftime the score was 1–1 with the Czechs still the better team, and even though Zito scored a goal for Brazil in the 69th minute, the Central Europeans continued to dictate the game. The tide of the game changed dramatically, however, in the 78th minute when Schroiff, who up to the final had been magnificent throughout the tournament, dropped a high ball that came across the goal mouth with the glaring sun behind it. Gleefully Vavá hit the gift ball into the back of the net. At that point the Brazilians took over the game, and when the final whistle blew Brazilians, both men and women, invaded the field, dancing, singing and crying as they carried off all the victorious players.

1962 WORLD CUP RESULTS:

GROUP 1

Uruguay 2, Colombia 1
Russia 2, Yugoslavia 0
Yugoslavia 3, Uruguay 1
Russia 4, Colombia 4
Russia 2, Uruguay 1
Yugoslavia 5, Colombia 0

Final Standings

	Won	Lost	Tied	Points
Russia	2	0	1	5
Yugoslavia	2	1	0	4
Uruguay	1	2	0	2
Colombia	0	2	1	1

GROUP 2

Chile 3, Switzerland 1
West Germany 0, Italy 0
Chile 2, Italy 0
West Germany 2, Switzerland 1
West Germany 2, Chile 0
Italy 3, Switzerland 0

Final Standings

	Won	Lost	Tied	Points
Germany	2	0	1	5
Chile	2	1	0	4
Italy	1	1	1	3
Switzerland	0	3	0	0

GROUP 3

Brazil 2, Mexico 0					
Czechoslovakia 1, Spain 0					
Brazil 0, Czechoslovakia 0					
Spain 1, Mexico 0					
Brazil 2, Spain 1					
Mexico 3, Czechoslovakia 1					

Final Standings

	Won	Lost	Tied	Points
Brazil	2	0	1	5
Czechoslovakia	1	1	1	3
Mexico	1	2	0	2
Spain	1	2	0	2

GROUP 4

Argentina 1, Bulgaria 0
Hungary 2, England 1
England 3, Argentina 1
Hungary 6, Bulgaria 1
Argentina 0, Hungary 0
England 0, Bulgaria 0

Final Standings

	Won	Lost	Tied	Points
Hungary	2	0	1	5
England	1	1	1	3
Argentina	1	1	1	3
Bulgaria	0	2	1	1

QUARTER-FINALS

Yugoslavia 1, West Germany 0
Chile 2, Russia 1
Brazil 3, England 1
Czechoslovakia 1, Hungary 0

SEMIFINALS

Brazil 4, Chile 2
Czechoslovakia 3, Yugoslavia 1

THIRD-PLACE GAME

Chile 1, Yugoslavia 0

FINAL

Brazil 3, Czechoslovakia 1

If the 1950 World Cup is still remembered by many as the series in which England was beaten by the United States, then the 1966 cup must be equally galling to Italians, for it was then that their star-studded Italian team, including such highly paid greats as Rivera, Mazzola and Bulgarelli, was beaten by eleven amateurs from North Korea, a country few Italians even knew played soccer. Before a wildly enthusiastic crowd of British well-wishers and stunned Italian fans, the small men from Korea scored the only goal of the game when Pak Doo Ik hit the ball past Albertosi, the Italian goalkeeper. When the Italians returned to Italy immediately after the game, they took a devious route to avoid the ugly crowd massing at Rome Airport. They landed at Genoa instead, only to be met by an equally unhappy mob who pelted them with overripe tomatoes.

The North Koreans also shocked the Portuguese in the quarter-finals, leading by the incredible score of 3-0 before Eusebio put on a display of high-powered shooting, scoring four goals as he led Portugal to its 5-3 win.

Another unexpected development had occurred before the 1966 World Cup—the theft, of all things of the World Cup itself. A few months before the tournament was due to open, the cup—the Jules Rimet Trophy—was put on exhibition in London's Central Hall; and despite the presence of six security guards assigned to protect it, the cup was stolen—or "nicked," as the London underworld would say. Nothing like this had ever happened in World Cup history, and although the cup had been insured for over $80,000 (it had cost only $6,000 when made in 1930), FIFA and the Football Association were both stunned. Many officials felt the trophy should never have been displayed in the first place, since in the past its whereabouts was usually a well-guarded secret. The theft was keenly felt by Dr. Barasi of the Italian Football Federation, who in World War II had buried it to prevent the occupying German army from taking it along with other booty stolen from Italy.

Fortunately, a man named Corbett and his dog Pickles went for a walk in a London suburb, where Pickles, with some fortuitous digging, unearthed the buried trophy. Thanks to Pickles, there would be no need for another cup to be made until the Brazilians won the Jules Rimet Trophy outright in 1970.

The Brazilians, hoping to win their third World Cup in 1966, brought to England an aging team, particularly in defense, where Djalma Santos, Bellini and Orlando had now entered the veteran stage. Pelé was still the most potent single force in soccer, but Didí was no longer around to push through those crackling passes, and Garrincha, recovered from a car crash, was but a shadow of the man of 1962. The Brazilians were to discover as the tournament got under way that the defensive tactics employed would be even more inhibiting than those in the 1962 cup; and even more depressing, they would encounter brutal tackling from both the Bulgarians and the Portuguese that would cripple Pelé, forcing him to drop out of the tournament.

England, the hosts; West Germany and Argentina were the favorites. England was managed by Alf Ramsay, a member of the English team that had lost to the United States in 1950, who was certain his team would win and said so publicly. His confidence was based upon a strong and rugged defense—a defense that included a terrierlike man, Nobby Stiles, only 5 feet 5½ inches and 145 pounds but a devastating tackler, who as the tournament progressed would be castigated by opponents for his allegedly dirty play.

Ramsay introduced a new variant of 4–3–3, one that did not use wingers; this tactical system did nothing to arrest the spread of defensive soccer, but proved effective for his team. England won its three games in Group 1 without conceding a goal, but it was uninspiring soccer, and it was only the nationalistic fervor of the home crowd that enabled England to leave the field at the end of each game to cheers.

In the quarter-final, the English found the going rough against an Argentinian team that seemed bent upon committing every kind of foul ever seen in soccer as well as some never seen before. These tactics backfired when the Argentinian center half and captain, Antonio Rattín, was ejected from the game, forcing the South Americans to play with ten men for the last fifty minutes. In the 77th minute, Geoff Hurst, later with the Seattle Sounders, headed the only goal of the game, to put England into the semifinal.

In the semifinal, England at last played splendidly, in a marvelous match against the Portuguese. Both sides concentrated on pure soccer, with none of the rough tackling and shirt pulling so prevalent in the tournament. England's Bobby Charlton and Geoff Hurst played extremely well, as did Nobby Stiles, who marked the Portuguese star forward, Eusebio, so closely throughout the match that the "Black Panther" was hardly noticed. England won the game by a score of 2 goals to 1, but it could have been by a much larger margin if all the scoring chances had been taken, particularly in the first half. Charlton scored 2 for the victors and Eusebio, considered Pelé's only rival as the world's finest striker, the sole Portuguese goal from the penalty spot.

England's opponent in the final was the West German team, a strong, fast side under its new manager Helmut Schoen, the successor to Sepp Herberger. Schoen, destined to become the most successful national manager of postwar soccer, was fortunate to take over the German team just as Franz Beckenbauer, the 21-year-old halfback and probably the best player of his time, was starting his international career. Together this shrewd manager and even shrewder player would be the most potent combination in world soccer for the next twelve years.

The Germans opened their World Cup play in devastating fashion, running all over the Swiss in a one-sided 5–0 victory. Beckenbauer—a right half in those days—scored 2 goals. Siggi Held, a potent young striker, got 1 and the splendid inside forward, Helmut Haller, the other 2.

A disappointing 0–0 tie with Argentina and a drab 2–1 win over Spain were both anticlimactic after Germany's fine showing against Switzerland. Even less impressive was the 4–0 win over Uruguay, as Germany gained ascendancy only after two Uruguayans were ejected—leaving only nine players to face stars of the caliber of Beckenbauer, Held, Haller and Seeler, all of whom scored.

The semifinal against Russia was yet another inferior game, very defensive and in no way a true picture of the talent resting in the German team. The Germans beat the Russians 2–1 with great difficulty, despite the Russians' having one player injured early in the game and another ejected. On the strength of this performance, an entertaining final between the Germans and the English seemed unlikely.

Surprisingly, the game, viewed by 100,000 fans at Wembley Stadium and 400 million via satellite TV, was superb. At once exciting, fast and open in style, it was an exceedingly pleasant contrast to the negative soccer displayed in most of the 1966 matches.

England was a goal down within thirteen minutes as Ramon Wilson, usually the safest of backs, headed a high incoming ball straight down to the feet of Haller, who had no difficulty in hitting it hard into the back of the net. Within six minutes the score was 1–1. Bobby Moore, the English captain, had taken a free kick quickly, before the German defense had organized itself, and sent a long ball down into the German penalty area, where an unguarded Geoff Hurst met the ball with his head, sending it screeching past goalie Tilkowski.

In the second half, England began to gain the upper hand, dictating the flow of the game through its strong midfield and the hard running of the young redheaded Alan Ball on the right wing. Peters scored for England to make it 2–1, and then Charlton missed a golden opportunity to add another goal. The English continued to attack throughout the second half, and with less than a minute to go the game seemed to be theirs. Then the Germans were awarded a free kick near the English goal. Emmerich, the German winger, took the kick, a hard shot right into the middle of the human wall of English defenders. It rebounded out, and Weber managed to get his foot to it, sending it into the net. There was but fifteen seconds left to play in regulation time.

The English lasted the grueling thirty minutes of overtime play far better than their opponents, and 2 goals by Geoff Hurst, who became the first man ever to score a hat trick in a World Cup Final, gave England its first World Cup. Although England was a worthy winner, there was some doubt whether it would have fared so well if Helmut Schoen had not played Beckenbauer in a purely defensive role—guarding Bobby Charlton. His shadowing of Charlton made it all the easier for the English to take over in the midfield, but Beckenbauer and Schoen's moment of triumph in a World Cup would come.

1966 WORLD CUP RESULTS:

GROUP 1

		Final Standings		
England 0, Uruguay 0		Won	Lost	Tied	Points

England 0, Uruguay 0
France 1, Mexico 1
Uruguay 2, France 1
England 2, Mexico 0
Uruguay 0, Mexico 0
England 2, France 0

	Won	Lost	Tied	Points
England	2	0	1	5
Uruguay	1	0	2	4
Mexico	0	1	2	2
France	0	2	1	1

GROUP 2

West Germany 5, Switzerland 0
Argentina 2, Spain 1
Spain 2, Switzerland 1
Argentina 0, West Germany 0
Argentina 2, Switzerland 0
West Germany 2, Spain 1

	Won	Lost	Tied	Points
West Germany	2	0	1	5
Argentina	2	0	1	5
Spain	1	2	0	2
Switzerland	0	3	0	0

GROUP 3

Brazil 2, Bulgaria 0
Portugal 3, Hungary 1
Hungary 3, Brazil 1
Portugal 3, Bulgaria 0
Portugal 3, Brazil 1
Hungary 3, Bulgaria 1

	Won	Lost	Tied	Points
Portugal	3	0	0	6
Hungary	2	1	0	4
Brazil	1	2	0	2
Bulgaria	0	3	0	0

GROUP 4

Russia 3, North Korea 0
Italy 2, Chile 0
Chile 1, North Korea 1
Russia 1, Italy 0
North Korea 1, Italy 0
Russia 2, Chile 1

	Won	Lost	Tied	Points
Russia	3	0	0	6
North Korea	1	1	1	3
Italy	1	2	0	2
Chile	0	2	1	1

QUARTER-FINALS

England 1, Argentina 0
Portugal 5, North Korea 3

West Germany 4, Uruguay 0
Russia 2, Hungary 1

Semifinals

England 2, Portugal 1
West Germany 2, Russia 1

Third-place Game

Portugal 2, Russia 1

Final

England 4, West Germany 2 (overtime)

The 1970 World Cup was held thousands of feet above sea level in Mexico, with most games scheduled to start at high noon to accommodate European television networks. These were obviously not the best conditions in which to play a stamina-sapping game like soccer, and most European teams expected their players to suffer dire consequences; but surprisingly, the quality of soccer was high, and except for those games which necessitated overtime, the players held up remarkably well. Three of the games were as good as one could ever want to see.

The first, a Group 3 match between Brazil and England, was an entertaining open game. England, up against a rejuvenated Brazilian side full of transcendent skills, was most unfortunate to lose 1–0, having missed two easy chances in the second half when Felix, the Brazilian goalkeeper, left his goal uncovered. At the other end, Gordon Banks, the world's top goalie, made one of the greatest saves in soccer's history when he dived backward and upward to knock a marvelous Pelé header over the bar.

The second superb match was the quarter-final between England and West Germany. England, playing a 4–4–2 formation with only two forwards—Hurst and Francis Lee, a small but lethal striker—was leading by a comfortable 2–0 score with less than twenty minutes of play left. The midfield, consisting of Mullery, Ball, Peters and Charlton, was in control, and it seemed that the game was all wrapped up. Beckenbauer had again been detailed to shadow Bobby Charlton, making it easier for the strong English defense to handle Ewe Seeler and the new German sensation, striker Gerd Müller.

The English were already wondering who their semifinal opponents would be when Schoen brought on a substitute, Grabowski, a speedy winger. At once the Germans became the aggressors, and with Grabowski causing left back Cooper all sorts of trouble with his speed and tight ball control, the English defense began to weaken. Beckenbauer ran through the middle of the English defense to score with a curling shot that went under the falling body of the English goalie, Peter Bonetti. Immediately after this setback, Ramsay, in what must be considered one of the biggest mistakes in modern soccer, took out Charlton, who at the time was having one of his best games in years. (In addition, Ramsay substituted a defensive player for atacking halfback Peters.) England's decision to switch to a defensive style did not stop Seeler from equalizing with a header to send the game into overtime. The Germans continued to attack in the extra period of play and won the game when the brawny striker Gerd Müller crashed in an unstoppable shot to put the World Champions out of the cup.

What made the game even more intriguing was the fact that Gordon Banks, far and away the best goalkeeper in the world, did not play, having come down with gastroenteritis—a virulent manifestation of what tourists know as "Montezuma's revenge." His replacement, Bonetti, who was later to play for the St. Louis Stars in the NASL, made two costly errors that enabled Beckenbauer and Seeler to score the first 2 German goals. Even today soccer fans still debate whether England would have lost that game if Banks had played.

The third masterpiece of the tournament was the semifinal between Germany and the Italians (or more specifically, the thirty minutes of overtime). After scoring an early goal, the Italians typically went into a defensive shell and held the lead until the last minute, when the Germans equalized. The exhilarating thirty minutes of overtime bore no resemblance to the stark, unimaginative defensive play of the previous ninety minutes as both teams threw everything into attack and for the first time in many years the world was allowed to see what brilliant attacking artists the Italians could be once released from their defensive chains. Forwards Boninsegna, Riva and Rivera, moving the ball incisively from man to man, all found the back of the net; even the uncompromising back Burnich raced up to score. The Germans could counter with only 3 goals, through Müller twice and Schnellinger once. Consequently, Germany joined England as spectators for the final game.

Meanwhile, the 1970 Brazilian team was reviving memories of its '58 squad with a joyous brand of attacking soccer in each of its matches. Pelé, enjoying this World Cup, was in brilliant form and combining well with Tostão, Gerson, Rivelino and Jairzinho as they swept through all opposition with ease, the one exception being the close game with England.

Rivelino, a masterly midfielder with a tremendous shot; Pelé and the superstriker of the 1970 cup, Jairzinho, scored all the goals in Brazil's victories over Czechoslovakia, Rumania and England.

Tostão scored twice and Rivelino and Jairzinho once each in the quarter-final win over the talented Peruvian team, and in the semifinal against Uruguay, Clodoaldo, Rivelino and Jairzinho all scored in an easy 3–1 victory.

After the Italians' sensational overtime performance against the Germans, it did not seem possible that they would revert to their old defensive strategy, but that's exactly what they did when they faced the favored Brazilians in the final. An early goal by Pelé should have impelled the Italians to add more players to the forward line in order to help the two strikers, Boninsegna and Riva; and if they had, perhaps the game would not have been so one-sided. Even when Boninsegna, taking advantage of a Brazilian defensive slip, scored the equalizer the Italians remained cautious.

In the second half the Brazilians hammered at their opponents' goal, and it was inevitable that eventually they would score. Pelé, Tostão, Gerson and Rivelino were outstanding in a memorable exhibition of open, attacking soccer that left the Italians nonplused and broken. Gerson put the Brazilians ahead with a tremendous shot. Then Pelé, who was everywhere, set up two goals, one for Jairzinho and another for Carlos Alberto. The Brazilians, who had made it all look so easy, won the World Cup for the third time and thereby gained permanent possession of the small but precious Jules Rimet Trophy.

1970 WORLD CUP RESULTS:

GROUP 1

Mexico 0, Russia 0
Belgium 3, El Salvador 0
Russia 4, Belgium 1
Mexico 4, El Salvador 0
Russia 2, El Salvador 0
Mexico 1, Belgium 0

	Final Standings			
	Won	Lost	Tied	Points
Russia	2	0	1	5
Mexico	2	0	1	5
Belgium	1	2	0	2
El Salvador	0	3	0	0

GROUP 2

Uruguay 2, Israel 0
Italy 1, Sweden 0
Uruguay 0, Italy 0
Israel 1, Sweden 1
Sweden 1, Uruguay 0
Israel 0, Italy 0

	Final Standings			
	Won	Lost	Tied	Points
Italy	1	0	2	4
Uruguay	1	1	1	3
Sweden	1	1	1	3
Israel	0	1	2	2

GROUP 3

| England 1, Rumania 0 | | Final Standings | | | |
Brazil 4, Czechoslovakia 1		Won	Lost	Tied	Points
Rumania 2, Czechoslovakia 1	Brazil	3	0	0	6
Brazil 1, England 0	England	2	1	0	4
Brazil 3, Rumania 2	Rumania	1	2	0	2
England 1, Czechoslovakia 0	Czechoslovakia	0	3	0	0

GROUP 4

| Peru 3, Bulgaria 2 | | Final Standings | | | |
West Germany 2, Morocco 1		Won	Lost	Tied	Points
Peru 3, Morocco 0	West Germany	3	0	0	6
West Germany 5, Bulgaria 2	Peru	2	1	0	4
West Germany 3, Peru 1	Bulgaria	0	2	1	1
Bulgaria 1, Morocco 1	Morocco	0	2	1	1

QUARTER-FINALS

Uruguay 1, Russia 0 (overtime)
Italy 4, Mexico 1
Brazil 4, Peru 2
West Germany 3, England 2 (overtime)

SEMIFINALS

Italy 4, West Germany 3 (overtime)
Brazil 3, Uruguay 1

THIRD-PLACE GAME

West Germany 1, Uruguay 0

FINAL

Brazil 4, Italy 1

There was some classical soccer in the 1974 World Cup, held in West Germany, and most of it was displayed by three teams: Holland, West Germany and Poland.

Led by the superstar of European soccer, Johan Cruyff, the Dutch were in exquisite form during the finals—particularly in the second stage of the tournament, when they beat the Argentinians, East Germans and Brazilians without conceding one goal. The team had a galaxy of stars. In addition to Cruyff, there were Johan Neeskens, probably the best player in the tournament; Wim Van Hanegem; Ruud Kroll; Johnny Reb and Rob Rensenbrink—all world-class players.

The Dutch tactical style was based upon a system called "total football" (or "total soccer," as we call it) in which there is a constant interchanging of positions, with everyone attacking or defending in a rotating wheel. It was an exciting revelation. But despite their artistry, technical ability and confidence, the Dutchmen did not win the cup.

It was the well-organized and strong West Germans who took the title— deservedly, if not for their individual brilliance then for their strongly coordinated teamwork.

A team that might well have beaten both West Germany and Holland was Poland. Winner of the 1972 Olympics, Poland, with a nearly identical team roster, eliminated England in the preliminary round, then in the early games of the tournament impressed everyone with its sparkling attacking play. Midfielder and captain Deyna was the inspiration of this fine team, with Garocha, Lato and Szarmach all splendid in attack. The Poles swept past Argentina, Italy, Sweden and Yugoslavia before losing to West Germany 0–1 on a waterlogged field in a game that should never have been permitted. The conditions made a mockery of this important game, and it will always be a matter of conjecture just what would have happened if Poland had faced the Germans on a decent field.

The format for the 1974 World Cup differed from previous years in that there were no quarter- or semifinals. Instead, the top two teams from each of the four groups were distributed into two more groups, the winner of each moving into the final. By beating Poland in the last match of Group B, West Germany went through to the final. In Group A, the decisive game was the Holland–Brazil match, which the Dutch won against a disappointing Brazilian team—a team lacking the brilliance of the 1970 World Cup winners. (Pelé, Gerson, Tostão and Clodoaldo were sorely missed.)

The 1974 West German squad, basically the same team that had won the European Nations Cup in 1972, was a group of highly skilled players, four of whom were world-class: Beckenbauer, now playing as an attacking sweeper—something quite new in modern soccer; Paul Breitner, one of the best backs ever developed in Germany; Uli Hoeness, the young scheming midfielder, and Gerd Müller. The Germans began the tournament as clear favorites, but were later displaced by the Dutch. If it had not been for the breathtaking style of the latter, the Germans would probably have gone down in history as great World Cup champions. Everyone paled in comparison with the Dutch, who, with their devil-may-care attitude, scintillating soccer and individual brilliance, were often as not thought the better team, even after losing the final to the West Germans.

From the kickoff it was clear that the Germans were going to try to eliminate Cruyff from the final by having Bertie Vogts, their right back, shadow him. Their plan worked, for Cruyff had a quiet afternoon. Nevertheless, he stunned the Germans in the opening seconds of play by running through into a good scoring position before being knocked down by Hoeness. The referee awarded a penalty, and Neeskens hit the ball hard for the first goal of the game. After this the Dutch made a strategic mistake: they spent the next twenty minutes playing defensively as if the game were already won.

Two German goals finally roused the Dutch. The first was scored from the penalty spot by Breitner after Hölzenbein was fouled. The second was scored in typical fashion by Müller. He met a cross from the right wing that fell to the right of him. Surrounded by Dutch defenders, he was still able to get to the ball, control it and kick it past the Dutch goalie, Jongbloed.

Switching back into high gear, the determined Dutch embarked on a nonstop bombardment of the German goal. For most of the second half the spectators in Munich witnessed an unusual sight: the Germans concentrating on defense. Maier, in the German goal, made save after save as wave after wave of orange-shirted Dutchmen came at him. For once the total soccer of the Dutch failed, and the Germans held out to capture their second World Cup.

1974 WORLD CUP RESULTS:

GROUP 1

West Germany 1, Chile 0
East Germany 2, Australia 0
West Germany 3, Australia 0
East Germany 1, Chile 1
East Germany 1, West Germany 0
Chile 0, Australia 0

Final Standings

	Won	Lost	Tied	Points
East Germany	2	0	1	5
West Germany	2	1	0	4
Chile	0	1	2	2
Australia	0	2	1	1

GROUP 2

Brazil 0, Yugoslavia 0
Scotland 2, Zaïre 0
Brazil 0, Scotland 0
Yugoslavia 9, Zaïre 0
Scotland 1, Yugoslavia 1
Brazil 3, Zaïre 0

Final Standings

	Won	Lost	Tied	Points
Yugoslavia	1	0	2	4
Brazil	1	0	2	4
Scotland	1	0	2	4
Zaïre	0	3	0	0

GROUP 3

Netherlands 2, Uruguay 0
Sweden 0, Bulgaria 0
Netherland 0, Sweden 0
Bulgaria 1, Uruguay 1
Netherlands 4, Bulgaria 1
Sweden 3, Uruguay 0

Final Standings

	Won	Lost	Tied	Points
Netherlands	2	0	1	5
Sweden	1	0	2	4
Bulgaria	0	1	2	2
Uruguay	0	2	1	1

GROUP 4

Italy 3, Haiti 1
Poland 3, Argentina 2
Argentina 1, Italy 1
Poland 7, Haiti 0
Argentina 4, Haiti 1
Poland 2, Italy 1

Final Standings

	Won	Lost	Tied	Points
Poland	3	0	0	6
Argentina	1	1	1	3
Italy	1	1	1	3
Haiti	0	3	0	0

GROUP A

Brazil 1, East Germany 0
Netherlands 4, Argentina 0
Netherlands 2, East Germany 0
Brazil 2, Argentina 1
Netherlands 2, Brazil 0
Argentina 1, East Germany 1

Final Standings

	Won	Lost	Tied	Points
Netherlands	3	0	0	6
Brazil	2	1	0	4
East Germany	0	2	1	1
Argentina	0	2	1	1

GROUP B

Poland 1, Sweden 0
West Germany 2, Yugoslavia 1
Poland 2, Yugoslavia 1
West Germany 4, Sweden 2
Sweden 2, Yugoslavia 1
West Germany 1, Poland 0

Final Standings

	Won	Lost	Tied	Points
West Germany	3	0	0	6
Poland	2	1	0	4
Sweden	1	2	0	2
Yugosalvia	0	3	0	0

THIRD-PLACE GAME

Poland 1, Brazil 0

FINAL

West Germany 2, Netherlands 1

In 1978 the World Cup is scheduled for Argentina, a debatable choice considering the state of militancy permeating that country's political climate. The military government, however, has guaranteed to FIFA that the cup will be an efficiently run tournament, and one can only hope so, since it will be the most open cup in years, with no one team clearly favored to win, although home advantage should give the talented Argentinians their first real hope of appearing in a World Cup final since 1930. Brazil, West Germany, Holland and Italy are other possible final contenders. As for the United States, knocked out of the preliminary qualification round by Canada a week before Christmas in 1976, there is always the World Cup of 1982, to be held in Spain, or the 1986 cup, scheduled for Colombia.

Chapter Five

The North American Soccer League

"This is a soccer ball."

The opening statement of Dick Walsh at the 1966
press conference announcing his appointment as
commissioner of the United Soccer Association

I doubt if any announcement in recent sports history caused more wide-spread disbelief than the one that came over the news wires in the spring of 1966 proclaiming that many millionaires wanted to invest in soccer—not in Brazil, England, Italy or any of the other hundred-odd countries that considered soccer their national sport, but right here in the United States. The public's first reaction was that someone devised a brilliant publicity gimmick. After all, why would anyone in possession of all his faculties willingly enter into competition with baseball or American football? What did Americans know about soccer, anyway? Here was a minor sport largely ignored by the press, radio and television except for the occasional satirical account of some foreign soccer riot. It was so completely a minor sport in the United States as far as the average American sports fan was concerned that it was quite often confused with rugby, lacrosse and even curling.

Overseas, foreign sports fans were also surprised, particularly when it was further announced that the game would be played in the summer, that hot, humid season when other countries dropped their love affairs with soccer to embrace cricket, baseball and other less energetic games. Even more inconceivable for foreigners was the news that the proposed American pro league and its eager investors would start with nothing more tangible than a legal document called a franchise. Now, everyone knew that the traditional pattern followed in forming a nationwide league was the tested British formula: First the amateurs paved the way with a few decades of missionary work—developing a national association, clubs, leagues, traditions and most importantly, a large body of dedicated soccer fans. Then, when the game was a national sport and paying its own way, the national association would permit the amateur clubs to reward their players financially. The metamorphosis from amateur to professional could take anywhere from a mere twenty years, as in Austria, to over sixty-five years, as in Holland.

Twenty years? Sixty-five years? The American investors must have chuckled to themselves. That was definitely not the way things were done in the United States of America. With all the marvels of the electronic age available, the persuasive methods of merchandising, marketing and advertising at their fingertips and unlimited capital in reserve, they planned to show the world how to build a professional soccer league overnight. And just to prove the tycoons were serious about the enterprise, they had already formed three different rival groups.

All three groups soon discovered that before they could organize their leagues they needed the approval of the national body, so some of the country's foremost sporting entrepreneurs headed for the small drab office of the United States Soccer Football Association at 320 Fifth Avenue in New York. The lucky group winning USSFA's approval would be recognized and accepted by all member countries of FIFA. As a part of FIFA's worldwide umbrella, the USSFA-approved league would be able to buy players from any of FIFA's 140 countries, participate in overseas tours and invite foreign teams to the United States.

The USSFA (now the United States Soccer Federation) was in actuality nothing more than a central office whose job was coordinating the various amateur and semipro leagues throughout the country with the twenty-seven state associations affiliated at that time. In addition, the five national high school and college groups were tied to it rather tenuously as associate members, but for practical purposes the schools went their own way, even so far as to have their own distinct set of rules. The USSFA, however, did have a good record of running the National Challenge Cup, Amateur Cup and Junior Cup and had been vitally involved in much of the pioneering work that had kept soccer alive since the organization's inception in 1913. Nevertheless, it seemed a most unlikely body to control and counsel the volatile business luminaries now demanding an instant decision.

It had but one full-time employee, Secretary Joe Barraskill, who at the grand age of 76 was a one-man walking encyclopedia of American soccer. The president of the association was Frank Woods, a police sergeant from San Rafael, California. Neither official was quite in the same league as Bill Bartholomay, owner of the Atlanta Braves; Lamar Hunt, owner of the Kansas City Chiefs; Jack Kent Cooke, owner of the Los Angeles Lakers, and Judge Roy Hofheinz, owner of the Houston Astros. But if Barraskill and Woods were out of their element, it did not take them and their fellow USSFA associates long to accustom themselves to their new importance.

That the transition from rags to riches would be easy was evident when the USSFA announced that any pro franchise would cost an initial $25,000 per club, plus a contribution of a further 4 percent of all gate receipts and 10 percent of any television income. With what they considered to be reasonable fees, the USSFA officials were going to ensure that their average annual income of $40,000 would be just a bad memory from that moment on.

The potential investors did not find USSFA's demands reasonable at all; in fact, they wondered why they should give the USSFA anything other than the paltry $25 a year the other so-called professional league was paying. This league, the American Soccer League, the successor to the famous one of the 1920s, was now only a semipro league at best, supported by the ethnic sports fans in the various cities on the East Coast.

One man who had resisted the demands of the USSFA was Bill Cox, a major figure in the early days of American pro soccer. He was the one who whetted the interest of the various sporting tycoons when he formed the International Soccer League in 1960. A summer tournament, the ISL brought many famous teams from Europe and South America to New York. By 1965 the ISL had spread to Chicago and Los Angeles, and it was becoming increasingly obvious both to the USSFA and to the American soccer public that Cox's avowed goal, a nationwide pro league, would soon become a reality as more and more of his business associates grew interested.

One fact of life that Cox and other American investors were to discover about soccer was that national soccer associations throughout the world are generally composed of elderly gentlemen who are steeped in the amateur traditions of the sport and view professionalism with some mistrust. Historically, the USSFA's officials have followed this pattern, so it was no surprise that Cox found his relationship with the American association a stormy one. In 1965 a dispute between the USSFA and Cox over the right to import teams resulted in a termination of the ISL tournament. Cox filed an antitrust suit against the USSFA and then proceeded to try again, this time with a pro league that would not rely, as the ISL had, upon imported teams.

Cox invited a number of prominent baseball and football club owners to a meeting in New York to discuss the idea of a nationwide league, and on May 10, 1966, he and Robert Herman of St. Louis held a press conference to unveil their plans for an 11-club league. Soon after, a group headed by Jack Kent Cooke and another combine headed by Richard Millen, who like Cooke was from Los Angeles, announced that they too could recognize a good investment when they saw one and were going ahead with their own leagues.

Even now, a decade later, one finds it difficult to understand what convinced these successful and shrewd businessmen that they could reap a profit from American soccer; and we must assume that profit was the motivating force behind the investments, rather than any noble altruistic vision of building soccer into a national sport. Perhaps it was the boom in sports franchises of the mid-'60s that spurred them on (when an investment in baseball, football, basketball or ice hockey was like money in the bank), or they may have overreacted to the very real growth of the sport among youth—which compared with the phenomenal boom in the '70s appears minute in retrospect—and to the enthusiastic reception American television viewers gave the 1966 World Cup Final, seen live here for the first time via satellite. Whatever the reason, those willing to put up the money were convinced that soccer was finally going to find its rightful place in the billion-dollar sports industry of America, and whoever received the USSFA's blessing would in fact be getting a license to print money.

Consequently, during the spring of 1966, the three groups headed for the small office of the USSFA. Slightly bewildered and more than a little flattered, the USSFA officials listened politely to the ambitious plans presented by personalties they had hitherto only read about in the society pages. When all the talking was over, the USSFA offered a simple solution: all three groups should amalgamate to form one league.

Each of the delegations in turn informed the USSFA that a merger was out of the question. There were, after all, duplicate franchises in New York, Chicago, Toronto, San Francisco and Los Angeles.

This refusal to compromise left the USSFA in a different position, since FIFA, and especially its president, Sir Stanley Rous, was insisting that the USSFA get the three leagues together quickly. It was clear to FIFA, as it was to the USSFA, that more than one league would kill whatever chance pro soccer had in the United States. To complicate matters, Bill Cox's group was claiming the support of Sir Stanley, while all three groups (although none had yet been recognized by the USSFA) were supposedly putting the finishing touches to lucrative deals with television networks.

The USSFA, faced with making the most momentous decision in its history, formed a committee to look into the sticky question of recognition. This committee was instructed to make its recommendation at the association's annual convention in June 1966, at which time the state associations would have the opportunity to vote on it. A few weeks before the convention, however, Cox's group announced it had gone ahead and formed the North American Professional Soccer League (NAPSL). Obviously piqued at this surprise move, President Woods stated again that no organization could be formed without the sanction of the governing body—the USSFA.

At the convention it was Cox and his associates' turn to be upset, for the USSFA voted to approve the committee's recommendation: an immediate recognition of the Jack Kent Cooke group (known later as the North American Soccer League—the NASL). This should have been the end of the controversy, but to the astonishment and chagrin of the USSFA, Cox's NAPSL and the third group (Millen's National Soccer League) were able to accomplish that which they had theretofore insisted was impossible—a merger. Once merged, the two former competing groups became known as the National Professional Soccer League (NPSL). It declared that it was going ahead with its own plans despite the USSFA's sanctioning of the NASL. Just to prove this was no idle threat, the NPSL added it would be kicking off in the spring of 1967, less than nine months away.

The official league, unwilling to ignore the NPSL challenge, announced it would also begin play in 1967 by bringing over complete teams from overseas to represent the 12 cities in the league. Teams like Cagliari of Italy, Cerro of Uruguay, Bangu of Brazil, Wolverhampton Wanderers of England and others of similar quality would do very nicely until the 12 clubs were able to acquire their own players for the 1968 season.

So the battle lines were drawn—with two leagues eager to tap their enormous financial resources in the struggle to win the loyalties of the soccer fans, both the existing ones and those who would be hastily converted.

Meanwhile, the part-time officials of the USSFA were wondering what to do next now that the association had within its jurisdictional territory an unauthorized league. Up to now the mere threat of exclusion from FIFA's worldwide network had been sufficient to discourage the formation of "private leagues," but the NPSL gave every indication that it had sufficient resources and willpower to confront FIFA, the USSFA, the NASL and any other body that stood in its way.

Despite the USSFA's threat that any player signing for the NPLS would be suspended by FIFA, a steady stream of foreign players began arriving in the United States eager to play for the NPSL. The caliber of the imports, however, was not as high as the soccer fans had hoped or as the NPSL was claiming in its exaggerated press releases; top international stars had no intention of risking suspension for an adventure with a pirate league. But the NPSL continued to plan its 1967 season, seemingly unconcerned that it was outside the official family of world soccer. Indeed, the pirate status even had its compensation: the franchise fees and other payments demanded by the USSFA could be ignored. And anyway, the real key to success was already theirs: a television contract with a national network. CBS had agreed to feature a weekly game in what was described as a "ten-year contract."

There was no network television contract for the official league, now calling itself the United Soccer Association. Discarding the NASL tag for something more distinctive, some clever soul had come up with the patriotic, all-American initials USA. By this time few soccer buffs—other than acronym addicts—could distinguish among the NPSL, NASL, NSL, FIFA, USSFA and now the USA. But even without television the USA, confident it would have better teams than the NPSL, was convinced the 1967 season would be a great success right from the opening whistle.

At first all indications suggested that the USA's bright forecast had been accurate. Before the opening of its first season, each of the 12 USA clubs offered tempting exhibition games featuring some of the best teams in the world. The attendance fluctuated between encouraging and enormous. A total of 33,351 spectators paid to see Real Madrid play West Ham of England at the Houston Astrodome; over 20,000 saw Benfica of Portugal face Manchester United in Los Angeles and 22,000 came to Toronto's Varsity Stadium for the Glasgow Rangers–Sparta of Prague match. League owners congratulated each other for investing in soccer. But once the regular season started, the figures dropped sharply. Respected first-division clubs like Sunderland and Stoke City of England; Hiberians, Aberdeen and Dundee United of Scotland; Bangu of Brazil and Cagliari of Italy drew a season average of less than 8,000 per game.

Over in the NPSL, the 1967 figures were even more uninspiring, averaging out to little more than 4,000 per game. Unlike the established teams guesting for the USA, the NPSL clubs were for the most part not much better than the semiprofessional clubs of ethnic America. Players with different nationalities, styles, experience and abilities had been hastily thrown together and then labeled international greats. Unknown Caribbean and African youngsters, swarthy Mediterranean veterans and overweight and sluggish Europeans and Latin American has-beens all formed part of the NPSL's "foreign legion." And in an effort to be free of discrimination against the natives, a few American college graduates were recruited. The NPSL managers were wise enough, however, to bring over a few names the experienced ethnic fans could recognize (of course, strong memories facilitated the recognition process): one-time leaders of world soccer like Bora Kostič, Milan Cop, Blagoje Vidinič and Dragon Sekularac, all four former Yugoslavian stars; Horst Szymaniak of Germany and Inter-Milan fame; Gerry Fraydl, the Austrian international goalie; Ladislao Kubala, the marvelous Hungarian forward, ostensibly the manager of the Toronto Falcons, but driven by despair to appear as a player before the season's end; the former Real Madrid star Juan Santisteban; Bill Brown, the Scottish international goalie; Salvador Reyes, a much-honored hero of Mexican soccer; Rubén Navarro of Argentina's 1962 World Cup team;

two Dutch internationals, Theo Laseroms and Co Prins; Brazilian center back Zemaria; Dennis Viollet, the former Manchester United forward; Phil Woosnam, a rare sight in British soccer, a star with a university education, and Siciliano, the famous Brazilian striker.

These and other aging personalties were a boon to Danny Blanchflower when he handled the color on the CBS soccer telecasts. The eloquent soccer raconteur needed all the interesting anecdotes he could recall from their varied pasts to enliven the telecasts when, as happened all too frequently, the players floundered in a morass of defensive soccer.

The dual 1967 seasons did have their moments of interest. The NPSL introduced the first change in soccer scoring since the mid-19th century. Instead of the customary 2 points for a win, 1 for a tie and none for a loss, the NPSL awarded 6 points for a win and a bonus point for each goal scored up to a maximum of 3 per team per game. This meant a team winning 3–2 would earn 9 points and the loser 2 points. Another innovation was the electric-age referee unveiled by the NPSL. Equipped with a hidden walkie-talkie, the cooperative ref was notified by the TV producer whenever an imaginary infringement should he whistled so that a commercial could be shown. Aided by some fine acting by NPSL players, this ploy worked until the middle of May, when an embarrassed NPSL and CBS admitted that they tried to tamper with soccer's nonstop action (one of its most appealing qualities) by creating the first official time-outs in the game's long history.

Excitement of a different sort occurred at the USA matches, when teams representing particular foreign cities attracted hyphenated Americans who clung to their ethnic traditions—making the games tests of national honor. The Chicago entry, Cagliari, seemed to incite more passion than any other team. Wherever the team traveled, the local Italian population, replete with Italian flags and banners, turned out in force to cheer for Italia. These "soccer fans" were instrumental in bringing about the termination of two of Cagliari's games before the full ninety minutes, once in New York, the other time in Toronto. On both occasions the referee was attacked by Cagliari supporters unhappy about his decisions.

Another unpleasant scene took place in Detroit, where the Irish players of Glentoran (representing Detroit) and the Brazilians of Bangu (representing Houston) fought in hand-to-hand combat aided by a few willing spectators.

As far as honors were concerned, the 1967 season ended with the Oakland Clippers beating the Baltimore Bays to take the NPSL title; and the Los Angeles Lakers (Wolverhampton Wanderers) won the USA title by edging out the Washington Whips (Aberdeen) 6–5 in an exciting goal-rich finale. This latter game was especially memorable as 4 goals were scored in a 3½-minute period. Even before these results were in, the owners had been busy scanning their financial statements, some of which were $500,000 in the red, trying to analyze what had gone wrong with their investments.

The owners wanted a simple explanation for their failure, and they found one. It was not the brand of soccer offered that had been responsible for the hefty financial losses, they reasoned. Nor was it the hurried planning or the numerous high-salaried administrators and advisers. Neither could it have been the inept recruiting of both players and teams. No, it was all too clear that the fault lay with the unnecessary competition of the two leagues, which had diluted the support of the many soccer fans. Give the country one pro league in 1968 and attendance would zoom.

The basic assumption that pro soccer would eventually succeed still was prevalent as the two leagues met to discuss a merger at the end of 1967. No doubt spurred on by an $18 million antitrust suit filed by the NPSL against the USA, USSFA and FIFA, the merger finally took place, producing the North American Soccer League—the original name adopted by the USA group back in 1966. It comprised 17 teams but did not include Pittsburgh or Philadelphia of the old NPSL, both of which— merger or no—had closed their doors after suffering losses of over $500,000 each.

1967 USA STANDINGS

EASTERN DIVISION

	Won	Lost	Tied	GF	GA	Pts
Washington	5	2	5	19	11	15
Cleveland	5	3	4	19	13	14
Toronto	4	3	5	23	17	13
Detroit	3	3	6	11	18	12
New York	2	4	6	15	17	10
Boston	2	7	3	12	26	7

WESTERN DIVISION

	Won	Lost	Tied	GF	GA	Pts
Los Angeles	5	2	5	21	14	15
San Francisco	5	4	3	25	19	13
Chicago	3	2	7	20	14	13
Houston	4	4	4	19	18	12
Vancouver	3	4	5	20	28	11
Dallas	3	6	3	14	23	9

CHAMPIONSHIP GAME

Los Angeles 6, Washington 5

TOP GOAL SCORERS

	Goals	Assists	Pts
Roberto Boninsegna (Chicago)	10	1	21
Henk Houwaart (San Francisco)	9	2	20
Paulo Borges (Houston)	6	3	15
Peter Dobing (Cleveland)	7	0	14
René Pas (San Francisco)	6	2	14

1967 NPSL STANDINGS

EASTERN DIVISION

	Won	Lost	Tied	GF	GA	Pts
Baltimore	14	9	9	53	47	162
Philadelphia	14	9	9	53	43	157
New York	11	13	8	60	58	143
Atlanta	10	12	9	51	46	135
Pittsburgh	10	14	7	59	74	132

WESTERN DIVISION

	Won	Lost	Tied	GF	GA	Pts
Oakland	19	8	5	64	34	185
St. Louis	14	11	7	54	57	156
Chicago	10	11	11	50	55	142
Toronto	10	17	5	59	70	127
Los Angeles	7	15	10	42	61	114

CHAMPIONSHIP GAMES

Baltimore 1, Oakland 0
Oakland 4, Baltimore 1
(Oakland won on aggregate of 4–2)

TOP GOAL SCORERS

	Goals	Assists	Pts
Yanko Daucik (Toronto)	20	8	48
Willy Roy (Chicago)	17	5	39
Eli Durate (Los Angeles)	15	5	35
Rudi Kolbl (St. Louis)	13	8	34
Manfred Rummel (Pittsburgh)	14	4	32

The 1968 season saw a vast improvement in the quality of soccer offered over the previous NPSL season. The Atlanta Chiefs, under the leadership of their general manager and player-coach, Phil Woosnam, won the championship by beating San Diego 3–0 in the final game of the season. Just how far American pro soccer had come in one year was illustrated when both Atlanta and the Oakland Clippers defeated the visiting English champions, Manchester City. Similarly, the Cleveland Stokers and the New York Generals both beat Pelé and his Santos team. Coaching the Generals in those days was one of England's brightest young soccer figures, Freddie Goodwin, who now runs the successful Minnesota Kicks.

The improved performances on the field, however, failed to increase the number of paying spectators at the box office. The 1968 average attendance was less than 4,500 per club. The only good news was that large crowds had been attracted by the touring teams from abroad. Over 36,000 watched Pelé and Eusebio face each other when Santos met Benfica; and nearly 30,000 turned out to see Santos play the Oakland Clippers in Oakland. Manchester City did well too, averaging 25,000 in each of its games against NASL clubs, proving that even without the magic of a Pelé or a Eusebio a quality team could bring out the American soccer fan.

As in 1967, there were many great names from the past on the American soccer circuit. A rotund Ferenc Puskás was at Vancouver in his first coaching position, and his old teammate at Real Madrid, Enrique Matéos, was trying to recapture some of his past glitter with the Cleveland Stokers. The Brazilian star of the 1958 World Cup, Vavá, was scoring goals for the San Diego Toros, while another veteran of the '58 Cup, Peter McPartland, saw action for the Atlanta Chiefs, along with former Welsh international Vic Crowe. Not all the big names on view were simply enjoying a second wind in the twilight of their careers. One international star still very much in the prime of his career was the Polish international John Kowalik. A year after playing for Poland against England, Kowalik was in Chicago playing for the Chicago Mustangs. The 23-year-old striker was the sensation of the 1968 season, scoring 30 goals in twenty-eight matches.

Another successful performer was Ilija Mitič. A former Yugoslavian first-division player, Mitič scored 18 goals in 1968 and has been one of the most consistent goal scorers in the league's history (he still tops the NASL all-time scoring chart).

The 1968 season concluded with clubs like St. Louis admitting to a $1½ million loss in less than two years. A mass exodus of club owners from soccer ensued as they returned to the sports from which they had come: baseball, football and basketball. But the league did not, as was generally expected, dissolve. Surprisingly, there were still a few club owners who believed in the long-term possibilities—particularly Lamar Hunt and Bill

McNutt of Dallas and Robert Herman and Ted Martin of St. Louis, all of whom were by 1968 confirmed soccer buffs. These four stalwarts of American pro soccer are the only club owners to have fielded the same teams throughout the NASL's history. They, along with the owners in Kansas City, Atlanta and Baltimore, voted to continue the soccer experiment in 1969.

1968 STANDINGS

EASTERN CONFERENCE

ATLANTIC DIVISION

	Won	Lost	Tied	GF	GA	Bonus Pts	Total Pts
Atlanta	18	7	6	50	32	48	174
Washington	15	10	7	63	53	56	167
New York	12	8	12	62	54	36	164
Baltimore	13	16	3	42	43	41	128
Boston	9	17	6	51	69	49	121

LAKES DIVISION

Cleveland	14	7	11	62	44	58	175
Chicago	13	10	9	68	68	59	164
Toronto	13	13	6	55	69	48	144
Detroit	6	21	4	48	65	40	88

WESTERN CONFERENCE

GULF DIVISION

	Won	Lost	Tied	GF	GA	Bonus Pts	Total Pts
Kansas City	16	11	5	61	43	47	158
Houston	14	12	6	58	41	48	150
St. Louis	12	14	6	47	59	40	130
Dallas	2	26	4	28	109	28	52

PACIFIC DIVISION

San Diego	18	8	6	65	38	60	186
Oakland	18	8	6	71	38	59	185
Los Angeles	11	13	8	55	52	49	139
Vancouver	12	15	5	51	60	49	136

PLAY-OFF RESULTS

Eastern Conference Atlanta 1, Cleveland 1. Atlanta 2, Cleveland 1 (sudden death overtime)
Western Conference San Diego 1, Kansas City 1. San Diego 1, Kansas City 0 (overtime)
League Championship Atlanta 0, San Diego 0. Atlanta 3, San Diego 0

TOP GOAL SCORERS

	Goals	Assists	Pts
John Kowalik (Chicago)	30	9	69
Cirilo Fernández (San Diego)	30	7	67
Ilija Mitič (Oakland)	18	12	48
Henry Klein (Vancouver)	20	4	44
Iris DeBrito (Toronto)	21	2	44

The 5 remaining clubs decided to limit their expenditures until a larger paying audience could be attracted to the sport. The groundwork for this growth had already been laid: clinics had been held, personal appearances made and two soccer seasons televised. Generating interest among the country's youth—the one positive accomplishment of American pro soccer in those two years—may have cost the club owners over $20 million, but it would prove money well spent by the mid-1970s. At that time the same youngsters, now soccer-viewing adults, would be a major source of soccer's success at the box office.

But for the 1969 season it was a matter of getting along with as little as possible. Big spending for imported stars was definitely out, and because of this decision to cut down on expenditures, more American players who had sat on the benches in 1967 and 1968 were now actively involved. Of the 18 players on the St. Louis Stars roster, 14 were Americans.

Kaizer Motaung of Atlanta, Pepe Fernández of Kansas City and Ilija Mitič of Dallas were the stars one read about in 1969—if one could find an American daily outside the five NASL cities that mentioned soccer. Kansas City won the championship, defeating the Atlanta Chiefs by one point. Attendances averaged around 3,000 for the shortest and shakiest season the NASL would experience. To further exacerbate the American soccer buff's frustrations, the U.S. World Cup team was eliminated by tiny Haiti.

1969 STANDINGS

	Won	Lost	Tied	GF	GA	Bonus Pts	Total Pts
Kansas City	10	2	4	53	28	38	110
Atlanta	11	2	3	46	20	34	109
Dallas	8	6	2	32	31	28	82
St. Louis	3	11	2	24	47	23	47
Baltimore	2	13	1	27	56	27	42

TOP GOAL SCORERS

	Goals	Assists	Pts
Kaizer Motaung (Atlanta)	16	4	36
George Benitez (Kansas City)	15	5	35
Ilija Mitič (Dallas)	11	4	26
Fons Stoffels (Kansas City)	8	7	23
Manfred Seissler (Kansas City)	8	6	22

Six teams competed in 1970. Baltimore had dropped out, but this was offset by the addition of 2 new franchises, the Washington Darts and the Rochester Lancers, both former members of the American Soccer League. The season was expanded from 16 games to 20, and the league owners exuded confidence, especially after it became known that New York would be entering a team in time for the 1971 season.

Rochester, winner of the Northern Division, and Washington, winner of the Southern Division, met in a two-game play-off, with the former emerging victorious on an aggregate of 4–3. The leading goal scorer was Kirk Apostolidis of Dallas, who scored 16 goals, followed closely by Carlos Metidieri of Rochester with 14. Attendance was up only slightly from 1969, but the performances on the field were vastly superior.

Pelé returned for a tour with his Santos team in 1970. Santos easily defeated the Washington Darts 7–4, with Pelé making 4 out of the 7 Brazilian goals, but found the NASL All-Stars much more difficult to beat. In a close 4–3 battle in Chicago, Pelé had to exert all his considerable skills to help his team win. Several other NASL teams performed well against foreign opposition: St. Louis beat Coventry City of England 2–1; Dallas surprised Monterrey of Mexico 5–2 and then edged Varzim of Portugal 1–0 and both Rochester and Washington also defeated Varzim, 3–2 and 3–1, respectively.

1970 STANDINGS

NORTHERN DIVISION

	Won	Lost	Tied	GF	GA	Bonus Pts	Total Pts
Rochester	9	9	6	41	45	39	111
Kansas City	8	10	6	42	44	34	100
St. Louis	5	17	2	26	71	24	60

SOUTHERN DIVISION

	Won	Lost	Tied	GF	GA	Bonus Pts	Total Pts
Washington	14	6	4	52	29	41	137
Atlanta	11	8	5	53	33	42	123
Dallas	8	12	4	39	39	32	92

PLAY-OFF RESULTS:

Rochester 3, Washington 0. Washington 3, Rochester 1

TOP GOAL SCORERS

	Goals	Assists	Pts
Kirk Apostolidis (Dallas)	16	3	35
Carlos Metidieri (Rochester)	14	7	35
Leroy DeLeon (Washington)	16	1	33
Art Welch (Atlanta)	12	8	32
Manfred Seissler (Kansas City)	11	7	29

In 1971 Dallas won the title as the league expanded to 8 teams with the addition of the New York Cosmos, the Montreal Olympics and the Toronto Metros and the loss of Kansas City. Carlos Metidieri led the goal-scoring chart with 19 goals in 24 games. Second was the "Rookie of the Year," Randy Horton, the huge New York striker, who netted 16.

It was a year of guarded optimism for the NASL. Attendances were still at a minimum, but the league had successfully reorganized itself and the league office, which was about to move back to New York after a two-year stay in Atlanta.

1971 STANDINGS

NORTHERN DIVISION

	Won	Lost	Tied	GF	GA	Bonus Pts	Total Pts
Rochester	13	5	6	48	31	45	141
New York	9	10	5	51	55	48	117
Toronto	5	10	9	32	47	32	89
Montreal	4	15	5	29	58	26	65

SOUTHERN DIVISION

	Won	Lost	Tied	GF	GA	Bonus Pts	Total Pts
Atlanta	12	7	5	35	29	33	120
Dallas	10	6	8	38	24	35	119
Washington	8	6	10	36	34	33	111
St. Louis	6	13	5	37	47	35	86

PLAY-OFF RESULTS:

Semifinals (best-of-three series)
Rochester 2, Dallas 1 (overtime). Dallas 3, Rochester 0. Dallas 2, Rochester 1
    (overtime). Atlanta 1, New York 0 (overtime). Atlanta 2, New York 0
Championship Games (best-of-three series)
Atlanta 2, Dallas 1 (overtime). Dallas 4, Atlanta 1. Dallas 2, Atlanta 0

TOP GOAL SCORERS

	Goals	Assists	Pts
Carlos Metidieri (Rochester)	19	8	46
Randy Horton (New York)	16	5	37
Casey Frankiewicz (St. Louis)	14	5	33
Jorge Siega (New York)	9	9	27
Manfred Seissler (Rochester)	10	7	27

In 1972, for the first time in five years, the composition of the league remained unaltered, with the move of the Washington franchise to Miami
the only change in the lineup. New York, with Randy Horton playing so
well, beat St. Louis 2–1 in the play-offs to take the championship: The
young, unlucky St. Louis Stars—mostly American-bred talent—conceded
a goal from the penalty spot four minutes from the end.

Randy Horton was the number one goal scorer with 9 goals, and Michael
Dillon of Montreal and Paul Child of Atlanta, tied with 8 apiece, were
runners-up.

A most encouraging development was the rise in league attendance to an average of 5,000 per game.

1972 STANDINGS

NORTHERN DIVISION

	Won	Lost	Tied	GF	GA	Bonus Pts	Total Pts
New York	7	3	4	28	16	23	77
Rochester	6	5	3	20	22	19	64
Montreal	4	5	5	19	20	18	57
Toronto	4	6	4	18	22	17	53

SOUTHERN DIVISION

	Won	Lost	Tied	GF	GA	Bonus Pts	Total Pts
St. Louis	7	4	3	20	14	18	69
Dallas	6	5	3	15	12	15	60
Atlanta	5	6	3	19	18	17	56
Miami	3	8	3	17	32	17	44

PLAY-OFF RESULTS:

Semifinals   St. Louis 2, Rochester 0
              New York 1, Dallas 0
Championship Game   New York 2, St. Louis 1

TOP GOAL SCORERS

	Goals	Assists	Pts
Randy Horton (New York)	9	4	22
Michael Dillon (Montreal)	8	2	18
Paul Child (Atlanta)	8	1	17
Warren Archibald (Miami)	6	5	17
Willie Roy (St. Louis)	7	2	16

Now we come to the breakthrough year for the NASL, and I say this not because I was fortunate enough to enjoy a successful first season with Dallas then but because 1973 was the year in which all the efforts of the past six years bore fruit. Attendance had nearly doubled since 1970, investors were inquiring again about franchises and the surge in youth soccer was at last recognized by the press. There was also a new team added: the Philadelphia Atoms.

The Atoms, coached by American-born Al Miller, was a prototype of the kind of team the NASL had been hoping to produce since 1969. It took off like a rocket, capturing the imagination of the soccer fans of Philadelphia and drawing over 21,000 fans to its opener. The Atoms went on to become the first expansion team in the history of the major American professional sports to win a national title in its first season. Miller went to Britain to bring back a group of "loan" players—fine players like Andy Provan, Jim Fryatt, Derek Trevis, Chris Dunleavy and George O'Neil. Joining them in Philadelphia were four of the best prospects ever to emerge from college soccer: Bob Rigby, Bob Smith, Casey Bahr and Barry Barto. This exciting team defeated my Dallas team in the championship game 2–0. Even though we had been favorites and were playing at home, we were well beaten. Our sole consolation was the healthy 18,825 attendance figure.

One interesting innovation in the '73 season was the change in the offside law for all NASL matches (an experiment made possible with FIFA's permission). The new offside rule stated that an attacker could not be offside until within 35 yards of his opponents' goal. An extra line running the width of the field was drawn at each end to mark the new offside zone. Once again overseas critics were quick to find fault with an American "gimmick." But within a short time it was clear that both the "blue line" concept and the controversial goal-bonus points, which forced the NASL teams to become attack-conscious, were the precise innovations needed to attract new spectators.

1973 STANDINGS

EASTERN DIVISION

	Won	Lost	Tied	GF	GA	Bonus Pts	Total Pts
Philadelphia	9	2	8	29	14	26	104
New York	7	5	7	31	23	28	91
Miami	8	5	6	26	21	22	88

NORTHERN DIVISION

	Won	Lost	Tied	GF	GA	Bonus Pts	Total Pts
Toronto	6	4	9	32	18	26	89
Montreal	5	10	4	25	32	22	64
Rochester	4	9	6	17	27	17	59

SOUTHERN DIVISION

	Won	Lost	Tied	GF	GA	Bonus Pts	Total Pts
Dallas	11	4	4	36	25	33	111
St. Louis	7	7	5	27	27	25	82
Atlanta	3	9	7	23	40	23	62

PLAY-OFF RESULTS:

Semifinals   Dallas 1, New York 0
              Philadelphia 3, Toronto 0
Championship Game   Philadelphia 2, Dallas 0

TOP GOAL SCORERS

	Goals	Assists	Pts
Kyle Rote, Jr. (Dallas)	10	10	30
Warren Archibald (Miami)	12	5	29
Andy Provan (Philadelphia)	11	6	28
Gene Geimer (St. Louis)	10	5	25
Ilija Mitič (Dallas)	12	1	25

By 1974 there was no longer any doubt that the league had successfully completed its period of stabilization. Now it was ready to expand nation-wide for the first time since 1968. New franchises were awarded to 8 cities: Los Angeles, San Jose, Seattle, Denver, Baltimore, Boston, Washington and Vancouver. Two teams dropped out—Montreal and Atlanta—leaving a total of 15 NASL clubs to enjoy the continuing rise in attendance during 1974. Over 1,181,000 spectators viewed the regular-season games—an average of 7,825 per game. A newcomer to the league, San Jose, enjoyed a phenomenal season as it drew a remarkable average of 16,576 fans to each of its games, many of which were sold out completely.

Another of the new franchises, the Los Angeles Aztecs, won the NASL title in an exciting play-off against the Miami Toros at the Orange Bowl in Miami. In the nationally televised match, the Aztecs won 4–3. The game stood at 3–3 at the end of ninety minutes and had to be decided in a special kind of overtime using a new tie-breaker procedure.

Believing that the American sports fans preferred a game to be decided one way or the other, the NASL introduced the tie-breaker concept in 1974 to implement a vote to do away with tie games. This concept, the latest of the NASL innovations, provided that whenever a game was tied at the end of the regular ninety minutes the game would be decided by penalty kicks, the teams alternately taking five turns each, and the winner would be the team scoring the most goals—or if a tie remains after five attempts, the team scoring more than the other after an equal number of additional attempts. Many soccer purists detested the manipulation of the rules, but the NASL persevered with it. Noting that over a million fans attended its games, the planners at the NASL concluded with no little joy that it must be doing something right. (In 1975 the tie-breaker penalty kicks would be preceded by fifteen minutes of "sudden death" overtime, divided into two 7½-minute periods. Then if the game was still tied the penalty kicks would be taken.)

Paul Child led the 1974 goal scoring, hitting 15 in only 20 games. Another English professional on loan, Peter Silvester, scored 14 in 17 games and was second on the goal-scoring chart.

1974 STANDINGS

NORTHERN DIVISION

	Won	Lost	Tie-Wins	GF	GA	Bonus Pts	Total Pts
Boston	10	9	1	36	23	31	94
Toronto	9	10	1	30	31	30	87
Rochester	8	10	2	23	30	23	77
New York	4	14	2	28	40	28	58

EASTERN DIVISION

	Won	Lost	Tie-Wins	GF	GA	Bonus Pts	Total Pts
Miami	9	5	6	38	24	35	107
Baltimore	10	8	2	42	46	39	105
Philadelphia	8	11	1	25	25	23	74
Washington	7	12	1	29	36	25	70

CENTRAL DIVISION

	Won	Lost	Tie-Wins	GF	GA	Bonus Pts	Total Pts
Dallas	9	8	3	39	27	37	100
St. Louis	4	15	1	27	42	27	54
Denver	5	15	0	21	42	19	49

WESTERN DIVISION

	Won	Lost	Tie-Wins	GF	GA	Bonus Pts	Total Pts
Los Angeles	11	7	2	41	36	38	110
San Jose	9	8	3	43	38	40	103
Seattle	10	7	3	37	17	32	101
Vancouver	5	11	4	29	30	28	70

(Baltimore and San Jose qualified for quarter-finals as "wild card" teams.)

PLAY-OFF RESULTS:

Quarter-finals   Dallas 3, San Jose 0. Boston 1, Baltimore 0
Semifinals   Los Angeles 2, Boston 0. Miami 3, Dallas 1
Championship Game   Los Angeles 4, Miami 3 (tie breaker)

TOP GOAL SCORERS

	Goals	Assists	Pts
Paul Child (San Jose)	15	6	36
Peter Silvester (Baltimore)	14	3	31
Douglas McMillan (Los Angeles)	10	10	30
John Rowlands (Seattle)	10	8	28
Steven David (Miami)	13	0	26

In 1975 the league had 20 clubs, 3 more than it had had in 1968. Chicago, Hartford, Portland, San Antonio and Tampa Bay were the new additions. Once again one of the newcomers—this time Tampa Bay, under the able direction of Eddie Firmani, the former star of English and Italian soccer—took the title.

Attendances were up everywhere. San Jose broke all records again as it finished the season with an average attendance of 17,927 fans. Seattle drew 16,830 spectators and Portland 12,816. Pelé's $4 million contract with the New York Cosmos brought the league national exposure and new attendance records as well, including a record 35,620 at the Washington Diplomats–New York Cosmos match at the RFK Stadium. Altogether a total of 1,695,651 fans viewed NASL soccer in 1975.

What the fans paid to see in 1975 was a vastly improved brand of soccer. Tampa Bay, Portland, Seattle, Boston, Chicago, New York and the nearly all-American St. Louis team all offered exciting styles, tactics and techniques. Tampa's trio of former first-division stars from England, Stewart Scullion, Clyde Best and Derek Smethurst, scored 35 goals among them as they led Tampa Bay to the league title. The championship game, now called the Soccer Bowl, was an exciting event played before a full house of 17,000 at San Jose's Spartan Stadium.

Tampa beat Portland 2–0 in a marvelous exhibition of skills and tactics. The game was evenly contested, and the score remained 0–0 until Haitian World Cup defender Arsène Auguste scored with a tremendous 30-yard drive. Clyde Best ensured Tampa Bay's victory in the 88th minute when he collected the ball on the halfway line, made a splendid solo run down the left wing, cut in and then hit a glorious swerving ball past goalie Graham Brown into the net.

There were now many classy players performing in the league in addition to the incomparable Pelé. Some of those who saw action in 1975 were Gordon Hill of the Chicago Sting, the dynamic winger destined later to return to England to enjoy great success with Manchester United and the English national team; veteran Peter Bonetti, England's 1970 World Cup goalie against Germany, who played so well for the St. Louis Stars that his club, Chelsea, restored him to first-team duty on his return to England; Mike England and Arfon Griffiths, the two famous Welsh internationals at Seattle; Peter Withe, the fine Portland striker; Wolfgang Sühnholz, the superb ex–Bayern Munich midfielder now with Las Vegas but who was playing for Boston in 1975, and Eusebio and Simões, the two Portuguese stars, both of whom were also performing for Boston in 1975.

The ever-improving quality of the imports continued to make it difficult for American-born players to attain starting positions with the NASL clubs. The one exception was the St. Louis Stars, still eager to employ familiar natives like Gary Rensing, Pat McBride, Al Trost, Denny Vaninger and Mike Seerey, who were, incidentally, quite capable of competing with the foreign talent in the NASL.

1975 STANDINGS

NORTHERN DIVISION

	Won	Lost	GF	GA	Bonus Pts	Total Pts
Boston	13	9	41	29	38	116
Toronto	13	9	39	28	36	114
New York	10	12	39	38	31	91
Rochester	6	16	29	49	28	64
Hartford	6	16	27	51	25	61

EASTERN DIVISION

	Won	Lost	GF	GA	Bonus Pts	Total Pts
Tampa Bay	16	6	46	27	39	135
Miami	14	8	47	30	39	123
Washington	12	10	42	47	40	112
Philadelphia	10	12	33	42	30	90
Baltimore	9	13	34	52	33	87

CENTRAL DIVISION

	Won	Lost	GF	GA	Bonus Pts	Total Pts
St. Louis	13	9	38	34	37	115
Chicago	12	10	39	33	34	106

	Won	Lost	GF	GA	Bonus Pts	Total Pts
Denver	9	13	37	42	31	85
Dallas	9	13	33	38	29	83
San Antonio	6	16	24	46	23	59

WESTERN DIVISION

	Won	Lost	GF	GA	Bonus Pts	Total Pts
Portland	16	6	43	27	42	138
Seattle	15	7	42	28	39	129
Los Angeles	12	10	42	33	35	107
Vancouver	11	11	38	28	33	99
San Jose	8	14	37	48	35	83

PLAY-OFF RESULTS:

Quarter-finals   St. Louis 2, Los Angeles 1 (tie breaker)
                 Miami 2, Boston 1 (overtime)
                 Tampa Bay 1, Toronto 0
                 Portland 2, Seattle 1 (overtime)
Semifinals   Portland 1, St. Louis 0
             Tampa Bay 3, Miami 0
Soccer Bowl   Tampa Bay 2, Portland 0

TOP GOAL SCORERS

	Goals	Assists	Pts
Steven David (Miami)	23	6	52
Gordon Hill (Chicago)	16	7	39
Derek Smethurst (Tampa Bay)	18	3	39
Peter Withe (Portland)	16	6	38
Uri Banhoffer (Los Angeles)	14	9	37

In 1976 league attendance went over the two-million mark for the first time in American soccer history—2,481,000, to be precise: not bad for an organization that five years earlier was unable to draw 400,000. Just how far the NASL had traveled since those days of retrenchment can be gauged by the average gates in such cities as Seattle (23,826), Portland (20,166), San Jose (19,282), New York (18,227), Tampa Bay (16,542) and Dallas (14,059). Overshadowing the phenomenal rise in attendance, however, was the sensational welcome Minneapolis afforded her recently acquired soccer team—formerly of Denver. Over 23,000 fans saw each of the Minnesota Kicks home games; the last three home games drew crowds of 42,000, 41,000 and 49,000.

Of course, not all the teams attracted large crowds in 1976. Boston and Philadelphia were lucky to pass the 3,000 mark for most of their games; the strong, entertaining Chicago Sting, winners of its division, ended its season with an average of only 5,803 and the Toronto Metros-Croatia, the eventual NASL champions, had a dismal average of 6,078 spectators.

But overall it was a thrilling season for pro-soccer fans. Pelé and his New York Cosmos colleagues broke attendance records wherever they traveled. At the Seattle Kingdome all previous U.S. soccer gate records were broken when 58,128 fans arrived to see Pelé and the Cosmos play the Seattle Sounders in a preseason exhibition. Other world-class players who helped to break the existing records included the massive but agile striker from Italy, Giorgio Chinaglia, who reportedly cost the New York Cosmos $500,000 to lure him from the Lazio club of Italy; Rodney Marsh, the artistic English international who added even more punch and finesse to Tampa Bay's marvelous forward line; the most famous European player of the late 1960s, George Best, formerly of Manchester United and now performing with the Los Angeles Aztecs; veteran English star Bobby Moore, now in his 30s but who played so well for San Antonio, and John Kowalik, the Polish striker, who returned to NASL soccer and the Chicago Sting after seven years in the Dutch first division.

This impressive lineup was more or less what the soccer fans had expected way back in 1967 when the pro leagues were formed. Although most of the big names performing for the NASL were forwards or strikers, the improving quality of play was not confined to the forward line. As the NASL took on all the trappings of success, it became more sophisticated. Individual skills and technique were at a new high for the league, and the pace was faster—all of which hastened the departure of the less skillful pros imported earlier. It was clear that the NASL no longer wanted veteran third- and fourth-division European players seeking comfortable havens in the autumn of their careers.

Freddie Goodwin, the new manager of the Minnesota Kicks and former coach of the old New York Generals in 1967–68, was pleasantly surprised by the progress American soccer had made when he arrived from England in 1976. He brought with him a fine array of talent including Geoff Barnett, Ron Webster, Alan Merrick, Frank Spraggon and Alan West. Along with these experienced British players came two young bright prospects, Alan Willey and Ron Futcher. The strength of his imports enabled Goodwin to build a team that not only was able to match the rising standards in the NASL but also was capable of beating any team in the league. The Kicks swept through the play-offs and were favored to win the Soccer Bowl held in Seattle's Kingdome.

In a fascinating game, the Kicks were upset by the Toronto Metros

3–0. Despite attacking most of the first half, the Kicks were down 1–0 at halftime after Eusebio hit a hard curving shot that rocked the crossbar before going into the net. In the second half Toronto scored two more goals through Lukacevic and Ferreira.

The Toronto team (its full name being the Toronto Metros-Croatia, despite the NASL's prohibition against ethnic names) had been a very dull defensive side until midway through the 1976 season when it was able to purchase Eusebio and Wolfgang Sühnholz from the financially pressed Boston side. Immediately it began to move up among the league leaders in rapid fashion and ended the season winning its last eight games, including play-off matches against Rochester, Chicago and Tampa Bay—all in a seven-day period. Eusebio—slower and less agile than in his prime but still a destructive force anywhere in the penalty area—had a fine season, as did the young Canadian back Robert Iarusci; Wolfgang Sühnholz, probably the best midfielder in the league, and Ivair Ferreira, the intelligent Brazilian striker.

In spite of Toronto's final success, it never captured the public's fancy as the New York Cosmos and Tampa Bay Rowdies did. Their scintillating scoring styles produced 123 goals between them, 65 for New York and 58 for Tampa Bay, in only 24 games each. It was this emphasis on attacking soccer which made 1976 a memorable season.

1976 STANDINGS

NORTHERN DIVISION

	Won	Lost	GF	GA	Bonus Pts	Total Pts
Chicago	15	9	52	32	42	132
Toronto	15	9	38	30	33	123
Rochester	13	11	36	32	36	114
Hartford	12	12	37	56	35	107
Boston	7	17	35	64	32	74

EASTERN DIVISION

	Won	Lost	GF	GA	Bonus Pts	Total Pts
Tampa Bay	18	6	58	30	46	154
New York	16	8	65	34	52	148
Washington	14	10	46	38	42	126
Philadelphia	8	16	32	49	32	80
Miami	6	18	29	58	28	63

SOUTHERN DIVISION

	Won	Lost	GF	GA	Bonus Pts	Total Pts
San Jose	14	10	47	30	39	123
Dallas	13	11	44	45	39	117
Los Angeles	12	12	43	44	36	108
San Antonio	12	12	38	32	35	107
San Diego	9	15	29	47	28	82

WESTERN DIVISION

	Won	Lost	GF	GA	Bonus Pts	Total Pts
Minnesota	15	9	54	33	48	138
Seattle	14	10	40	31	39	123
Vancouver	14	10	38	30	36	120
Portland	8	16	23	40	23	71
St. Louis	5	19	28	57	28	58

PLAY-OFF RESULTS:

Qualifying Round	New York 2, Washington 0
	Dallas 2, Los Angeles 0
	Seattle 1, Vancouver 0
	Toronto 2, Rochester 1
Quarter-finals	Tampa Bay 3, New York 1
	San Jose 2, Dallas 0
	Toronto 3, Chicago 2 (overtime)
	Minnesota 3, Seattle 0
Semifinals	Toronto 2, Tampa Bay 0
	Minnesota 3, San Jose 1
Soccer Bowl	Toronto 3, Minnesota 0

TOP GOAL SCORERS

	Goals	Assists	Pts
Giorgio Chinaglia (New York)	19	11	49
Derek Smethurst (Tampa Bay)	20	5	45
Pelé (New York)	13	18	44
Mike Stojanovič (Rochester)	17	7	41
Alan Willey (Portland)	16	7	39

The 1977 season opened with 18 teams competing in the NASL, Philadelphia and Boston having dropped out and three other clubs having moved: Miami to Fort Lauderdale, San Antonio to Hawaii and San Diego to Las Vegas.

Prior to the opening game, Phil Woosnam, the league commissioner, prophesied that it would be the most successful season yet, but even he was staggered by the extent of the success as the season progressed. The first 60,000 crowd in American soccer history flocked to the Giants Stadium to see the Cosmos play Tampa Bay on June 4. The new attendance record lasted for less than ten weeks. On August 14, 77,691 fans saw the Cosmos beat Fort Lauderdale in a play-off game at the Giants Stadium and a week later nearly 74,000 returned to the same stadium to see the Cosmos eliminate Rochester in a semifinal game.

Over 3½ million fans watched the NASL teams in action during 1977 and there was a rise of 31 percent in the average attendance to 13,555 per game. These were thrilling figures for Woosnam and his former assistant, Clive Toye, now the Cosmos' president, both having survived the nightmare days of the 5-team league of 1969 and its 2,000–3,000 gates.

Some other statistics that brought joy to their hearts were the average attendances of many of the clubs: Cosmos (34,142), Minnesota (32,771), Seattle (24,226), Tampa Bay (19,492), San Jose (17,739 despite stadium remodeling), and Dallas (16,551).

The player most responsible for the league's fairy-tale growth and acceptance, Pelé, ended his three-year sojourn in the NASL on a happy note, helping the Cosmos beat Seattle 2–1 to win the NASL title at the Soccer Bowl in Portland. The Pelé-inspired Cosmos had finished second to the surprise team of the season, Fort Lauderdale, in the strong Eastern Division but hit top form during the play-offs, winning all six games. Much of their improved performance was due to the arrival of Franz Beckenbauer, one of the world's greatest players, and Carlos Alberto, the masterly Brazilian international defender.

In the Soccer Bowl Seattle was most unlucky to lose to the Cosmos in a thrilling game. Cosmos' Steve Hunt, a fast skillful winger, scored the first goal, stealing the ball from an unsuspecting Tony Chursky, the Seattle goalkeeper, who had rolled the ball along the ground not realizing Hunt was right behind him. Within minutes Seattle equalized with a goal from former Cosmos player Tommy Ord following some beautiful one-touch interpassing. The winning goal was a deftly executed header by Chinaglia, his ninth play-off goal, a record for the league. Seattle theatened to equalize right up to the final whistle but the Cosmos' defense, with Alberto outstanding, held on so as to earn the Cosmos a 2–1 victory and to enable Pelé to retire knowing he had been a member of a winning side in every league or cup tournament in which he had ever played.

In addition to being delighted to see Pelé walk victoriously off the field at Portland, I was very happy to see my former coach at Dallas, Ron Newman, voted Coach of the Year, a just reward for molding a weak Miami Toros side into the potent Fort Lauderdale Strikers. It was also good to see Steve David recapture his 1975 form and top the goal-scoring chart again. He was helped greatly by the skillful distribution of Georgie Best and Charlie Cooke, both playing as midfielders. It was also gratifying to see Franz Beckenbauer win the Most Valuable Player award for all who saw him in action had to be awed by his transcendent artistry.

The 1977 season saw the NASL devise yet another way to insure that no game ended in a tie. To replace the tie-breaking penalty kick, the league introduced the shootout, a one-on-one duel between the kicker, standing on the 35-yard line, and the goalkeeper, on the goal line. When the referee blew his whistle the kicker had five seconds to shoot at goal and he and the goalie could move anywhere they pleased. Although the shootout caused many a soccer purist to complain it was making a circus out of soccer, the majority of the fans seemed to find it an exciting innovation.

1977 STANDINGS

NORTHERN DIVISION

	Won	Lost	GF	GA	Bonus Pts	Total Pts
Toronto	13	13	42	38	37	115
St. Louis	12	14	33	35	32	104
Rochester	11	15	34	41	33	99
Chicago	10	16	31	43	28	88
Connecticut	7	19	34	65	30	72

EASTERN DIVISION

	Won	Lost	GF	GA	Bonus Pts	Total Pts
Fort Lauderdale	19	7	49	29	47	161
Cosmos	15	11	60	39	50	140
Tampa Bay	14	12	55	45	47	131
Washington	10	16	32	49	32	92

SOUTHERN DIVISION

	Won	Lost	GF	GA	Bonus Pts	Total Pts
Dallas	18	8	56	37	53	161
Los Angeles	15	11	65	54	57	147
San Jose	14	12	37	44	35	119
Hawaii	11	15	45	59	41	106
Las Vegas	11	15	38	44	37	103

WESTERN DIVISION

	Won	Lost	GF	GA	Bonus Pts	Total Pts
Minnesota	16	10	44	36	41	136
Vancouver	14	12	43	46	40	124
Seattle	14	12	43	34	39	123
Portland	10	16	39	42	38	98

PLAY-OFFS RESULTS:

Qualifying Round   Rochester 1, St. Louis 0 (shootout)
                    Cosmos 3, Tampa Bay 0
                    Los Angeles 2, San Jose 1 (overtime)
                    Seattle 2, Vancouver 0
Quarter-finals   Rochester 1, Toronto 0. Rochester 1, Toronto 0
                    Cosmos 8, Fort Lauderdale 3. Cosmos 3, Fort Lauderdale 2
                    (shootout)
                    Seattle 2, Minnesota 1 (overtime). Seattle 1, Minnesota 0
                    Los Angeles 3, Dallas 1. Los Angeles 5, Dallas 1
Semifinals   Cosmos 2, Rochester 1. Cosmos 4, Rochester 1
                    Seattle 3, Los Angeles 1. Seattle 1, Los Angeles 0
Soccer Bowl   Cosmos 2, Seattle 1

TOP GOAL SCORERS

	Goals	Assists	Pts
Steven David (Los Angeles)	26	6	58
Derek Smethurst (Tampa Bay)	19	4	42
George Best (Los Angeles)	11	18	40
Giorgio Chinaglia (New York)	15	8	38
Mike Stojanović (Rochester)	14	5	33

After ten years of pro soccer it seems reasonable to assume that the NASL will continue to grow. The only question worrying many interested observers is will the league get too big? League Commissioner Phil Woosnam, always optimistic, seems set on having a 40-city circuit within the next five years, and many people fear the NASL's administrative capacity is insufficient to handle such a large number of franchises. The question of loan players may well decide just how big the NASL becomes over the next few years. Many English clubs have complained that the loan players do not get back in time for the beginning of the English soccer season (mid-August), and there is a growing reluctance on the clubs' part to release players for an American summer. Of course, a drying-up of the English source would hasten the complete Americanization of the NASL and open the door to the hundreds of collegiate soccer players who graduate every year.

Certainly there is a pressing need for more American-born players. Although the league rules provide that six Americans must be on the seventeen-man roster, few are regular starters. This is a major weakness of the NASL, and a growing voice heard in American soccer is demanding a more equitable integration of native and foreign players. No one would argue that the fans do not appreciate seeing superior foreign talent performing in the NASL, but the exclusion of Americans is obviously restricting the progress of American soccer. A happy medium, I think, would be to allow each team a maximum of five non-Americans. Perhaps at first this rule would affect the standard of play, but I am certain that as more and more Americans enjoy professional experience it would rise again.

In Chapter Thirteen I outline some other suggestions for the NASL as well as American soccer development as a whole, but it seems to me that any basic improvement in the quality of American soccer can come about only when there is greater participation of Americans in the NASL. I, for one, am convinced that the NASL will solve this and other problems and that the next decade will be an exciting one both for the NASL and for all those interested in American soccer.

Chapter Six

The Stars of the First Ten Years

Although compiling lists of names for best-ever teams is a favorite pastime for soccer fans everywhere, publication of such lists has always been risky if not downright foolhardy. Most choices are hotly disputed, and in some countries the individual compiling the list may well find his life threatened if he has omitted any local or national favorite. Thankfully, soccer is still a sport in the United States, not yet having reached that frenzied stage at which it is no longer a game but a matter of life and death, so I feel confident that I can stick my neck out and select players for a best-ever NASL team without fear of retribution—at least, not of the physical type.

Selecting players for this best-ever team will not only be an enjoyable task but also provide me with the perfect opportunity to review some of the many talented individuals who have left a lasting impression on the NASL in its first ten years.

However, before proceeding to review these various players I must solve the problem of how to rate the many world-famous players who arrived in the league late in their careers. To simplify my task, I am going to judge these players not on their overall careers or on the reputations they earned in their prime, but solely on their performances in the NASL. This decision means that the dashing 23-year-old Vavá of the 1958 Brazilian World Cup will not be considered in my evaluations; rather it is the Vavá who played for San Diego in 1968—still dangerous in the penalty area, but at the age of 33 too slow to be an effective striker. Likewise many other famous names of international soccer will now be excluded from my list. Players of high caliber like Salvador Reyes, the Mexican star who played for the 1967 Los Angeles Toros; former Hungarian forward Laddie Kubala of the Toronto Falcons; Horst Szymaniak, the onetime strong man of German and Italian soccer who played for the Chicago Spurs; former Welsh international Vic Crowe of the Baltimore Bays; Dennis Viollet, the former Manchester United and English international (later the coach of the Washington Diplomats), and Phil Woosnam, player-coach for the Atlanta Braves (now the commissioner of the league) were all in their mid to late 30s and mere shadows of their former selves when they first appeared for NASL teams.

On the other hand, some veterans show few signs of aging. Three who come immediately to mind are Mike England, who was 33 in his first NASL season; Pelé, who came here when he was 34, and Franz Beckenbauer, approaching 32 when the Cosmos spent nearly $2 million to bring him to America in 1977. All three have played extremely well here, and even though the NASL standards are rising every year, it will be some time before such skilled and experienced players can be overlooked in the compilation of an NASL best-ever team.

One of the easier spots to fill in my all-star team is that of goalkeeper, for no other goalkeeper in the history of the league was as consistently good throughout an NASL season as was Peter "The Cat" Bonetti in 1975. His sensational displays for St. Louis will never be forgotten by any of us who were fortunate enough to see them. Considered over the hill at the age of 32, he came to St. Louis after being relegated to the reserve team by his English club, Chelsea. He played so well for St. Louis that Chelsea recalled him to its first team upon his return to England.

If Bonetti had not arrived in 1975, I would have had no hesitation in selecting our own Kenny Cooper at Dallas for the goalkeeper spot. Kenny has been one of the top goalies in the NASL ever since his debut in 1970. He is at once acrobatic, courageous and tough as nails. A goalie of many talents, Kenny is just as good at catching high balls as he is at collecting ground balls. But despite his versatility, I have to be objective and stick with Bonetti, for what he meant to the St. Louis team.

Other goalkeepers on my short list of contenders included Eric Martin, the entertaining Scottish goalkeeper of Washington, and the two top American goalies, Arnold Mausser of Denver and Los Angeles' Bob Rigby, both young, strong and worthy of comparison with the best of the foreign goalkeepers in the league.

If we go back a few years, there were others who excelled between the posts. In the early 1970s the Washington Darts' Lincoln Phillips was considered the best in the NASL. Another who deserves recognition, even though he played in only one Detroit Cougars season (1968), is Jim Standen. An exceptional goalie, Standen starred with the artistic West Ham team of England in the mid-'60s before going to Detroit. One more figure from the past, Mirko Stojanovič, the Yugoslavian goalie, would probably be most soccer buffs' first choice on any best-ever NASL list. Tall, strong and agile, Stojanovic was a brilliant goalkeeper with the Oakland Clippers from 1967 to 1969; after the club's demise, with our Dallas team and finally with San Jose. He is the only goalkeeper in the NASL to be selected for three annual all-star teams.

One area of NASL soccer in which American players have been able to compete with the foreign imports is defense. Americans like Bobby Smith of New York, Neil Cohen and Steve Pecher of Dallas, Alex Skotarek of Chicago, Jim Pollihan of Rochester and Werner Roth of New York have all played sufficiently well to be considered alongside such international stars as Franz Beckenbauer and Mike England.

Of the four defensive positions, the two center backs are the easiest to fill. Franz Beckenbauer and Mike England are my choices, rather than their younger and speedier rivals, for three reasons. First, they dominate any game in which they play with their tactical expertise, general skills and verbal control of the play. Secondly, in defense they are powerful tacklers, superb in the air and difficult to elude. And lastly, in attack their passes are crisp and accurate. Franz Beckenbauer in particular distributes passes like few others in the game.

Choosing experienced players for my center backs—Beckenbauer was selected 103 times for West Germany, while Mike England played 42 times for the Welsh national team—means I have to omit Chicago's talented Alex Skotarek and our Steve Pecher, who are, I feel, the two outstanding American center backs in the league. A former midfielder and forward, Alex is a cool and creative defender, always prepared to join in attacking moves. He was an all-star at Michigan State and upon graduation in 1970 did something that was unheard of at the time in American soccer when he traveled to Europe to play for the Maastricht team in Holland. Up until that time the soccer-player traffic between the Continent and America had been very much one-way and in the reverse direction. Alex also played for the Belgian club Diepenbeek before returning to his hometown, Chicago, and the Sting in 1975.

Steve took quite a different route to the NASL, coming straight from Florissant Valley College in St. Louis, where he was a sophomore, to seek a tryout at Dallas. He joined the team as a free agent and made a big impact in his very first season. Unlike Alex, Steve is more of a stopper. A relentless terrierlike defender, Steve storms around the penalty area, pressuring opponents constantly. He already has the quickest feet for a man his size that I have ever seen, and I am confident that with his potential Steve will become the best defender in the league within a few years.

Other center backs I have had to omit from my team include such NASL stalwarts as Keith Eddy of New York, a former English first-division player from Sheffield United; his rugged teammate Werner Roth, captain of the U.S. national team in the mid-'70s, and John Best, who has played such a vital role in the NASL since he first was engaged by the Philadelphia Spartans in 1967. In 1968 he joined the Cleveland Stokers, then in 1969 joined our Dallas team and was the hub of the defense until he moved to Seattle in 1974 as its coach. Selected five times for the NASL all-star team, John is now the manager of the Vancouver Whitecaps.

A teammate of his at both Philadelphia and Cleveland who figures high on my list of center backs is the Argentinian Rubén Navarro. A destructive and at times ruthless tackler, Navarro, like John, was a difficult player to beat. But neither Best's nor Navarro's fine performances in the early NASL days can persuade me to change my selection of Beckenbauer and England. For that matter, neither can the performances of such big stars as Juan Santisteban, the ex–Real Madrid star who played for the Baltimore Bays, and Milan Cop, the Yugoslavian star of the Oakland Clippers.

For my two outside backs I must select players who are not only tenacious tacklers but also extremely fast. I also want these two backs to be skillful in overlapping—that is, taking the ball down the wing ahead of their midfielders and forwards. The aforementioned requisite, speed, enables me to quickly drop from my list those foreign backs who arrived here as older veterans. It also gives men the opportunity to place at least one American-born player on my best-ever team: Bobby Smith of the New York Cosmos, my unequivocal choice for the right-back position. Bobby has tremendous speed, is one of the best tacklers in the league and never stops pressuring those opponents who are unlucky enough to get anywhere near him with the ball at their feet. An automatic selection for the U.S. national team, Bobby is undoubtedly one American who has proven himself equal to any imported star on view in the NASL.

In choosing Bobby I am forced to leave out many deserving players. Regrettably, there is no place for either Robert Iarusci of the Cosmos, considered by many to be the best young back in the NASL today, or Tommy Smith, the muscular but splendidly mobile former English international of Tampa Bay. Neil Cohen of Dallas is another back I wish I could have included. This young American discovery, improving every season, is blessed with an abundance of natural talent, and I expect him to become one of the big stars of the NASL in future years.

As for the other flank, I find it difficult to choose between two exceptional left backs: George Ley of Dallas and Chicago's John Webb. George Ley has never played a poor game for Dallas, and from a sentimental standpoint I should give him the nod, but on the strength of his past performances against us in each of the many Dallas–Chicago matches since 1975, my vote has to go to John Webb. A fourth-division player when he came to Chicago in 1975, Webb blossomed into the best attacking back in the league under the guidance of Coach Bill Foulkes, who was himself a former international back for England. I consider Webb to be the exemplar of what the modern back should be: strong in the tackle, creative with the ball and fast with or without the ball. Webb in full flight dashing up to the opposing team's goal line is one of the most exciting sights to be seen in the NASL.

Two other left backs I considered were Bob McNab of San Antonio (now called Team Hawaii) and Gabbo Gavrič. McNab was, of course, a more famous player than either Webb or Ley. A former English international, he was a member of the 1970 Arsenal team which won the "double" in England. A majestic defender who read the game well, McNab was, however, in his 30s and no longer possessed the speed of his younger days.

Gabbo Gavrič is the ageless wonder of our league. Now nearing 40, he still plays an occasional game for San Jose even though he is the team coach. It was with the Oakland Clippers in 1967 that he made his league debut after playing first-division soccer in Yugoslavia. A complete defender who can play in any position, Gabbo has the knack, common to all top backs, of timing his tackles perfectly, and when he tackles it feels as if a steamroller has run over one's foot. I know that many strikers in the NASL are breathing easier now that Gabbo's coaching responsibilities at San Jose preclude his playing regularly.

There are a host of good American candidates for the three midfield positions; but once again I am forced to pick non-Americans, for how could any reasonable selection omit Rodney Marsh, Wolfgang Sühnholz or Ilija Mitič from any NASL best-ever team?

Marsh, a striker with Manchester City and the English national team, has functioned as a midfielder for Tampa Bay. Undoubtedly the most talented player in the 1976 season, Marsh can do things with the ball that the rest of us can only dream about. But besides his exceptional ball control, he has a terrific shot and has to be considered, along with Pelé, a superstar of American soccer.

Sühnholz, less of a showman than Marsh, is a midfielder of outstanding ability. Strong in defense and creative in attack, Sühnholz distributes the ball with devastating effect, and he can best be described as a midfield general without equal in the league.

Ilija Mitič, now at the end of his long career but still an important figure in the NASL, is included not just because he is the leading overall NASL goal scorer but because no matter how classy the opposition he faced in his nine years in the NASL he has always managed to be a commanding figure on the field. He is a truly great NASL player and I cannot omit him from my team.

Four other worthy midfielders, all foreign internationals, should be mentioned here: Ramón Miflín, the former Peruvian star now with the New York Cosmos; his former New York colleague David Clements of Ireland; Scotsman Charlie Cooke of Los Angeles and Antonio Simões, the Portuguese veteran, now at San Jose. All are exciting players to watch, and many fans will wonder how I could pass over them. Similarly, leaving Luis Marotte out of my team will cause many fans to shake their heads.

Like the previous four, Marotte has marvelous ball control, is imaginative and passes the ball with pinpoint accuracy.

Two St. Louis midfielders, Pat McBride and Al Trost, are also worthy of consideration for any NASL best-ever team. Both are products of the flourishing St. Louis youth-soccer system and have excelled for the U.S. national team. McBride, the only player in the league still with the same club since 1967, is one of the finest players ever produced in the United States. His teammate tall and powerful Al Trost has a phenomenal work rate enabling him to play all over the field—one moment, in defense; the next, moving into a scoring position to take a shot at goal. Scoring goals has been one of Al's special abilities since he moved into American pro soccer with St. Louis in 1970. I can still remember Al's memorable 20-yard shot that rocketed past the Polish goalie in 1973 when the U.S. team beat the Polish national team 1–0, an upset that compares with our victory over England in the 1950 World Cup.

Other midfielders whom I admire include the elegant and highly talented Julie Vee of San Jose, who did so well for Team America in the Bicentennial games of 1976; Alan West, the brilliant star of the Minneapolis Kicks; Bobby Hope, the Scottish international now at Dallas and a most inventive and artistic player; Ronnie Sharp of Fort Lauderdale, probably the hardest-working midfielder in the league, and little 20-year-old Jimmy Kelly of Chicago, an immaculate ball handler and clever dribbler, who had a sensational first season in the NASL in 1976. There are many more fine midfielders in the league, and I wish it were possible to include more than three in my best-ever team.

With four defenders and three midfielders chosen, all I need to do now to complete my 4–3–3 formation is to pick three forwards, two of whom will be strikers and one, a winger. For the wing position I am tempted to pick the irresistible Georgie Best of Los Angeles, who had such a successful debut in the NASL after retiring from English first-division soccer in 1972. If he had played in the NASL while at the height of his career, there would be no question that he would be my choice; but as good as he was in 1976 and 1977, his performance was overshadowed by that of Gordon Hill, the Chicago winger, in 1975. Hill, now firmly established back in England with Manchester United, was a phenomenon during his brief stay in the NASL, captivating fans wherever he went with his magical ball control, ferocious shooting and high-speed dribbling. Even the marvelous Polish national team, fresh from its third-place finish in the 1974 World Cup, was unable to stop Hill from turning its defense inside out in an exhibition game in Chicago in 1975. Twice he was brought down illegally when he was about to score, and few people who witnessed his sparkling display that night will complain about my choice for the wing position on my team.

Jimmy Kelly of Portland, who stands only 5 feet 6, is another winger who has thrilled American soccer fans with his magic along the touchlines. Jimmy's fancy footwork and swift acceleration are feared by every defender in the league. Unlike Best and Hill, he is not a goal-scoring type of winger but more of a schemer who sets up goal-scoring opportunities for others. Kelly's new teammate at Portland, Stewart Scullion, the former first-division player from England, has been one of the most effective NASL forwards in the last few years while with the Tampa Bay Rowdies. Fast and able to make long penetrating runs into the penalty area, Scullion is a delight to watch in action.

Jorge Siega of New York and Warren Archibald are two other fine wingers who have made their mark in NASL history. Archibald was one of the first players to sign up with the league in 1967, playing for the New York Generals until its demise, then moving on to Washington and Miami. Yet another small figure, at 5 feet 7 (smaller players seem to gravitate to the wing position), Archibald has speed, fluid ball control and the ability to score goals. He is, in fact, the second-highest goal scorer in the NASL overall scoring chart. Jorge Siega, on the other hand, has not been a prominent goal scorer in his six-year stay in the NASL, but he certainly could have claimed the title of best winger in the league until his knee injury in the mid-1970s. Tricky and accurate in his passing, the Brazilian-born star was one of the most popular players in the league.

It would be unfair not to mention one other winger: 5-foot-6-inch Ivan Grnja. It was this speedy Yugoslavian who, upon joining Toronto midway through the 1976 season, transformed Toronto's goal-shy forward line into a potent goal-scoring machine. Unfortunately, this highly skilled, old-fashioned winger did not return to the NASL in 1977.

Now we come to the most challenging part of this selection process: whom, out of the many top-class players who have appeared in the NASL, to pick for the two striker positions. A plethora of famous names have played in the NASL since 1975. On the East Coast we have had not only Pelé, but also Chinaglia. The famed Portuguese great Eusebio has played at Boston, Toronto and Las Vegas; Chicago was fortunate to have the former Polish international John Kowalik; in Seattle, England's 1966 World Cup hero, Geoff Hurst, led the attack in 1976, and down in Tampa Bay, Derek Smethurst continues to score goals at an extraordinary rate. In addition we have players—lesser known perhaps, but just as valuable to their teams—of the caliber of Paul Child of San Jose; Peter Silvester of Washington; Clyde Best, so long a fixture at Tampa Bay but now with Portland; Steve David, the stylish striker at Los Angeles, and the powerful but classy Mike Stojanovič of Rochester.

Further complicating my choice are the many fine strikers who played in the earlier years of the NASL. Willy Roy of Chicago, Kansas City and St. Louis, the 1967 Rookie of the Year, did enormously well for an American player. Another Rookie of the Year, this time in 1968, was Kaizer Motaung, an important member of the 1968 Atlanta Chiefs championship team. An unusually clever dribbler, Kaizer went on to score many goals for Denver after the Atlanta club folded in 1973. Then there was Carlos Metidieri, a small, speedy striker who was nearly impossible to stop, once he received the ball, as he darted between much bigger opponents with impunity to score marvelous goals. He was the NASL Most Valuable Player in 1970 and 1971. He was also the leading scorer in both of those years and still remains the third-highest overall scorer in the league.

A fourth veteran, Pepe Fernández, began his NASL career quietly in 1967 with Los Angeles, where he displayed no more than average talent. But in 1968 with the San Diego Toros he became, along with John Kowalik, one of the two most feared strikers in the league. He scored 30 goals in twenty-nine games and proved to be one of the fastest strikers in all of NASL history. When San Diego folded in 1968 he moved on to Kansas City and Seattle.

I could go on citing many more worthy strikers, but it would make little difference to my final selection, since I am convinced my two choices are to be found among five players: Pelé, Chinaglia, Kowalik, Hurst and Smethurst. I do not believe any other strikers in the league—past or present—reach their high standards in skill and technique or can claim more experience.

Looking at the five candidates and remembering the original guideline that I set myself—judging the individual player not on his past reputation but on his performance in the NASL—I might be tempted to pick Chinaglia and Smethurst, for each has scored a high number of goals, as a striker must. Chinaglia topped the 1976 scoring chart in his first season, and Smethurst came in third in 1975, his first NASL season, and second in 1976. Moreover both have played as well in the NASL as they have in the rest of their careers.

Kowalik also has been in top form in most of the years he has seen action in the NASL, but his goal scoring in 1976 and 1977 was not up to past high standards. Geoff Hurst performed most effectively for Seattle. His shooting was still powerful and accurate, and he headed the ball as well as he ever did. However, his acceleration off the mark had been reduced considerably, and speed is important to his style of play.

Pelé presents me with a unique problem. Even "The King" himself would admit that the Pelé of the NASL is at least 25 percent less a player than the Pelé of the 1960s. But 75 percent of the former Pelé, possibly the best player ever to touch a soccer ball, is still the equal of anyone in the NASL. As reluctant as I am to pass over either Chinaglia or Smethurst, and even though I do not think Pelé has been quite as potent a goal scorer as either of them, I cannot see how I can have an NASL best-ever team without him, for he still has the same unmatchable effect on any game in which he plays. His arrival in 1975, which conferred his immense prestige on American soccer, opened the door permanently for other top foreign players to enter American soccer, players who hitherto had been unwilling to risk their careers and reputations in the uncertain world of the NASL. Another compelling reason to include Pelé in my NASL team is the lasting impression he has left on all of us who have played with or against him in the NASL. His gentlemanly conduct, kind disposition, warm friendly smile in the heat of a game and genuine love of people will linger in our memories long after he has left American soccer.

So Pelé is in, and either Chinaglia or Smethurst must be omitted. Which one? Well, since Pelé and Chinaglia combined so well together for New York, I feel I should leave out Smethurst so that my best-ever team will have that extra degree of understanding. Moreover, in my opinion, Chinaglia should have the edge on Smethurst anyway as he is probably one of the best strikers in the world today.

All in all, I believe my team would prove a match for any team. It has a strong defense, a formidable midfield and a forward line that would cause problems for the best of defenses. I for one would love to see the following eleven step out onto the soccer field:

		Bonetti		
Smith	England		Beckenbauer	Webb
	Sühnholz	Marsh		Mitič
	Pelé	Chinaglia	Hill	

I do, of course, feel sad that so many fine players are not included in this best-ever team, and to reduce my guilt feelings I am going to pick a second-choice best-ever team—a team that I believe would prove a worthy opponent to my best-ever NASL all-star team:

		Cooper		
Iarusci	Skotarek		Navarro	Ley
	Simões	Trost		West
	Smethurst	Kowalik	Best	

Pelé scores Brazil's third goal in the 1958 World Cup Final despite an acrobatic leap by Svensson, the Swedish goalkeeper. (WIDE WORLD PHOTOS, INC.)

Joe Gaetjens, the Haitian-born center forward, receives a hero's welcome from admiring Brazilian fans after scoring the goal that defeated England in the 1950 World Cup upset. (WIDE WORLD PHOTOS, INC.)

Watched by a bemused Eintracht Frankfurt defense, Alfredo di Stéfano scores Real Madrid's first goal in the superb 1960 European Cup Final. (WIDE WORLD PHOTOS, INC.)

Seen here playing for Blackpool in the historic 1953 English Cup Final, Stanley Matthews beats Bolton center half Barrass with a flick of his right foot. Known as the "Matthews Final" because of his dazzling display, the 1953 game was won by Blackpool 4–3. (THE PRESS ASSOCIATION)

Tommy Lawton rises high to head past French goalkeeper Darui in England's 3–0 win over France in 1947. (THE PRESS ASSOCIATION)

With a hostile nonchalance usually reserved for passport photos the Harrow School team of 1867 poses reluctantly for a group photo. (RADIO TIMES HULTON PICTURE LIBRARY)

England attacks the Scottish goal in the 1875 international held in London. The game ended in a 2–2 tie. Note the tape instead of crossbars, and the lack of nets. (RADIO TIMES HULTON PICTURE LIBRARY)

A merry style of soccer as played in Crowe Street, London, in 1721. (RADIO TIMES HULTON LIBRARY)

Football in London's Strand in the 18th Century. (RADIO TIMES HULTON PICTURE LIBRARY)

Two of the all-time greats meet. Dixie Dean, England's center forward, rushes Ricardo Zamora, the Spanish goalkeeper. This 1931 international proved to be a disaster for Zamora, who let in seven goals in England's 7–1 victory. (RADIO TIMES HULTON PICTURE LIBRARY)

The well-dressed soccer player of 1891, William Julien, the Arsenal captain. (RADIO TIMES HULTON PICTURE LIBRARY)

The incomparable Pelé juggles the ball before flipping it over his head for teammate Terry Garbett to run onto. (BILL SMITH)

I get the better of old friend Alex Skotarek of the Chicago Sting. (BILL SMITH)

The late Miro Rys of Chicago rises above bearded Bobby Smith of the Cosmos in a courageous header. (BILL SMITH)

It seems clear I'm going to lose the ball to Benny Alon, Chicago's midfield star. (BILL SMITH)

Steve Pecher rests against the goalpost as he waits for the Philadelphia Atoms to take a corner kick.

George Ley, my teammate at Dallas, running with the ball.

Our star goalie at Dallas, Ken Cooper, makes a diving save, and Dallas' star winger Jim Ryan dribbles through the St. Louis defense.

Dallas' elegant midfielder Bobby Hope takes on two Hartford Bicentennials in a 1976 game. (PHIL STEPHENS)

Eusebio (Las Vegas Quicksilvers)

Antonio Simões (San Jose Earthquakes)

John Mason (Los Angeles) pushes the ball with the outside of his foot in perfect textbook style. (JULIAN BAUM)

eorge Best plies his magic against Antonio Simões of San Jose. (JULIAN AUM)

Giorgio Chinaglia (Cosmos), with Tom McConville (Washington) in attendance, running into an open position to receive a pass.

Cosmos' Fran Beckenbauer (#6) in action against Tampa Bay.

Pat McBride (St. Louis) heads the ball against Portland.

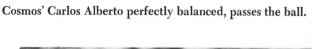

Cosmos' Carlos Alberto perfectly balanced, passes the ball.

St. Louis midfielder Bob O'Leary tackles John Stremlau (#15) of Dallas.

Defender Roger Verdi (#6) clears the ball off the line with goalkeeper Len Bond beaten.

St. Louis defender Gary Rensing heads the ball out of danger.

San Jose defender Buzz Demling (#2) tackles Steve Moyers of St. Louis.

Seattle's Paul Crossley (#11) races past San Jose defender John Rowlands. (MARCIA EDELSTEIN)

Paul Child of San Jose controls the ball with the outside of his foot as Mike England (#5) of Seattle prepares to tackle him. (FRED MATTHES)

St. Louis' strong striker Denny Vaninger leans over the ball as he shoots at goal.

Tampa Bay's prolific goal scorer Derek Smethurst jumps high to beat Ray Lugg of Fort Lauderdale. (ROD MILLINGTON)

Tampa Bay defenders Arsène Auguste (#4) and Stewart Jump (#13) watch as George Best moves away with the ball. (DORI HOWE)

An unusual sight in American soccer—the brilliant Rodney Marsh (#10) has the ball taken away from him. (ROBERT T. SPANN)

Jimmy Kelly
Forward
Portland Timbers

Bob Rigby
Goalkeeper
Los Angeles Aztecs

Werner Roth
Defender
New York Cosmos

Robert Iarusci
Defender
New York Cosmos

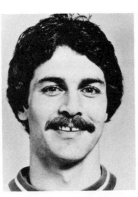

Shep Messing
Goalkeeper
New York Cosmos

Ramón Miflín
Midfielder
New York Cosmos

Al Trost
Midfielder
St. Louis Stars

Alan West
Midfielder
Minnesota Kicks

Patrick "Ace" Ntsolengue
Midfielder
Minnesota Kicks

Ron Futcher
Forward
Minnesota Kicks

Mike Flater
Forward
Minnesota Kicks

Steve Litt
Defender
Minnesota Kicks

Mike Stojanovič
Forward
Rochester Lancers

Alan Mayer
Goalkeeper
Las Vegas Quicksilvers

Geoff Hurst
Forward
Seattle Sounders

Tommy Ord
Forward
Seattle Sounders

Bruce Wilson
Defender
Vancouver Whitecaps

Les "Buzz" Parsons
Forward
Vancouver Whitecaps

Gordon Banks
Goalkeeper
Fort Lauderdale Strikers

Ivair Ferreira
Forward
Toronto Metros-Croatia

Zeljko Bilecki
Goalkeeper
Toronto Metros-Croatia

Eric Martin
Goalkeeper
Washington Diplomats

Peter Silvester
Forward
Washington Diplomats

PART TWO

Chapter Seven
The Team in Action

The most essential attribute of a modern soccer team is teamwork. This term, as far as soccer is concerned, can best be defined as joint action by a team in which each individual player subordinates his own preferences in tactics and style to the coach's.

No matter how big the star, there is no place in modern soccer for the player who dribbles just for the sake of it, tackles halfheartedly, shoots when he should pass or—probably the worst of all sins according to most coaches—is plain lazy. Of course, to have good teamwork one must first have players talented enough to carry out the coach's wishes. Trapping (stopping the ball dead), shooting, heading, ball control, screening, passing and dribbling are just some of the skills and techniques players must master, and throughout the second half of this book I will attempt to describe them. But first of all, let's take a quick look at the anatomy of the game.

Soccer is played on a field measuring anywhere from 100 to 130 yards long and from 50 to 100 yards wide, with the length always greater than the width. The preferred size is 115 by 75, but NASL teams using football stadia have played on fields as small as 105 by 55. The game is played in two forty-five-minute halves and there are eleven players on each team, one of whom, the goalkeeper, might appear to be participating in the wrong game, since he uses his hands and arms and his teammates do not. They are restricted to using their feet, legs, chests and heads in manipulating the ball.

The object of the game, of course, is to score more goals than one's opponents, but soccer's real fascination lies in what takes place along the meandering, indirect and often tortuous route to the back of the net. Goals are hard to come by in soccer—at least, this holds true when the teams are closely matched—but this has not prevented the game from being the most thrilling of all sports for both player and spectator.

The first thing a newcomer to soccer notices is the nonstop action—the constant movement of both ball and players up and down the field, with frequent changing of possession and no time-outs. As one spends more time watching, it also becomes evident that there are few set plays, as the fluidity of the action effectively prohibits most preplanning. Consequently, the player in possession has to make instant decisions. His options are many: a pass to a teammate, a shot at goal, a change of direction, a quick dribble or even a pass back to his goalkeeper. (Passing the ball in any direction in either half of the field is legal.)

Some of the actions that are illegal are kicking, tripping, striking, holding or pushing an opponent and charging an opponent, unless it is a fair shoulder charge, and even this, if done too violently, will be penalized. Infringements in soccer are penalized by free kicks. A direct free kick is awarded for the more serious infringements and an indirect for the lesser. Goals can be scored from direct free kicks, as the name implies. Any direct free kick awarded in the defender's penalty area automatically becomes a penalty kick. In this situation the ball is kicked from the penalty spot, 12 yards from the goal, and only the goalkeeper may attempt to stop it; all the other players from both teams remain outside the penalty area. This one-on-one confrontation is always exciting, but stacked heavily in favor of the kicker, who has the large 8-foot-high by 24-foot-wide goal to shoot at from a nearly point-blank range.

In indirect free kicks, someone other than the player taking the kick must touch the ball before a goal can be scored. The complete rules (the Laws of the Game) can be found in Appendix G, but a brief review of the offside law would be appropriate here, for no other rule of soccer causes so much confusion.

The confusion over the offside law stems from two problems. The first is that fans and players often fail to read the law properly. As I noted in Chapter Two, the offside law states that an offensive player must have two opponents between him and the defender's goal line when the ball is played toward him. The law does not say "when the player receives the ball" but "when the ball is played toward him." The other problem is that soccer's speed and fluidity make it nearly impossible for everyone to concur on just when the ball is played toward the player. The only opinion that matters in the end is the referee's, but even the most reasonable of players will argue vehemently with referees over offside calls. Not that arguing with the referee is a profitable exercise; few referees ever change their minds, and their authority on the field is absolute.

Once the general concept of the offside law is understood, the following three exceptions to it are simple to comprehend. A player cannot be offside:

1. In his own half of the field. (In the NASL, as we have seen, this has been extended to a line drawn 35 yards from the opponent's goal.)

2. When the ball comes to him after an opponent has touched it or played it toward him.

3. Whenever he receives the ball directly from a goal kick, corner kick or throw-in or when it has been dropped by the referee.

Although he is assisted by two linesmen, the referee has the complete authority to decide whether or not a man is offside. He may consult with them if he deems it necessary, but does not have to accept their opinions. Quite often when a linesman's flag is raised to indicate an offside infringement, the referee, disagreeing, will disregard it and shout out, "Play on!"

Seldom, however, will the referee question the linesmen's decisions relating to a ball that has gone out of play (over the touchlines for a throw-in and over the goal line for a goal kick when last touched by an offensive player or a corner kick when last touched by a defensive player). Nevertheless, the linesmen's decisions can often be another source of controversy, for many soccer fans fail to remember that all of the ball must cross the line before it is out of play, or "dead."

And yet most newcomers to soccer still find the game easy to understand. Having only 17 rules facilitates the learning process and is unquestionably one of the major reasons the sport is enjoyed throughout the world. As all the other contact sports see their rule books get thicker as the years go by, soccer fans see theirs nearly unchanged from what it was in the 19th century.

As in the days when Mr. Thring published his *Simplest Game,* soccer remains basically simple despite all the advances in coaching. The fundamental axiom formulated in the late 19th century still rings true: when in possession you are attacking; when possession is lost you are defending. Modern soccer, however, has refined the axiom somewhat. It now reads: when in possession *everyone* attacks; when possession is lost *everyone* defends. This emphasis on constant movement—with and without the ball—is the one thing that clearly distinguishes today's game from the days when the players turned out for soccer wearing high-top boots and knee breeches.

Although I suspect admirers of these great terms of the past may object, there is no doubt in my mind that the Scottish "Wembley Wizards" of the late 1920s, the star-studded Arsenal machine of the '30s and even the Hungarians of the early '50s would be run into the ground by a team employing today's ninety-minute style of nonstop running as practiced by advocates of total soccer. I do not mean to say that extraordinarily physically fit players necessarily make a better team when a team is viewed as a collection of individual skills, for no one could surpass such gifted ball handlers as Alex James, Stanley Matthews and Alfredo di Stéfano. But when a team is viewed as an effective unit, then the modern team is the best team yet devised.

Today's talented player no longer has the freedom to express himself in an individualistic exhibition of dribbling skills, or stroll around the field waiting for a pass. In the 1970s each player has one, two and sometimes three specific duties and must move up and down the field constantly; whereas in the past he would have stayed in his assigned position in one part of the field, and thus been able to take a breather whenever the ball moved out of his area.

Although the total soccer of the '70s demands that a player be capable of defending one moment in his own goal mouth and attacking the next in his opponent's, there are still eleven team positions in soccer. The traditional names for them have virtually disappeared from the vocabulary of many a pretentious modern coach, but pros and amateurs alike still use the familiar old names like fullback, halfback and inside forward. Listed here are all the names, both old and new, with the "old-fashioned" shown in *italics*.

goalkeeper

sweeper

right fullback	*center half*		*left fullback*
right back	right center back	left center back	left back

right half			*left half*
right midfielder	central midfielder		left midfielder
right linkman	central linkman		left linkman

inside right		*inside left*	

outside right	*center forward*		*outside left*
right winger	central striker		left winger
right flanker	targetman		left flanker
right striker			left striker

The whole question of terminology can be simplified if one merely thinks of the soccer field as divided into three areas of responsibility: defense, midfield and attack. With this in mind, let's take a closer look at the team positions.

In direct contrast to modern soccer's trend toward the all-purpose player, one who can handle all positions with equal competence, the goalkeeper's role as the only specialist on the team remains unchanged. He is still the only player on the team who may use his hands, and although the skills he employs are different from those of the rest of the team, he continues to be the vital key in the defensive structure. Indeed, a top-class goalie can often compensate for the rest of the defense's being inadequate. Conversely, many a fine team has been let down dramatically by weak goalkeeping—the Hungarians of 1966, for example. A splendid artistic team, full of creative ideas, the Hungarians in the World Cup could have gone all the way but for the one weak link in the team: goalkeeper Gelei.

The goalie's responsibilities, as we will see later in Chapter Eight, are not limited to leaping, diving and making courageous saves in front of the 8-by-24-foot goal. He, like the rest of the team, is an integral part of the offensive structure, since he can start attacking moves every time he kicks or throws the ball to a teammate.

The goalkeeper stands behind his backline, usually four players: a right back, two center backs and a left back. Some defenses use a sweeper behind the center backs for additional insurance, but whether there are four or five defenders their main task is to keep the approach to goal closed to unfriendly traffic. In his auxiliary role, however, each outside back must move up into attack along the flank whenever the opportunity arises, and the center back must move up to help the midfielders. Some progressive teams also encourage one of their central defenders to move up too, the best example being Bayern Munich of the mid-'70s with Franz Beckenbauer striking for goal despite his being a sweeper.

The outside backs are usually extremely fast in order to match the speed of fast wingers. They play out near the touchlines, guarding their opposing winger, and their objective is to ensure that attacks from the wings do not outflank the defense. The two center backs are more concerned with the direct approach to goal, and they are generally the tallest players on the team, so that they will be more likely to head the many high balls that come into the penalty area and the goal mouth.

All four defensemen must be strong tacklers—tackling in soccer meaning taking the ball away from an opponent by using the feet and perhaps a hefty shoulder charge (the only legal charge) as well. The defenders must also be prepared to cover for one another, so that if a teammate is beaten, the opponent will be quickly confronted by another defender. At Dallas our defenders are constantly rotating as they support one another and overlap our midfield into attack. If it weren't for the numbers on their shirts, it would be practically impossible for new spectators to decide which positions they were playing.

The midfielders are the heart of the team, pumping out endless energy in an effort to link the defense with the attack. Depending upon a team's tactical deployment and style of play there may be two, three or even four midfielders. The more defensive a team's style the more midfielders there will be, for even though a midfielder is expected to defend and attack, his first duty lies in assisting the defense until the pressure is relieved.

The midfielder's dual duties of defending and attacking mean that he must be ruthless in the tackle, creative in distribution of the ball and quick to spot any goal-scoring opportunities. Above all, he must possess and maintain a superhuman level of physical fitness, for the midfielder does more running than any other member of the team.

The modern forward's role is probably the most difficult, as he must score goals against packed defenses. Normally the player in the center of the attacking line—the striker, or center forward—is the one who is relied upon to do most of the scoring, and because of this he is the most closely guarded or, to use a soccer expression, marked. The outside strikers, the wingers, have more room to maneuver out by the touchlines, but once they move in, they too are surrounded by defensemen.

A winger also has his share of defensive chores and is expected to move back along the flank to assist his teammates when they are under pressure, but the central striker, on the other hand, usually stays upfield to act as a targetman when the ball is played out of defense. Many a successful counterattack is made possible by the center striker's collecting a long ball before his opponent's defense has had time to regroup.

No matter in which positions the coach places his ten field men, the basic requirement for successful teamwork in modern soccer is having a balanced formation—that is, equal strength in defense, midfield and attack, based on the styles and abilities of the available players. A good example of this was England in 1966 when Alf Ramsey developed a system without wingers in order to get his best team on the field.

Once a balanced formation is achieved and a system of support is developed, the next objective for any team should be to develop understanding between the three divisions so that there will be support from all teammates at times of defensive pressure, midfield activity and offensive action.

In defense situations, the midfielders and any forwards who have come back to help must not only pressure the opponent with the ball but also keep a wary eye open for other opponents moving in toward goal.

When there is midfield activity or an offensive situation, it is vital that those players without the ball position themselves in such a way that the teammate in possession will have various options open to him when he is ready to release the ball. Ideally he should have at least three players willing to accept a pass. The secret of winning soccer is, after all, having more players near the ball than your opponents whenever you are in possession. Getting there to be that extra man means a great amount of running without the ball in order to move into an unguarded area, or space as it is called in soccer. It also requires an unselfish attitude. Bobby Hope on our Dallas team is always willing to support the man in possession; he buzzes around him constantly, trying to be as conspicuous as he can so that the player with the ball can spot him. Many times he acts as a decoy, running solely in an effort to confuse our opponents. This is heartbreaking work, for he must cover a tremendous amount of yardage without receiving the ball, but it is a job that has to be done.

Proper support should enable an attacking team to retain possession of the ball for as long as it takes to move into a scoring position, but should also enable a defending team to stall the opposition until it can regain possession.

Once balance is achieved and support is developed, the team must concentrate on the style of play to be adopted. Until recently, a particular style of play was typical of a certain geographical area. The British and the Germans enjoyed soccer heavily seasoned with hard physical contact. Fast running, long passing, hard shooting and bone-jolting charging was their idea of good masculine fun. Austrians, Hungarians and other Central Europeans preferred a more delicate and sophisticated style built around the short pass. The South Americans emphasized ball skills above all else. They too shunned the hefty shoulder charge and the virile tackling of the British and the Germans. What was considered a fair tackle in Northern Europe could incite a riot if performed in the Southern Hemisphere.

The South Americans' ball skills were further refined by the Brazilians, especially the black players. Adding a rhythmic beat of their own, they pirouetted, leaped and swayed with bodies so supple and elastic they could have been performing a modern dance. This uninhibited, joyous style, as aesthetically sublime as it was, could not last in the pragmatic world of modern soccer. Nor could the gentle Central European style. Slowly at first in the early 1960s, then at a mad gallop by the decade's end, the geographical differences had faded. That harsh taskmaster, commercial success demanded a faster tempo. The exotic tango, the romantic waltz and the carefree samba all fell victims to the frill-less new quickstep of modern soccer with its diminution of individual freedom and cynical approach to the sport in general.

Yet top professional soccer today is still not completely homogeneous. In warmer climates the game is still played at a slower pace than in Northern Europe, and Latin America continues to produce players with amazing ball control. There is also a distinct difference between European and South American rhythms. The Latins tend to change gears more often than the Europeans. They like to freeze the ball at times, moving it from man to man casually, then suddenly explode with a series of one-touch lightning moves. The Europeans, on the other hand, quite often play at top speed throughout a game.

It is interesting to reflect on the difficulties the multinational players presented to the NASL coaches of the 1967–68 period. Trying to devise one style to suit five or six different nationalities was a nearly insurmountable task. Today, ten years later, the only significant problem NASL coaches are having with the mixing of nationalities is that the Latin Americans find it hard at first to adapt to the speed and work rate of the NASL. Our league's employing the European hard-running style is not surprising when one remembers that the majority of coaches and players are British. Consequently, anyone entering the NASL not in prime physical condition is in for an unhappy and certainly painful experience. Even those of us who like to think we are in great shape find the speed of the NASL style completely exhausting, particularly since we play most of our games in the summer months, sometimes when it is 90 degrees or more. Our players often lose 10 or more pounds per game.

Probably the most important element of style, at least as far as the spectators are concerned, is the degree of commitment the team has made to offensive action. No matter how well organized a team is or how many games it wins, it will never capture the imagination or support of the true fan without a fair measure of attacking inventiveness and flair. Thankfully, we have in the NASL many teams committed to attacking soccer, and one need look no further than the New York Cosmos' and the Tampa Bay Rowdies' fans to see how they respond to goals.

In 1976, New York scored 65 goals and Tampa 58 in the 24-game season, an average per team of over 2.7 and 2.4 respectively. Not far behind were Minnesota, 54 goals (2.25); Chicago, 52 (2.17); San Jose, 47 (1.95), and Washington with 46 (1.91). These offensive-minded teams are remarkable in an era of decreasing goals. To illustrate the commitment to attacking soccer by these and other NASL teams, let's compare the average number of goals scored per NASL game with the average number of goals scored per game in some European countries. In the 1976 season West Germany led the European professionals with an average of 3.29 goals scored (combined scores of both teams) per game. The English first division could muster only 2.66 and the Italians, 2.25. Whereas in the NASL the average was an encouraging 3.40, surely an indication of American professional soccer's health.

Chapter Eight

The Lonely Breed

"The bigger they are the harder they fall" notwithstanding, most coaches today prefer their goalkeepers big—big, that is, for soccer—and strong. One only has to look at the top goalies in the world today to see that the majority are tall, muscular men, strong enough to take the bruising treatment meted out by aggressive opponents in the goal area. Sepp Maier of Germany, Dino Zoff of Italy, Ray Clemence of England and Pat Jennings of Northern Ireland are all over 6 feet.

The top goalkeepers in the NASL are quite often the tallest and strongest players on their teams. Arnold Mausser of Denver is 6 feet 2, as are John Jackson of St. Louis, Merv Cawston of Chicago and Eugene DuChateau of Hartford. Even taller at 6 feet 3 are Jimmy Joerg of Team Hawaii and Dave Jokerst of St. Louis; and standing way above the rest of his teammates at Seattle is Mike Ivanow at 6 feet 4.

There is little doubt that height is an advantage for catching or punching high balls. And there is hardly any doubt that a larger frame and longer arm span leaves less of the goal as a target. What is debatable, however, is whether or not a tall man is slower than his shorter counterpart when he goes down for the low shots, especially when it means diving suddenly to stop them. I think he is. Most tall goalkeepers overcome this natural disadvantage not only by working hard on agility exercises but also by relying more on anticipation than on reflexes.

Anticipation in soccer means keeping one step ahead of the developing action. All great goalkeepers seem to have the knack of standing in exactly the right place when the ball is hit toward them. Quite often new soccer fans will comment on how lucky they are, not realizing that the goalkeeper has developed an ability to foresee what will happen. If a goalkeeper has properly mastered the art of anticipation, the necessity for split-second emergency diving will be reduced. Ken Cooper, my colleague at Dallas, has an uncanny ability to "read the game." Many times when he runs out to block an opposing striker coming through alone he will make his move even before the striker has broken through our defense. He also seems to know when a striker is going to shoot and when he is likely to pass. Many a game has been won for Dallas by Ken's sixth sense.

The value of good anticipation has increased in modern soccer, since so many high balls come in from the wings across the goal. Usually the goalkeeper must decide where the ball is going and move out to reach it before one of the opposing forwards gets a head or foot to it. But sometimes he may decide that the ball has been purposely spun so that it will curl away from goal, and in this case he must remain on his goal line.

Probably the most gifted anticipator is the goalkeeper who foresees all the possible dangers, especially mistakes on the part of his teammates. And teammates do make mistakes. A defender may head a ball toward his own goal after miscalculating its swerve or miskick a pass back to his goalkeeper so that the ball heads straight for the back of the net. Pity the poor goalkeeper who fails to anticipate these errors, for as the last line of defense he is the one who usually gets the blame.

Closely tied to anticipation is the technique of narrowing the angle. Where to position oneself to meet the ball is, after all, the next logical decision to make after deciding from which direction the ball will come. In its simplest form, narrowing the angle means moving off the goal line in the direction of the approaching player who has possession in order to offer the least possible area of the goal open to the opponent. If the goalie were to stay on his line in the center of the goal in a one-on-one situation, he would leave his opponent an inviting target 24 feet wide. Of course, if a goalkeeper advances too far from his goal line he leaves himself vulnerable to a dropping chip shot. The goalkeeper must combine his skills at anticipation and at narrowing the angle in order to determine how far out he should go. The taller the goalkeeper is, the farther he can safely move away from his line, but any distance over 6 yards must be considered risky.

Another skill that all goalkeepers—even the tallest—must perfect is punching. Catching a high ball in a crowded goal area is becoming increasingly difficult in modern soccer. Many top goalies consider punching a poor substitute for a clean catch, but even they resort to punching in crowded goal areas where opponents and defenders alike make it nearly impossible to reach the ball with both hands. It is far easier to punch the ball away from the goal mouth, but unless the ball is sent far enough away from the goal, it may well come straight back. The other disadvantage of punching is that the goalkeeper does not get possession.

Whenever possible, a goalkeeper should attempt to punch the ball with both fists in the direction from which it comes. However, if he can get only one hand to the ball he should try to punch the ball in the same direction in which it is going. This is quite often simply a matter of helping the ball on its way. The goalkeeper's aim should be to make the ball go high, wide and away from the goal mouth.

Deflecting the ball over the crossbar is another way of clearing the ball with one hand. It is the safest way to deal with high balls coming so close to the crossbar that a punch may be dangerous. Most top goalies use the palm of the hand and the fingers to guide the ball to safety. Whatever a goalkeeper commits himself to—be it catching, punching or deflection—he should never change his mind with his hands in midair, for any indecisiveness can be fatal.

There is, of course, much more to the art of goalkeeping than merely developing anticipation and studying positioning. First and foremost, a goalkeeper must perfect his agility. Body rolls, back arches and somersaults are all part of a day's work for a goalie trying to stop the variety of shots coming at him. Few who witnessed the 1970 World Cup game between Brazil and England will ever forget the amazing agility shown by England's Gordon Banks when he stopped what should have been an unstoppable header from Pelé. When the ball zoomed off Pelé's forehead toward the vacant corner of the net, Banks, completely out of position at the other end of the goal, somehow dived across the goal to flick the ball over the bar with his right wrist. Pelé said later it was the greatest save he had ever seen.

Pelé was the catalyst again when the Cosmos met the Chicago Sting in 1976. This time he forced Merv Cawston to leap backward in order to flick the ball around the post. On both occasions, the goalkeeper's endless hours of training and experience saved the day.

Even though he may make miraculous saves, a goalkeeper cannot help feeling he is on his own. Eventually a goal will be scored against him, and no matter how poor his defenders are, he will be the one held responsible. It's an extremely lonely position as well as a dangerous one, and for most of the time a thankless job, too; small wonder that goalkeepers in soccer have the reputation of being slightly mad. This reputation is, of course, more satirical than factual, but what is certainly true about goalkeepers is that only courageous types seem to want the position. Personal safety is a luxury few goalkeepers permit themeselves as they go throwing themselves in front of onrushing opponents or diving through a sea of legs and arms. Seldom does a professional goalkeeper back off from danger, and because of this he is liable to suffer the most serious injuries of any player on the team.

In 1931 Scotland's top goalie, Johnny Thompson of Glasgow Celtic, was killed while diving at the feet of Sam English, the Glasgow Rangers' center forward. (His replacement in the Celtic goal was none other than Joe Kennaway, the Fall River goalie.)

The history of soccer is full of incidents of goalkeepers' sustaining serious injuries while diving, particularly in the one-on-one situation when fast-moving forwards are unable to avoid hitting the advancing goalie. In 1976, America's bright young hope goalie Bob Rigby of the Cosmos (now with Los Angeles) spent most of the season on the sidelines recovering from a broken collarbone, the result of a heroic save against the Washington Diplomats.

What makes the goalkeeper's job even more dangerous is the fact that he keeps his body behind the ball whenever possible, as he has been taught to do ever since his first practice session. Even when making flying dives, a top goalie will try to get his body in the way of the ball. This precaution saves many shots that otherwise would enter the net when the hands or arms have missed the ball. Any part of the body will do as a back-up: chest, waist, legs or feet.

The duties of the goalkeeper are not limited solely to stopping the ball from entering the net. Once the ball is in his hand, his team has possession and like everyone else on the team he becomes an attacker. His style should be similar to that of a basketball rebounder initiating a fast break. The distribution should therefore be accurate and designed to begin a series of moves that will send the ball into the opponents' penalty area. Making a throw to an unguarded teammate and kicking a volley (kicking a ball before it touches the ground) are two methods of starting a counter-attack.

Employing the short bowling-style throw is the safest and most accurate way to distribute the ball to a field player. A ball thrown this way does not go very far, but the receiving player is able to collect it without having to concern himself with controlling a high or bouncing ball. If the goalie were to use the overarm throw or basketball throw, the ball would go farther, but both result in balls that have to be brought down, or trapped.

Goalies often choose to use the long volley kick, for it causes the ball to go deep into the opponents' half. Merv Cawston of the Chicago Sting used this dangerous kick to advantage in 1976 when he would aim for the heads of the tall twin strikers from England, John Lowey and Geoff Davis, causing many problems for the Sting's opponents.

Bill Foulkes, the former Chicago Sting coach, enjoys recalling a most unusual volley kick that he witnessed when he was playing as a center back against Tottenham Hotspur in the English first division on a very windy day. He was standing just outside his own penalty area guarding the Tottenham striker, Alan Gilzean, when Pat Jennings, the Tottenham goalie, kicked a long volley. Both Foulkes and Gilzean prepared themselves for a header, but the ball, swirling in the wind, continued over their heads toward the Manchester goalie, Alex Stepney, who was standing by the penalty spot. It bounced in front of Stepney and much to his horror rebounded like a tennis ball way above his head into the back of the net, providing goalkeeper Jennings with a 90-yard goal.

The goalkeeper also has the responsibility (at least on most teams) of taking the goal kicks (taken within the goal area after the ball has gone over the goal line and was last touched by an offensive player). Although a dead ball does not travel as far as a volleyed ball, it can still be kicked over the halfway line by most professional goalies. Not all goal kicks have to be long, however. A useful alternative is the short kick that travels just outside the penalty area to a teammate. The teammate can then advance with the ball or pass it back to the goalie, who can then pick it up and either throw or volley it.

When the goalie collects the ball, either after making a save or as a result of a pass from a teammate, he is permitted only four steps before he must release the ball. Until 1967 he could take as many steps as he wished provided he bounced the ball after every four. The law was then changed because goalkeepers were slowing up the game. Today the goalie often circumvents the new rule simply by momentarily releasing the ball, then picking it up again for another four steps. Some goalies do this indefinitely while waiting for their strikers to get into position or to stall near the end of a game. However, the goalie must be cautious if opponents are near when he attempts this time-wasting maneuver, for it is quite legal for them to go for the ball once the goalie releases it.

Present-day goalkeepers who practice this tactic must consider themselves fortunate, for in modern soccer the charging of goalkeepers by aggressive forwards has practically been eliminated. Although the law still permits the goalie to be charged when he is holding the ball, few referees will permit it.

With or without the ball, the goalkeeper must be in command of his penalty area. Facing the direction of play at all times, he is in the best position to see everything that is happening, and his defenders expect him to warn them of any dangerous developments. Because of this, a goalie does a lot of shouting and expects to be heeded by his teammates. He may point out the appearance of an unguarded opponent in the penalty area or yell at a teammate who is allowing a striker too much room. The frequently repeated warning "Keeper's ball!" is one call teammates instinctively react to, for when a goalie decides to take an incoming ball, anyone standing in his way may well find himself crashing to the turf with the goalie on top of him.

Bravado, machismo, arrogance; call it what you like—but whatever it is, the goalkeeper must have it if he is to command the penalty area. His domination is best seen in a dead-ball situation in which the opponents are

awarded a free kick near or in the penalty area and a human wall of defenders is formed to block off one part of the goal. At Dallas, Kenny
Cooper keeps up a stream of instructions to our defense until he is certain
the wall is to his satisfaction and that he will see the ball when it is kicked.
Usually the wall is formed to cover the side of the goal closer to the ball
(the near post), leaving the goalkeeper the responsibility of protecting the
area around the far post.

In addition to worrying about the way in which the wall is formed, the
goalkeeper must also be alert to an unguarded opponent's moving up at
the time of the free kick. A pass to such an unmarked player not only
would bypass the wall but would present an opportunity for a close shot
at goal.

Despite all the efforts of goalkeepers, more and more goals are being
scored from free kicks taken near the goal. The human wall of four or five
players lined up 10 yards from the ball may look impenetrable, but goalkeepers are only too well aware of the increasing number of players, in the
last ten years, who are able to spin a ball so that it will drop or curve
around the wall. The Brazilians have been driving goalies to despair for
years with their accuracy in "bending" the ball; Pelé and Rivelino in particular have tormented most of the world's top goalies at one time or
another, and before them, the great Didi amazed opponents and teammates alike with his swirling "dry leaf" shot.

At Dallas our skillful winger Alan Hinton can bend the ball from right
to left, and defender George Ley can bend it the opposite way, from left
to right. My ex-teammate, that ace goal scorer of the NASL, Ilija Mitič can
also bend the ball, but his speciality is to "top-spin" the ball so that it goes
into the air, then sinks quickly. Of course, sheer power and speed will
sometimes beat a goalkeeper, as Geoff Barnett, the Minnesota goalie, will
attest. In the 1976 NASL final, neither he nor the wall in front of him could
stop Eusebio from scoring with a tremendous drive from 25 yards out.

One other dead-ball situation that can unnerve a goalkeeper is the
penalty, or penalty kick. Trying to save a penalty is, as I have noted, a
seemingly impossible task, particularly since the goalie is not permitted to
move until the ball is kicked, and even worse, the penalty spot is only 12
yards from the goal line. One would have to agree that under these conditions the awarding of a penalty is tantamount to the awarding of a goal.
And yet, as befits a game that is full of surprises, penalty kicks are saved—
quite often, in fact.

Many goalkeepers use a simple method to deal with penalty kicks: they
simply decide before the kick is taken which way they are going to dive,
about half of the time to the right and half of the time to the left. This

50–50 system can be acutely embarrassing for the goalkeeper, for he can look ridiculous if he dives one way and the ball goes the other. Other goalies try to analyze penalty kicks in depth and keep a record, whenever possible, on the opposing kicker's past penalty kicks: in which direction he usually shoots, whether he prefers high or low shots and whether he usually employs a hard drive or a soft chip. Of course, many of those players taking penalty kicks have done similar homework on the goalie's past performance, so it becomes a game of cat-and-mouse, with each player trying to outguess the other. Whatever the outcome, the tension and drama of the penalty-kick situation make it one of the great moments in soccer.

In most of the exciting incidents in soccer, the goalkeeper is in the center of the action. Probably this is why so many players want to play in the position, despite the general thanklessness of the job and the physical risks involved. Perhaps they are slightly mad—but without them, soccer would be a far less interesting game.

Chapter Nine

The Modern Defenders

The 800 million people around the world viewing the 1970 World Cup final held in Mexico City saw Carlos Alberto score the final goal in Brazil's 4–1 victory. Alberto, storming into an open space on the right side of the Italian penalty area, ran onto a lateral pass from Pelé and then unleased a terrific 20-yard shot. It was a beautifully executed goal—but of more interest was the fact that Alberto was the right back on his team. Tall, elegant and extremely mobile, he bore little resemblance to what ten years earlier had been thought of as a typical back. In those days a back was usually the big, brawny type, slow on the turn and, so it seemed, constantly being made a fool of by fast, tricky wingers.

Today the backs, or defenders, as we call them now, are as fast as or faster than wingers. As agile and technically accomplished as the best strikers, the professional defenders can play in any position. Indeed, with the advent of total soccer there is less and less distinction being made between defenders and the players in other positions.

As I have already noted, modern defenses are generally built around a four-man backline. The outside backs—right and left—and the two center, or central, backs are spread across the entire width of the field. Some defensive-minded teams, seeking the ultimate in security, use a sweeper. Stationed behind the defense and not having any opponent to shadow or guard, the sweeper is held back in reserve, ready to pounce on any opponent or ball that penetrates the backline. Incidentally, the inclusion of a sweeper does not always mean that a team is playing a five-man defense, for quite often the sweeper's role is assumed by one of the center backs. In this case, the center back is simply withdrawn behind the three other defensemen. At Dallas, whenever we use a sweeper he is almost always a withdrawn center back.

Many teams reverse the sweeper role by playing him in front of the backline instead. Called a free man, a *libero* or a defensive shield, the man in front devotes his energies to making the first challenge to any opposition attack.

Most pro teams use either man-to-man marking or a zonal system of defense. The man-to-man method is more defensive, since it restricts the movement of the defenders, particularly where the marking is extremely tight. It is, however, easier for a defender to master than the more subtle

142

zonal system, in which each defender is given a particular area to guard. Many teams in the NASL use a combination of the two systems—using the zonal in midfield and man-to-man as the opposition advances close to the penalty area.

All teams utilize the man-to-man whenever they face an exceptional striker or some other recognized "danger man." Pelé has spent most of his career being tightly marked, many times by two opponents.

Georgie Best is another forward who can always expect special treatment. In 1976 he had a marvelous season with the Los Angeles Aztecs after a long layoff from soccer, but in one game he found the tenacious marking of Ron Webster of Minnesota frustrating. Wherever he went, even as far back as his own penalty area, he was shadowed by Webster. The tactic was effective, for Best was chained, and Minnesota won 1–0, but it did mean that Webster was unable to contribute to his team's offensive buildup.

Another problem with the man-to-man system is that when a defender is beaten, another defender must leave his assigned player to take up the challenge, and unless there is a sweeper or another free man playing in defense, trouble is likely.

In the zonal defense system, on the other hand, the defender is assigned essentially to cover his zone rather than to shadow a particular opponent. This system has all but eliminated the dangerous need defenders have in the man-to-man system to follow their assigned opponents away from defensive positions, but it does give an opposing forward more room in which to maneuver before he is challenged.

In a combined man-to-man and zonal defense, each defender has a zone to patrol and an opponent to mark. It is up to the defender to stay close to his particular opponent whenever he comes near or into the penalty area.

At Dallas we have used both systems, but we don't use man-to-man unless our opponents have some outstanding players like a Pelé, a Chinaglia or a Best. When we play against such a team, we withdraw a midfielder back into defense to ensure that every time a "danger man" goes for the ball he is challenged quickly, preferably before he even gets the ball. For most free kicks and corner kicks, however, we switch to man-to-man, since each opponent must be tightly guarded in all dead-ball situations.

Although we don't stress the offside game at Dallas, we still expect our defenders to keep alert for any possible offside situations. Too many offside calls can ruin any game of soccer, and few fans want to see the game revert back to the offside stoppages of the early 1920s, but the judicious use of the offside law can be an effective tool for defenders. Certainly nothing is likely to unsettle a team more than to find themselves constantly offside, particularly at the beginning of a game. A good example of how a team can be knocked off its stride occurred in the 1976 Soccer Bowl when Toronto caught the Minnesota Kicks offside four times within the first ten minutes. It was enough to make the Kicks worry every time they got the ball that they would be offside, causing the team to lose confidence and eventually the game.

One basic element of any defense is cover (support of teammates). Defenders try never to commit themselves to challenging advancing opponents unless their colleagues are nearby to cover for them. Of course, in a desperate situation the defender has to go in for the tackle, but in most cases, if he jockeys or stalls his opponent, help will arrive before he is forced to make his move.

The best time for a defender to challenge an opponent for the ball is before his opponent gets possession. Experienced international defenders like Franz Beckenbauer and Mike England are skilled at intercepting passes intended for opponents. They may both be slower than the younger defenders in the league, but they both have an ability to think rapidly and react quickly to any new situation which thoroughly compensates for any lack of speed. A defender's ability to read the game enables him to anticipate many passes, thus making his job that much easier, for once an opponent brings the ball under control a defender has to be wary. If he rushes into the tackle he may well find himself beaten with some clever footwork or a feint; instead, he should bide his time, running with his opponent, pressuring him into making a mistake or forcing him to go in a desired direction. Of course, if the opponent overruns the ball the defender will tackle immediately, but generally the emphasis is more on containing an opponent than on tackling him, particularly in those teams which have adopted the retreating defense—a system in which defenders move back to their penalty area before defending en masse. This noncommitment of defenders is a feature of modern soccer, and although it is obviously not as exciting as the full-blooded lunge at the ball, it is now accepted by thoughtful fans as good tactics.

Whenever a defender is beaten, it is his responsibility to run back into the defensive line in order to maintain a numerical balance and assume the position originally held by the teammate who has moved in to challenge the approaching opponent. This interchanging between defenders continues until possession is gained or the ball goes out of play. Complete understanding and a great amount of running off the ball are essential if this covering system is to work effectively. What the defenders try to forestall, of course, is the situation in which there are more attackers than defenders. A two-on-one or three-on-two encounter can be disastrous for the defending team, especially if it is close to goal, where there is little space left for containment. In such a dire circumstance there is almost no choice for the defender but to tackle.

The old-fashioned lethal tackle is still a forte of many top defenders. Tommy Smith, who played for Tampa Bay in 1976, was probably the strongest tackler ever seen in the NASL. This former English international usually got the ball whenever he decided to go for it. The secret of his success was his determination. There's an adage in soccer that the player who tackles halfheartedly is the one who always gets hurt. The formidable Nobby Stiles of England's 1966 World Cup team was a firm believer in this saying. Only 5 feet 5½ inches tall and weighing 145 pounds, he was the most feared tackler of the tournament. At one time during the tournament there was an outcry against his tackling, and many wanted to see him dropped from the English team. But Stiles' tackling was not illegal, though it was certainly powerful. Stiles would move close to his opponent, shift his weight to his standing leg and block the ball with a powerful swing of his other leg.

There are various forms of tackling. The two most commonly used are the front block and the slide tackle. Both must be timed perfectly or else the defender will be kicking at the air or, worse, lying on the ground. Positioning is also all-important, for if the tackler is too far away from the ball his tackle will lack power.

The slide tackle, the most exciting of all, is best reserved for a do-or-die situation, because if the tackler is unsuccessful he is left on the ground for a few precious seconds while his opponent continues on his way. Two players who effectively use the slide tackle are Clive Griffiths of the Chicago Sting and my teammate at Dallas, Roy Turner.

Another form of tackling is the shoulder charge. Even though goal-keepers are seldom the targets of a shoulder charge, the rest of the team certainly receive their full share. However, for a shoulder charge to be legal the ball has to be within playing distance and the tackler's shoulder must come into contact with his opponent's shoulder. The tackler's arms must be straight and his elbow may not be used (not that my ribs haven't had their share of elbow digs).

Heading is another skill all defenders must acquire early in their play-ing careers. The center backs especially must master heading, as they do more than anyone else on the team. Getting up high to guide the ball out of the danger zone is a constant chore for center backs, particularly in dealing with corner kicks and high crosses (high balls coming into the goal mouth from the wing). Anytime a high ball comes into the penalty area and the goalkeeper stays on his goal line, it is up to the center backs to get to the ball before the opposing strikers. As I noted before, this heading requirement usually forces coaches to seek tall men for the center-back positions. Mike England, Steve Pecher and Peter Nover of Hawaii are just three of the many NASL center backs whose height advantage makes them that much more skilled at heading.

The correct way to head a ball is with the forehead, the flattest and strongest part of the head. The neck should be taut and the eyes open, so that a late change in direction or spin will not result in a misdirected header. Power for the header comes from the snap of the stomach and neck muscles as the head hits the ball—the ball should never be allowed to bounce off the head. The defender tries to head the ball up into the air, over the heads of the attacking opponents. Conversely, the striker attempts to head the ball downward when trying to score, since it is harder for goalkeepers to stop a low ball.

As I mentioned earlier, a defender in modern soccer is expected to think offensively as soon as he gains possession. The outside backs have the additional duty of moving up and overlapping (running along the flanks). At Dallas, since we use only one winger in our 4–3–3 formation (the other two forwards are central strikers), we push up our backs, Neil Cohen, Bobby Moffat and George Ley, all fast and extremely skillful, in order to exploit this vacant space along the wing. We also have our backs send passes into this empty space for our strikers to run into. We've always prided ourselves on having a strong defense, but once our backs get the ball they go all out for goals.

Teams that employ only one winger, or even no wingers at all, must use their backs to fulfill some of the formations of a winger, such as taking the ball down to the corner flag and then crossing it into the goal mouth, or racing down the flank to pick up a pass from a midfielder and running in to score the way Carlos Alberto did in the 1970 World Cup. Italy's Rocca impresses me as the composite fullback of this fast-paced style. Total-soccer advocates have even taken this mobility one step further by having backs and forwards rotate their positions for periods of the game, either to confuse the opposition or for strategic purposes.

The additional offensive duties defenders perform in recent years have certainly enlivened the game. Not only does the modern defender pass the ball to a midfielder after gaining possession, but he also runs into a forward position to receive the return pass. By assuming these tasks, he enables his team to have an extra forward and quite often numerical superiority in the place where it counts: the opponent's penalty area.

But even when he is in the opponent's half, the defender must be prepared to defend. Once his team has lost possession, he must drop back quickly or, if he is near the action, try to harass or pressure the opponent with the ball. It possible, though, he should let his own forwards do this defensive work so that he can withdraw behind them as the final defensive cover.

Catastrophe can strike if the defender has moved up into attack without making certain that his position in the defensive line is covered by a teammate. If he fails to have his position covered, the loss of the ball in the opponent's half might well result in a swift counterattack in the area he has vacated. To ensure that this will not happen, most defenders attempt to reach a mutual understanding about covering. The Bayern Munich defense of the mid-1970s displayed remarkable flowing movements into and out of positions, reflecting an understanding of the highest order. That Franz Beckenbauer could move away with such ease from his sweeper position into attacking territory without detracting any strength from Bayern's defensive line was one of the wonders and strengths of soccer in the '70s. Luckily for Americans, he is now organizing the same kind of flexibility for the Cosmos, and I urge any budding defender to make an effort to see him play.

Chapter Ten

The Fluent Technicians

A quick way to judge a team is to take a look at its midfield, or halfback line as it was once called. If the midfielders are creative and talented ball-players, it is almost guaranteed that the side will play intelligent soccer; if the midfielders are strong tacklers but lack finesse, the team will almost certainly play a defensive-minded game. These rules of thumb have taken on even greater significance in recent years with the growing importance of the midfield in the presently popular 4–3–3 and 4–4–2 systems.

No longer simply the link between defenders and forwards, midfielders today defend in the penalty area, score goals at the other end and are still expected to control the midfield. Their stamina must be limitless to enable them to cover all three areas of the field, their tackling must be sharp and direct, and their ball control must be exceptional.

It is in the midfield that the tempo and rhythm of the game are decided. Skillful midfielders are able to dictate the pace of the game, speeding up the offensive movements when necessary or slowing down the game to a stop-go rhythm when opponents are applying the pressure. The speed at which a team plays, or permits its opponents to play, is an important tactical consideration anywhere in the world, but in the United States it is extremely significant, since we play our games in the summer. If a team permits its opponents to dictate a frantic pace for very many games in hot weather, its players will burn themselves out in the first half of the season. Losing 8 to 10 pounds a game is not exceptional in the NASL, and when we have back-to-back games there is little time to replenish our energy supply even if it is possible to replace our body fluids through a high in-take of liquids.

One of the major tasks of our midfield line at Dallas is to see that we don't play under pressure at full speed for a long period in any one game. Roy Turner, Bobby Hope and Kevin Kewley are all former British pros accustomed to playing the perpetual-motion style of soccer popular in the cooler British climate, but like other British imports they soon learned how to adjust their style to the rigor of American summers.

The midfielder gets his feet to the ball more than anyone else on the team, and because the guarding (or marking) of players in the midfield is looser than in the penalty areas, he also has more time to work the ball and more opportunity to display his ball skills than his teammates. The ball control of Charlie Cooke, a midfielder for the Los Angeles Aztecs and a former Scottish international winger, is matched by only a handful of players in the world. He traps a ball effortlessly with either his feet, thighs or chest or even with his head. His ability to control the ball upon contact with any part of his body is dazzling.

Not only midfielders but all soccer players must learn how to trap a ball with precision. The correct way to trap an approaching ball at any height is to relax the part of the body being used. This action cushions the ball, which will be either slowed down or stopped, depending upon what is required. A player being challenged by an opponent will normally want to keep the ball moving so that he also can keep moving. This is best accomplished by a stop-push motion of the foot. The thigh or chest trap, on the other hand, requires a two-touch action. First the ball is cushioned; then when it drops to the ground, the foot takes over. Trapping with the head is probably the most difficult of all, but here again the idea is to cushion the ball so that it drops quickly down to the feet.

Possession and penetration, the two keys to successful soccer, are possible only with skillful ball control and accurate passing by the midfielders, for most games are determined by which team dominates the midfield. If the team winning the ball is able to control it for long periods through good ball handling and passing, it will have a greater chance of breaking through the opposition to score. But if its passing is weak, unadventurous or too obvious, penetration will probably be a long time in coming.

The safest and simplest pass is, of course, the short one. There is no reason why a team cannot retain possession through the use of short passes indefinitely. Unfortunately, it is difficult to counterattack quickly with this form of passing. Thus teams try to develop the ability to execute both the short and the long styles of passing.

The chief disadvantage of the long pass is that it is risky. The longer distance it has to travel gives opponents more time to react, and even the most accurate long pass can be intercepted by alert opponents. What makes a 30–40-yard pass so valuable, however, is the fact that when it is employed accurately it packs both surprise and speed. Two or three such passes can move the ball within a matter of seconds from one penalty area to the other.

Although professional teams vary their use of the short and long passes, there are some that favor one over the other. As we have seen in Chapter Seven, South American and Central European teams traditionally have favored the short pass, and this preference still lingers. Similarly, the British continue to employ the long pass more often than most other countries. In Italy too, the long pass is seen frequently in the fast counter-attack out of the thickly packed defense. Generally, however, the trend today is toward a slow buildup in the midfield based upon short passes, with midfielders offering themselves as targets for the man with the ball. This is the method Minnesota Kicks coach Freddie Goodwin prefers. "The ball is too precious to be lost in midfield" is his attitude. Bill Foulkes, the former Chicago Sting coach, feels the same way, whereas San Jose coach Gabbo Gavrič and John Sewell, the coach of St. Louis, like to see their teams break out of defense quickly. At Dallas we vary our passing, with emphasis on the short pass. When we do hit long balls, our coach, Al Miller, prefers that we keep them on the ground, directed either to one of our teammates' feet or into space for a teammate to chase. I prefer the ball to come head high, since heading is one of my strong points, but as a team player I realize controlling high balls is far more difficult than controlling those which arrive at ground level. The ground approach is also more accurate.

Whatever style is used, it is vital that a pass be made in such a way that the receiver can control it quickly. A ground pass would obviously be more easily trapped than, say, a lofted spin pass. The need for accuracy has multiplied in recent years with the increased speed of the game. Many times it is impossible for a receiver to attempt to control a pass because of pressuring opponents. In this situation he must be proficient at first-time passing (also called one-touch passing), which requires a high degree of skillful ball manipulation.

The most effective way of passing and maintaining possession is through triangular movements, which require at least three players' moving with the ball. Triangular movements offer depth as well as a variety of angles for the ball to be moved into. They give the man in possession the option of passing backward if any avenue of approach is blocked, and more importantly, they minimize the use of that most predictable of all passes, the lateral, or, as it is called in soccer, square pass.

Although the triangular passing formations are pretty to watch and most effective in building an attack out of a defensive situation, there are times when midfielders will want to use the long pass, especially when their opponents have overcommitted themselves by sending too many players up into the attack. A wonderful example of the efficacy of the sudden long accurate pass was seen in a game between the Los Angeles Aztecs and the Seattle Sounders in 1976. Miguel Lopez, the young Aztec defender, won the ball in his own penalty area. Seeing Georgie Best standing on his own in the Seattle half of the field, he hit a 40-yard ball. Best, taking advantage of the unsettled Seattle defense, passed quickly to the former Welsh international Ron Davies and then ran on toward goal. As he reached the penalty area, Davies flicked a 15-yard return pass to Best, who scored with a beautifully curved shot in the upper left side of the net. From the time Lopez made his incisive pass until the goal was scored, not one Seattle player touched the ball, and just as important, none of the Sounders was able to get back in time to reinforce the Seattle defensive line.

In addition to winning the ball and distributing it, the midfielder must also be ready to run ahead of his strikers to receive a pass. Goal-scoring opportunities arise frequently for midfielders in modern soccer because when they break through the opposition they, unlike the tightly guarded strikers, are quite often able to get close to goal before they are challenged.

Midfielders are constantly aware of their changing responsibilities. When the team is not clicking, it is in the midfield that coaches are likely to introduce a change. If the forward line is failing to penetrate, quite often a coach will convert a midfielder into an extra striker. Conversely, if an opponent is proving too elusive for the defense, the coach may withdraw one of the midfielders to work in concert with a defender to double-mark the "danger man." Switching positions during a game can be successful only if the midfielder has all-around soccer skills.

In the NASL, the best example of a player possessing all the necessary skills is Wolfgang Sühnholz of the Las Vegas Quicksilvers. A former Bayern Munich, Boston Minuteman and Toronto Metros midfielder, Sühnholz was the inspiration behind Toronto's winning streak which gave the Metros the 1976 NASL title. A superb craftsman, Sühnholz acts like a general in the midfield, controlling the speed and rhythm of the game like few others in the NASL.

Probably the greatest midfield player of the past twenty-five years was the late Duncan Edwards, the tall, powerful superman of English soccer until his tragic death in the Manchester United airplane crash at the age of 21. Edwards, who played for the English national team when only 18, was, according to Bill Foulkes, his teammate at Manchester, "the nearest thing to perfection in what a midfielder should be. His 40- to 50-yard passes had to be seen to be believed. He had strength, a tremendous shot in either foot and amazing ball control and balance for a big man."

Today Bill Foulkes's eyes are on a much different type of midfielder, little Jimmy Kelly. Only 5 feet 6 and weighing 145 pounds, Kelly was brought to Chicago from Manchester United by Foulkes when only 19 and has proved to be the most elegant young midfielder in the league.

Two other splendid midfielders worth watching in the NASL are Ramón Miflín of the Cosmos and Rodney Marsh of Tampa Bay. Both are former internationals: Miflín played for Peru in the 1970 World Cup in Mexico and Marsh was a star of the English national team in the early seventies.

Before leaving the subject of midfielders we should look at the throw-in, a traditional responsibility of midfielders. Although most pro teams today expect the closest man to the ball whenever it goes over the touchline to take the throw-in, the midfielder is still the specialist. He's the one who does the throwing at practice sessions when new plays are tested.

The throw-in, one of the simplest skills to learn in soccer, is often poorly executed, even by the pros. Perhaps because it is so easy, experienced players get careless. Instead of using the opportunity to start an attack, many players quite often throw the ball to teammates unthinkingly, either too high or too far away for them to have more than a 50–50 chance of keeping possession. Generally, the thrower should aim for his teammate's head or feet, so that no time will be lost in trying to control the ball and the receiver will be in a position to send it right back to the thrower if necessary. Of course, if a teammate can find an empty space to run into, then the ball should go to him even if it means throwing it yards away from him.

Professional teams devote much time to practicing decoy runs which they hope will confuse and spread out defending opponents at throw-ins. In one such decoy run the thrower waits for one teammate to run, then throws the ball into his vacated space so that a second teammate may rush in and receive it. During these decoy runs there is constant movement of players as they interchange positions, so unless there is complete understanding between the thrower and his teammates the ball may well be sent straight to an opponent.

During a throw-in, each defender attempts to guard his nearest opponent so that no opponent is free. This will be impossible if the throw-in is carried out quickly before the defenders have a chance to regroup. This is why it is important for the nearest player to the ball when it passes over the touchline to take the throw-in.

Some teams possess a player who is endowed with sufficient strength in his upper back and arms to catapult a "long throw" from the touchline all the way into the goal mouth. Unlike the ordinary 10–20-yard throw, the long throw has little chance of surprise, unless it is the first time the defending team has encountered the player who is throwing. Most long throws in the opponent's half of the field are like free kicks or corner kicks, since the ball travels as far. Most players who throw the 30–40-yard ball try to hit a targetman near the goal or aim for an empty space away from the goal for a striker to run into to meet the ball.

In the NASL, Mike Flater is the man goalkeepers keep an eye out for whenever the ball goes over the touchline. His ability to throw past the penalty spot has proved very profitable for Minnesota; many goals have resulted from his long throws, including a particularly fine one against Washington in 1976 when Peter Short, rising high to meet Flater's throw-in, headed it to Alan West, who in turn deflected it into the Washington net.

Throw-ins, passing, shooting, defending, attacking—a good midfielder is expected to excel in every department; so it should not be surprising that midfielders often switch positions during their careers and become successful defenders and attackers.

Chapter Eleven

The Priceless Gems

Scoring goals is unquestionably the most difficult task in modern soccer. The introduction of the two center backs, the sweeper, retreating defenses and other refinements in defensive play has enabled the defensive side to get the upper hand in recent years. It is, therefore, not surprising that a striker who can consistently score goals in top pro soccer is now worth his weight in gold (a cliché presently more literal than figurative, considering the spiraling prices paid for strikers. John Cruyff of Holland and Giuseppe Savoldi of Italy were each traded for over $2½ million).

Agility, balance, speed and power are the four basic requirements for an effective striker. He may, however, have more of one than of the others. If he has a powerful shot he will be welcomed by most teams even if his agility and speed are somewhat average. Similarly, a place in the team will always be found for the striker whose ball control is so masterly he can maintain possession under extreme pressuring despite his weaknesses in some other department.

Agility and balance are especially vital for the central striker to have as he acts as a targetman, the player his teammates look for when they hit a long ball out of defense. Most times such a long ball will be lofted, arriving at the striker's head or chest with the striker facing the wrong way—that is, toward his own goal. Controlling the ball while being tightly guarded is not easy, and when the striker tries to turn, his task becomes increasingly harder. Under these circumstances he will have to screen the ball by keeping his body between it and the defender. The secret of good screening is to control the ball with the foot farther away from the opponent. Geoff Hurst, the former English World Cup and Seattle star, is a superb screener of the ball and nearly impossible to dislodge once he gains possession. Ilija Mitič of San Jose is another player whose screening and turning with the ball are top class.

Of course, a striker does not have to turn when he receives the ball. Some targetmen never turn when opponents are breathing down their necks; instead they counter by hitting the ball first-time to a teammate or running back toward their own half of the field before passing and then, once free of the ball, running into an open space for a return pass.

"Space" is what the striker spends most of the game trying to find. There are two ways of getting space in soccer. Running into an unguarded area is one. In midfield this is easy enough, but as the striker gets closer to his opponent's goal he will find less room; indeed, it gets so crowded at times he is lucky if he can move, let alone find space. The other way to get space is to create it where none exists. This is possible when a teammate moves away from a spot—say, near the penalty spot—taking his shadowing opponent with him, so that another teammate can move into the area vacated.

There are times, of course, when the striker, alone with no help in sight, has to make his own way to goal. It is here that the striker must call upon his dribbling skills. In soccer, dribbling means controlling and moving the ball with soft strokes of the feet combined with body feints, acceleration and change of pace. There are few sights in the sporting world that compare with that of a dribbling Stanley Matthews, a Pelé or Georgie Best weaving through desperate defenders, eluding tackles and obstructions effortlessly with a farrago of feints, tantalizing twists and varying rhythms. Unfortunately, these great moments are rarer than they once were, owing to changes in the style of play. Most coaches today frown upon excessive dribbling even if it is executed with great skill, since it slows up the game and enables opponents to get players back into defense. It also tends to frustrate those players who do a great amount of running off the ball but never receive a pass.

Yet when dribbling is used sparingly it can be one of the most successful means of breaking down the best of defenses. Carl Humphrey of the St. Louis Stars showed just how destructive to defenses controlled dribbling can be in a game against Rochester in 1976. He was all alone just outside his opponent's penalty area near the goal line when he picked up a long pass. Two defenders rushed him, but he beat both of them within a space of three yards, twisting and turning with miraculous balance. He maneuvered the ball past them and shot from an acute angle by the goal line, scoring a marvelous goal in the far top corner of the net. If Humphrey had played it safe by passing the ball back when he saw he was outnumbered or by shielding the ball until help arrived, the defense might well have nullified the St. Louis scoring attempt. This is an excellent example of where on the field a player can risk dribbling by opponents: in the attacking zone.

Another way of penetrating tight defenses is to spread the defenders out by attacking across the whole width of the field. Teams with wingers do, of course, play on a wide front, but as we have seen, many teams in the 1960s played without wingers, and it was up to the midfield to give width to attack. Today, however, wingers are coming back into favor again, a trend that I hope will continue. As a striker, I know how much easier they make it for me and other strikers when they cause trouble out on the wings.

Few teams, however, can afford to have two wingers, unless they play 4–2–4, but even with one winger there is more opportunity to outflank the strongest defense. A winger can open up a defense by going down to the corner flag with the ball, then "cutting" it back (a reverse pass into the penalty area) for a striker or incoming midfielder to shoot first-time. Just as valuable a method of opening up a defense is for the winger to beat the outside back and get behind the defense. Even if he is unable to beat the outside back, his just being out there on the wing means a defender has to be allotted to mark him, which again helps to spread out the defense, making close covering more difficult for the defenders.

Wingers—and strikers too—are expected to drop back to help out in midfield when the ball is lost. Many modern wingers are in fact a combination of midfielder and forward, devoting equal time to the two roles. A winger can no longer stand on the touchline waiting for a pass, as Stanley Matthews and other earlier wingers used to; he must go back and try to win the ball like other midfielders. And when he is attacking, he is just as likely to be seen running through the middle of the defense as on the wing, since interchanging of positions among forwards is the dominant characteristic of modern soccer.

Another distinctive change for wingers playing today is that now they must be able to shoot with power. The days have gone when players like Stanley Matthews could dribble and pass but never score. Everyone in the forward line—indeed, everyone in the team—must be able to kick with power and accuracy.

Shooting at goal requires basically the same action as making a pass or clearing a ball out of defense, except that the player usually hits the ball so that it stays low. The instep and the outside-of-the-foot kicks are the two accepted kicks for shooting at goal. The other basic kick, the inside-of-the-foot kick, although the most accurate, does not have sufficient power and is generally used only for short passes. To keep the ball low, a player kicks with his knee and body over it. To add height, a player keeps his body farther back from the ball and leans back.

Strikers when they do shoot for goal must do it quickly with as little backswing as possible, though not to the extent that there is no power in the kick. The extra split second taken to exaggerate a backswing may be all the time necessary for a defender to either block the ball or steal it. Because of the tight marking and crowded conditions in the penalty area, the striker must be prepared to hit the ball no matter how it comes to him: on the ground, waist high, chest high or even head high. Pelé has often delighted his fans by scoring goals from nearly impossible positions. In 1976 he scored against the Miami Toros when Cosmos midfielder Terry Garbett crossed a high ball from the right wing into the Miami penalty area. Pelé, his back toward the Miami goal and surrounded by defenders, met the ball with a spectacular overhead volley, launching himself up high with his legs crisscrossing as his right foot hit the ball. The ball rocketed into the far top corner of the goal as Pelé fell to the ground. Cosmos coach Gordon Bradley claimed it was the best goal he had seen in his twenty-four years of soccer.

One way to avoid the congestion in the penalty area is to take long shots. Many goals are scored from 20 to 30 yards out; such goals are more likely to occur if the goalkeepers are surprised by sudden shots. However, long-range shooting requires enormous power, which only a few players, such as Pelé, Eusebio, Chinaglia, Best, Mitič and a few other strikers in the NASL possess.

Heading is another way to evade a crowded defense. Tall strikers quite often score more goals with their heads than with their feet, and many can hit a ball equally hard either way. Anyone who has seen Derek Smethurst's headers zooming into goal will know what I mean. Geoff Hurst is another marvelous header of the ball. Besides great power, he has a talent for deflecting the ball—he allows the ball to slide off his head at an oblique angle which makes the goalie's job that much more difficult.

After a player learns the correct way to head the ball, he concentrates on timing and jumping, since both the many defenders in the penalty area and the goalkeeper are obstacles when he attempts a header for goal. The proper way to head the ball here is to jump up high and hit the ball at the peak of the jump. To do this correctly, the player must have mastered anticipation. Geoff Hurst showed how it should be done in a game against San Antonio in 1976. His teammate Davey Butler took the ball out to the right wing and started a long run down the touchline. Upon seeing Geoff Hurst running toward the near post, Butler drove the ball across toward the goal mouth. Hurst, timing his run perfectly, reached the ball at the apex of his jump and nodded the ball into the net. It was such a well-executed goal that the 30,000 fans at the Seattle Kingdome stood on their feet and applauded for nearly five minutes.

The heading abilities of a forward line are best put to the test at corner kicks, since most corner kicks are hit into the air so that strikers can attempt to score. There are many variations of corner kicks, but most high ones are aimed far enough away from the goal so that the goalie will not come out and intercept them. Some are aimed so that they will drop short of the near post in order that the ball can be flicked to a teammate who will attempt to score; others, so that they will travel only a few feet to a teammate standing near the corner flag, who will then chip a high ball into the goal mouth for another teammate to head.

Strikers have to watch for the spin imparted to the ball at the time of corner kicks. The inswinger kick will spin the ball toward the goal; the outswinger, away from the goal. As most strikers are well aware, a miscalculation of the spin can result in the ball's being headed in the wrong direction.

Heading—like anything else in the penalty area—calls for a great amount of courage, much more than anyone who has not played competitive soccer may realize. Fear of flying legs and bruising physical contact has kept many a potentially talented player from reaching the top, particularly budding young strikers entering pro soccer. The powerful tackling in the NASL comes as quite a shock to the rookie drafted from college. As I was soon to learn in 1973, pro soccer is a great proving ground for courage, with the ultimate test coming as one enters the penalty area.

A striker must try to hide his fear and pain from his opponent. No matter how many knocks he takes or how many times he is kicked in the ankles or legs, the striker must keep going, for as soon as he shows his opponent any weakness he can be certain the opponent will take advantage of it. Unfortunately, there is many a defender in pro soccer, both here and abroad, who will try to intimidate a striker at the beginning of a game, either with some verbal threat or by violent physical contact. Such a defender hopes not only to scare the striker but to put him off his game and thereby ruin his concentration, without which no striker can be effective in modern soccer. The experienced striker learns to take all these threats with a grain of salt, but it can be a frightening experience for the rookie.

Bravery and determination are unteachable. So is opportunism. All three are, of course, related, and because they are so instinctive few of us can ever expect to achieve the success enjoyed by Gerd Müller, the amazing West German opportunist. Short and stocky, with legs like tree trunks, Müller scores goals from half chances. When others wouldn't attempt or even consider a shot at goal, Müller does, and with a high degree of success. He is perhaps not very elegant and certainly not a classical player like Pelé or Cruyff, but he is effective.

Most opportunists are good readers of the game. They are constantly aware of what is happening around them and usually have excellent peripheral vision—that human precursor of the wide-angle lens. They have to think and act quickly and, of course, have the courage to chase every ball that comes into the penalty area and take a quick shot, an overhead volley, a diving header or whatever action is needed to score.

The striker is also expected to do his fair share of defensive chores. At Dallas my job is to make certain that the opposing center backs do not move into our half of the field without my going with them. I also guard any opposing back who tries to overlap against us down the wing I might be covering, and I always rush back to my defensive position for corner kicks and free kicks, usually to guard the tallest opposing defender who has moved up. In addition to all this, I am expected to try to regain possession as soon as it is lost in the opponent's half—seldom possible when I am outnumbered but still a necessary duty of every striker, because it allows my teammates time to drop back in defense.

In the NASL we have a variety of types of strikers with varying styles, and who would want to say which is the preferred? Heavyset 190-pound, 6-foot-1 Giorgio Chinaglia, with his great shooting power and heading ability, is very different from, say, John Kowalik, who at 5 feet 7 and 145 pounds is nimble, can turn on a dime and has amazing acceleration. Georgie Best at 5 feet 8 scores just as many goals as the massive Clyde Best does at Portland, and Denny Vanninger of St. Louis is no better a striker for his 30-pound advantage over Paul Child of San Jose or Dallas' Jim Ryan. All types can be strikers in the NASL, but all must possess those four qualities I talked about at the outset—agility, balance, speed and power—plus that extra attribute: courage.

Chapter Twelve

Team Tactics

On November 30, 1872, in Glasgow, the English fielded eight forwards in the first English–Scottish international. When the same two teams met on May 27, 1972, only two English players were forwards. Yet two years later in the 1974 World Cup, the Dutch were playing total soccer with eight forwards again—at least, so it appeared at times. Such is the changing pattern of soccer tactics. How and why team formations have fluctuated so over the past hundred years is what I will attempt to trace in this chapter.

At the time of the Football Association's formation in 1863, soccer was basically a "team game for individuals," with each player trying to gain possession of the ball and run with it as far as he could. This "dribbling" style saw the man with the ball being chased not only by opponents but also by his own teammates, all trying to get the ball once he lost it. Apparently the English sporting gentlemen of the time never considered the option of passing the ball to one another. Instead, they battled through a mass of players, most of whom enjoyed nothing more than knocking to the ground the man in possession or, if this was not possible, at least hacking him in the shins.

A partial explanation for this unscientific style is found in the influence of the early offside law which prohibited an attacking player's going in front of the ball and also the ball's being passed forward. But even with this law, passing laterally or backward could have spread out the game if it had been tried.

The Scots were the first to see the benefits of passing. The famous amateur Scottish team Queen's Park of Glasgow (still an amateur team today and still competing against the pros in Scotland's second division) was the initiator of the passing game and used two backs, two halfbacks and six forwards—in modern parlance a 2–2–6 lineup. By interpassing, Queen's Park showed how the whole of the field could be used in its "modern" game based upon teamwork. It remained unbeaten for the first nine years of its existence, and not a single goal was scored against it in the first three.

As I noted in Chapter Two, this Scottish style spread to England after Scotland's national team had inflicted a series of defeats on the English in the late 1870s. Preston North End of England built a memorable team based upon the Scottish short pass, which became even more effective after Preston withdrew one of the six forwards to form a 2–3–5 lineup. This extra halfback became the center half, who was primarily an attacking halfback but was expected to help in the defense whenever needed.

In the 2–3–5, or "pyramid," system, the two fullbacks, or backs, guarded the penalty area. The two flanking halfbacks (also called wing halves) helped out in defense, permitting the center half to move up into the attack, while the five forwards were spread across the field. Although 2–3–5 was the favored system for nearly fifty years, variations in each player's duties were common. In most countries by 1925 (when the offside law was changed) the two wing halves had become more like present-day midfielders, free to move up in support of the forward line. The two inside forwards also acted as midfielders whenever necessary, withdrawing behind the three other forwards to provide more depth in the attacking formation. (Even in those days it was clear that a line of forwards strung across the width of the field was not as effective as an echelon formation.)

The offside trap of the early 1920s brought about the change in the offside law, with the magic number of opponents being reduced from three to two. In the avalanche of goals that resulted from the change, center forwards broke all scoring records: Dixie Dean scored 60 goals in 39 games in England's first division; George Camsell of Middlesbrough broke the second-division record with 59 in 37 games; and up in Scotland, J. Smith of Ayr United hit 66 goals in 38 games. The emergence of the "stopper" center half soon put an end to this goal glut.

When the attacking center half was moved back to meet the opposing center forwards, it was the first time in soccer's history that the forwards did not outnumber the defenders. Five forwards now faced five defenders, and if one counts the goalkeeper the forwards were actually at a disadvantage numerically.

For over twenty-five years attackers tried to find an answer to the stopper center half, who was the linchpin of the new defensive formation—now called the W–M system because of its resemblance to the two letters when the players lined up. The rest of the defense pivoted around the center half, so that a balanced or diagonal defense was formed with him in the middle. For instance, if an attack came from the right wing, the center half would move across to assist his back while the other back would drop behind the center half to cover him in case he engaged the opposing winger. The three defenders would thus be in a diagonal line, as in Diagram E. By careful covering, each of the defenders had a backup man in case he was beaten. Highly skilled defenders were able to use this W–M system to advantage, but many teams thought it too defensive-minded, and some teams, especially Latin American, stayed with the attacking-center-half, or 2–3–5, system until the late 1930s.

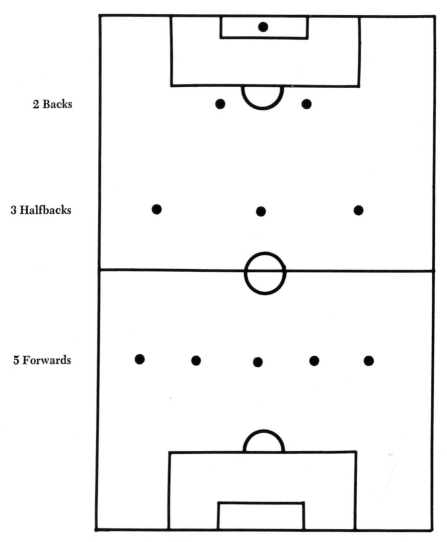

2 Backs

3 Halfbacks

5 Forwards

The backs stayed in or near the penalty area and marked the opposing inside forwards. The right half and the left half assisted the backs by marking the opposing wingers, while the center half—when he came back into defense—marked the center forward. The five forwards attacked in a straight line.

In later years the two wing halves and two inside forwards would link up in midfield as in Diagram D.

DIAGRAM B
DEPTH IN ATTACK

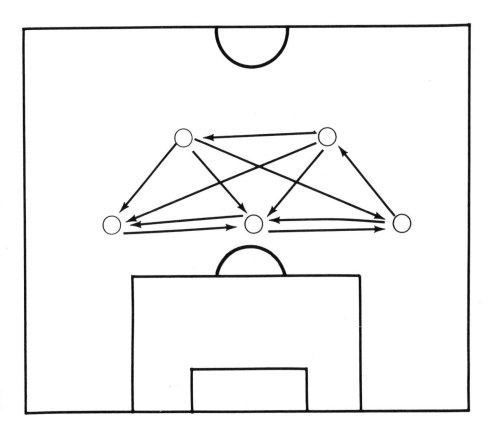

When the two inside forwards dropped back, they opened up the way for a variety of passing options. Even today, this triangular passing pattern is the method most often used for advancing the ball.

DIAGRAM C

OFFSIDE

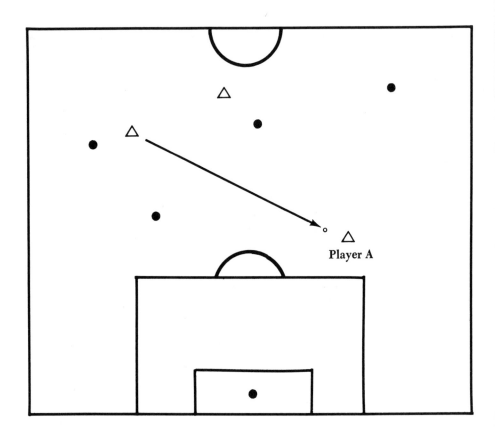

Player A is offside, since there are not two opponents (depicted by circles) between him and the opponent's goal line at the time the ball is played toward him.

DIAGRAM D

THE W-M FORMATION OR 3-4-3

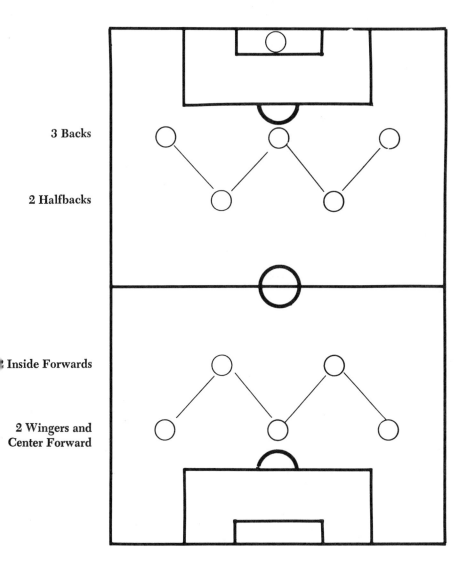

The center half has dropped back to play alongside the two backs. In modern day terms this could be described as a 3–4–3 system.

DIAGRAM E

THE BALANCED LINE

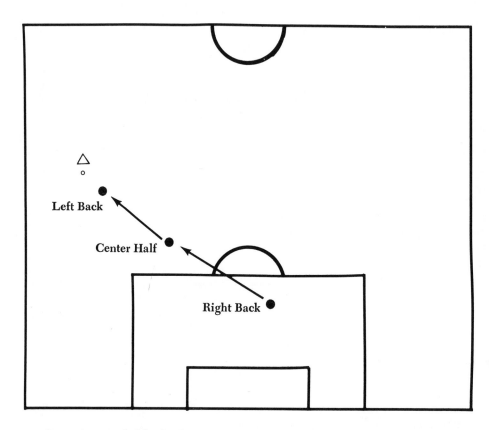

Cover is provided by backs pivoting on the center half so that a balanced or diagonal line is maintained whenever an opponent approaches the goal. In this diagram notice how the center half covers his left back while the right back, moving away from his touchline, has dropped behind the center half.

The secret of the success of the W–M, or third-back, system was that the center half was stationed permanently in the middle of the defense, blocking the direct route to goal. When the Hungarians showed the world how to move this obstacle, by drawing the center half out of his position through the use of the withdrawn center forward, the W–M system was doomed.

The next step in the evolution of soccer strategy came about in the late 1950s when an additional defender was placed in the center of the defense so that two center halfs or center backs could effectively solve the problems caused by the withdrawn center forward.

In the 1958 World Cup we saw the Brazilians use two center backs in a 4–2–4 lineup, instead of the one center half of the W–M system, who in effect had been a center back for over twenty-five years. The 4–2–4 system consisted of four backs; two halfbacks, or midfielders, and four forwards. The fullbacks no longer pivoted on the one center back but stayed out on the wings while the two center backs covered each other.

Actually, many teams had played a form of 4–2–4 for many years without calling it such. The double center forward had been tried, as had the two center halfs, but not in the organized style of the Brazilians, nor with the brilliant array of talent that they were able to call upon to perfect the new system. Especially important to the success of a 4–2–4 system are first-rate midfielders, and Brazil was indeed lucky in 1958 to have both Didi and Zito, certainly two of the greatest midfielders ever. Other top teams in the late 1950s and early '60s were to find 4–2–4 too hazardous simply because they did not have the right men for the two midfield positions.

It soon became clear to teams lacking the right players for the two midfield positions that 4–2–4 could be made easier if a third midfielder were added to assume some of the work load. And so in the early 1960s, 4–3–3 came into favor. The game was now tilted unequivocally toward defense— or was it? Seven men in defense with only six in the attack (if one counted the midfield men in both contingents) certainly seemed a step backward. In actual fact, 4–3–3, when played with a great deal of running off the ball, overlapping by backs and midfielders' going up into the forward line, can be as offensive as any system yet devised; but here again it depends upon the players available. As modern coaches have discovered, systems can work well only if they are built around talented players. If players are forced to work in a system that does not fit their capabilities, the results are usually disastrous.

The majority of the teams in the NASL use a flexible form of 4–3–3 with an emphasis on pushing the midfielders up into attack. Many teams also

DIAGRAM F

THE WITHDRAWN CENTER FORWARD

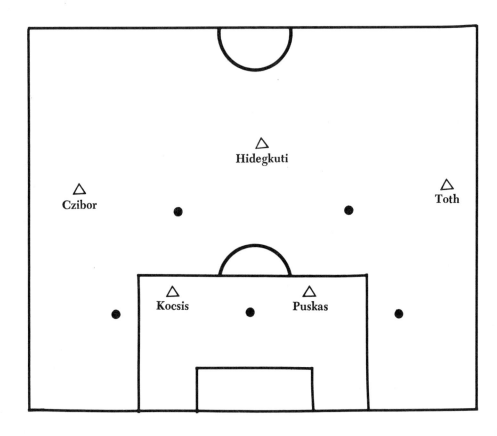

The Hungarians of the early 1950s played Hidegkuti behind their two inside forwards, who in actual fact could have been described as the first twin center forwards of modern soccer. The wingers, Czibor and Toth, were also withdrawn to play behind the two inside forwards, Kocsis and Puskas.

Against England in 1954 the two wingers were able to draw the English backs far away from their center half, causing large gaps to appear in the English defense.

DIAGRAM G
THE 4–2–4 FORMATION

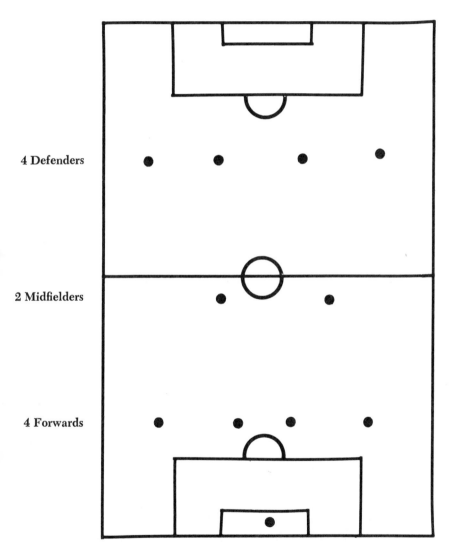

4 Defenders

2 Midfielders

4 Forwards

In this system two center backs replace the center half, and two backs stay out on the touchlines and no longer pivot on the center half. The two wingers are of the orthodox style—speedy players who hug the touchlines and provide the twin center forwards, or strikers, with passes.

DIAGRAM H

THE 4–3–3 FORMATION

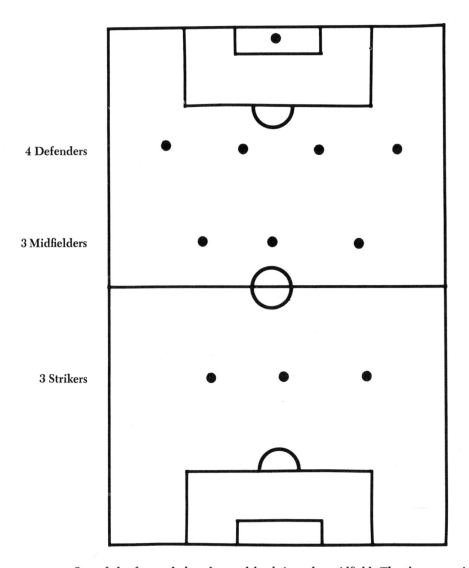

4 Defenders

3 Midfielders

3 Strikers

One of the forwards has dropped back into the midfield. The three remaining forwards can be used in various combinations: two wingers and one striker, two strikers and one winger or no wingers at all with three strikers spread out across the width of the field.

use one or more midfielders as auxiliary wingers—the midfielder assuming the winger's position in the empty space along the touchline when it has been left vacant because the team plays with only one or no wingers. At Dallas, as in the majority of NASL clubs, we attempt to build up our attacking movements in such a way that our midfielders can participate from the time we gain possession until we try to score. This continuous use of midfielders as additional helpers in attack is what makes 4-3-3 attractive. If, on the other hand, they are used mostly as defensive players, 4-3-3 can be a great bore. I believe the NASL style of attacking soccer has proved that 4-3-3 can be attractive and entertaining.

In the late 1960s an ultradefensive system was developed: the 4-4-2. Thankfully, it's seldom seen in the NASL—our bonus-points sytsem makes it foolish for even the most defensive-minded coach to consider utilizing it. In 4-4-2 the two strikers are expected to go for goals alone against four or more defenders, or else to slow up the game until their midfield players arrive to help. (It should be noted that once a game starts, these modern soccer formations are difficult to recognize. The interchanging of positions and the constant movement of the players make it difficult to see whether, for instance, there are four backs or eight, or two forwards or six. But after a reasonable period of "formation watching" fans can usually tell what system the coach is using.)

Probably the most definitive of all defensive systems is *catenaccio*, which mercifully has been confined for the most part to Italian soccer. The most prominent characteristic of *catenaccio* is the role played by the sweeper, or *libero*, who patrols the last line of defense, stationed as he is behind the back line. His singular job is to challenge anyone who gets past the backs. To further bolster this precautionary system, many teams withdraw the majority of their players to defensive positions, so that formations like 1-4-4-1 are not uncommon sights in Italy.

The monotony of *catenaccio* and 4-4-2 have been relieved in the last few years by the appearance of total soccer. The Dutch and West Germans are the prime exponents of this nonstop style of play, in which the strong, energetic aspects of German and English soccer are mixed with the high degree of technical skill commonly associated with the talented South Americans. The origins of total soccer can be traced to Alf Ramsay and his wingless 4-3-3 World Cup team of 1966—a team whose "work rate" was phenomenal as the players increased their running off the ball to compensate for the lack of wingers. The distinction among the three zones on the field—defense, midfield and attack—was dimmed as individual players switched from one zone to another. Fullbacks Cohen and Wilson in particular overlapped as they ran down the touchlines as auxiliary for-

DIAGRAM I

THE 4–4–2 FORMATION

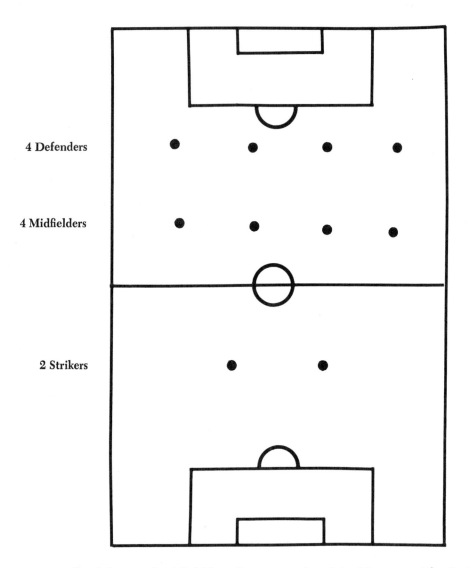

4 Defenders

4 Midfielders

2 Strikers

The defense and midfield have been strengthened in this system. The diminution of the forward line is mitigated somewhat by the movement of some of the midfielders into attacking positions whenever possible.

DIAGRAM J
CATENACCIO

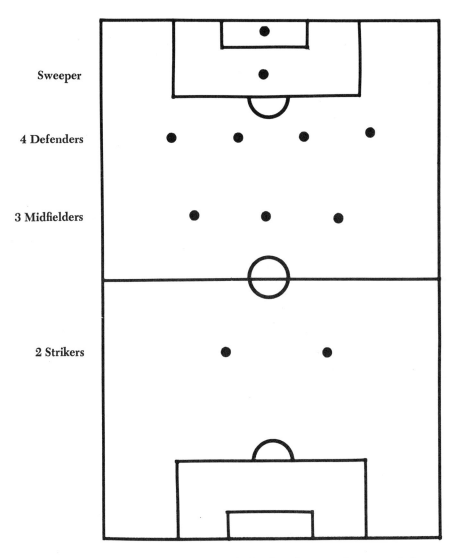

Sweeper

4 Defenders

3 Midfielders

2 Strikers

In this system a sweeper stays behind a three- or four-man defense, and at least two of the midfielders are assigned defensive duties. Man-to-man marking is very tight, allowing opposing forwards little room to maneuver. The forwards are expected to function effectively on breakaways. Some defensive-minded teams in Italy play a 1–3–5–1 formation, leaving just one striker upfield to act as a targetman.

wards. Midfielders Peters, Charlton and Ball also moved away from specialization as they assumed increasing striking duties.

In the early 1970s, the Dutch and then the West German national teams went one step further than the English team of 1966, giving all team members (other than the goalkeeper, of course) the opportunity—indeed, the responsibility—of switching from any of the three zones to another to meet the demands of the immediate game situation. Their players were now expected to be sufficiently skilled and fit enough to handle any of the ten field positions, notwithstanding their actual team position. Without these all-around players total soccer would be a disastrous system, and this is the reason why so few teams have adopted it.

I think, however, that as more players are introduced to it, total soccer, with its elasticity of positional play and all ten field men trying to score goals while at the same time trying to stop opponents from scoring, will be the style of the future. A player will obviously have to be in perfect physical shape for total soccer—probably fitter than any other sporting athlete, for he must spend most of his time on the field running, either with the ball or in support.

No matter what tactical disposition a team uses, without outstanding individuals it will never be great, for despite all the changes over the past hundred years, soccer is basically still a "team game for individuals." It is not a sport in which pro athletes can be programmed to carry out detailed instructions by rote. Every moment of the game a player has to make swift subjective decisions which must be carried out with a combination of skill, agility and sheer good luck—all too unscientific for any computerization of the sport. Thankfully, soccer will always belong to the individual, and that is what makes it the best of all team sports.

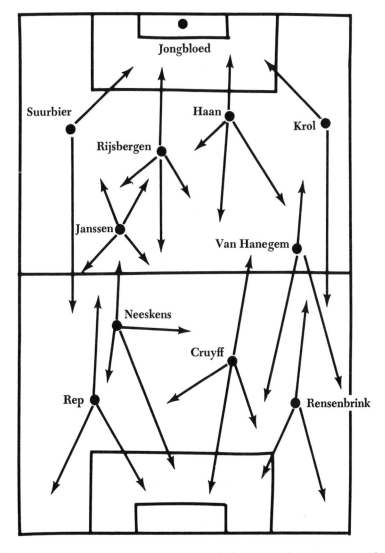

DIAGRAM K
TOTAL SOCCER

In this system there is nonstop movement of players, and cover is provided by teammates' interchanging positions as the situation dictates; for example, whenever a defender or midfielder moves out of position someone is expected to move into his slot.

In the 1974 World Cup, as the arrows indicate, Suurbier and Krol were constantly switching with Jansen and Van Hanegem as they moved up into attacking positions. Meanwhile Cruyff, Neeskens and Rensenbrink dropped back to cover for Van Hanegem and Jansen when they moved out of position. Everyone on the team, other than goalkeeper Jongbloed, moved up, down and across the field, attacking one moment, defending the next. The system was fluid, effective and total.

PART THREE

Chapter Thirteen

The Future of American Soccer

"The United States will be the center of world soccer within ten years."
Phil Woosnam, Commissioner of the NASL

If someone had suggested ten years ago that I would one day be writing a book on soccer, I would have considered the person slightly insane. I had never watched a real game of soccer played and probably would have continued playing football in the fall, basketball in the winter and baseball in the summer if pro soccer had not come to Dallas in 1967. Like many other high school students in Dallas and other NASL cities, I watched the pros and liked what I saw. The 1967 Dallas team was actually Dundee United, guesting as the representative for the Dallas Tornado in the old United Soccer Association setup (before the merger of the USA and the NPSL). Dundee played a strong, physical and fast game that certainly impressed me.

The arrival of the pros in 1967 brought soccer to the attention of youngsters like me and added a new phrase to the American vocabulary: youth soccer. In Dallas and other NASL cities like Atlanta, Baltimore, Los Angeles, Oakland, San Francisco, Cleveland and San Diego, youth soccer expanded seemingly overnight despite the lack of interest of the adults at the box office. The growth at the youth level continued at a rapid rate even in 1969 and 1970, the weakest years of the NASL.

The late 1960s and early '70s also saw a mass movement by colleges into soccer. In 1959 when the National College Association organized the first nationwide tournament there were 100 college teams. In 1967 there were 250, and by 1972, 600 were fielding varsity teams.

Even though many college teams in the past sought success by importing foreign students on scholarship, by the mid-1970s more and more Americans were filling the ranks of the better teams. Not all, of course, who might have wished to. Even today there are college coaches who would rather win games with foreign students than risk losing games with homegrown players. Three powerhouses of the collegiate scene, Howard,

Clemson, and the University of San Francisco, are prime examples of schools heavily laden with foreign talent. The top "Americanized" schools are to be found around the St. Louis area: St. Louis University, ten-time winner of the national championship since 1959; Missouri–St. Louis; Southern Illinois University; Quincy and Indiana University, whose team included only one foreign student when it lost the 1976 championship (by the only goal of the match) to the University of San Francisco. The success of Indiana University and the St. Louis teams in recent years augurs well for the future of both American college soccer and professional soccer.

The tremendous growth in college soccer is matched by the rapid strides made in youth soccer. In 1968 there were 1,770 high schools fielding soccer teams. In 1972 there were 2,800, and today there are so many no one can really say with any certainty how many there are. Trying to compute the number of park-district, YMCA, boys'-club and grammar school teams is also beyond the capabilities of state and national soccer bodies. In 1977 a reasonable estimate was that over 2 million youngsters were playing in organized soccer.

Undoubtedly, the most amazing development of all in the youth soccer explosion has been the success of the American Youth Soccer Organization (AYSO) in the Western states. Formed in 1964 by a group of California parents with a motto of "Everyone Plays," the AYSO had 11,000 youngsters playing in California by 1972. Today there are over 100,000 boys and girls participating in 18 states.

Along with the growth of soccer have come distinct improvements in coaching, at both the high school and college levels. The United States Soccer Federation (USSF) can claim credit for the advances made. Its nationwide coaching schools have been instrumental not only in improving existing coaching but also in inspiring young coaches to stay with soccer, especially those in high schools where the job of coaching soccer was traditionally given to the P.E. instructor with the least tenure. American coaches today really know their soccer. Many of them, like Al Miller, who had a glittering career with Hartwick College before coming to Dallas, have written books on the game. Indeed, so many coaches and sportswriters are authoring soccer books that only the most ardent of fans would consider buying all of them. In 1976, for example, there were twenty-one soccer books published in the United States, the majority of them in hardcover. Who would have thought ten years ago when I first tried to find a soccer book in the stores that Americans would eventually have such a choice or would be willing to spend $10 or more for one?

On the adult level, the ethnic semiprofessional leagues continue to thrive as they adjust to the new influx of American-born players. Out West, the oldest of all the existing leagues, the Greater Los Angeles Soccer League (GLASL), founded in 1902, remains one of the top semiprofessional circuits in the country. Representative of the high standard of play seen in the GLASL are such teams as the Los Angeles Kickers, the Yugoslavia-Americans, South Bay United and the Los Angeles Maccabees.

There is also top semiprofessional soccer in another old league, The San Francisco Soccer League, founded in 1904. Some of its stronger teams are the San Francisco Athletic Club, the Greek-Americans, the Sons of Italy, Concordia and the San Francisco Scots.

Probably the most organized of adult soccer leagues is the National Soccer League of Chicago, comprising over 100 teams, prominent among which are the Lions, Schwaben, Croatans, Eagles, Kickers and Maroons.

Around New York, the best semipro league is the fifty-five-year-old German-American Football Association (GAFA), another league whose ethnicity has diminished in recent years. A league that continues to expand, the GAFA now has over 50 adult teams as well as nearly another 50 youth teams. Some of its top clubs include Croatia, German-Hungarians, Inter Giuliana, Elizabeth, Dalmatinac and New York Hungaria.

Many NASL players have been recruited from these four semiprofessional leagues, but some return to play semiprofessional soccer for their old clubs during the NASL off season.

The best-known professional league next to the NASL is the American Soccer League (ASL). Not to be confused with the old ASL of the 1920s, the present American Soccer League was founded in 1931 and until the 1970s was based on the Eastern Seaboard. In the last few years it has expanded to the Middle West and the West Coast and now includes the following teams:

California Sunshine (Orange County)	New England Oceaneers
Cleveland Cobras	New Jersey Americans (Freehold)
Connecticut Yankees (Milford)	New York Apollo
Los Angeles Skyhawks	Sacramento Spirits

Although the league has had some measure of success in a few cities, the expansion has not convinced anyone that the ASL is presently a serious rival to the NASL as America's leading pro soccer league. Nevertheless, the ASL commissioner, Bob Cousy, the former basketball star, states that the league plans to expand to many more cities in the next five years. If this happens and the clubs are successful I think the NASL will be forced to sit down and discuss a merger with the ASL, for if there is one thing American professional soccer has learned in the last ten years it is that rival soccer leagues spell financial ruin.

In reviewing the strides made in youth and adult soccer over the last ten years, one can see the clear-cut trend which substantiates the claims, oft thought exaggerated, of soccer's phenomenal growth. And now there are other signs which point to a quickening of the pace. One significant indicator is that for the first time top young athletes are entering soccer now that it has become a fashionable sport for American youth. The other and more revealing indicator is the stressing of soccer in high schools and colleges, not only because it is less expensive and safer to play than football but also because it has come to be recognized as the best of team sports for physical conditioning. The fact that anyone can play regardless of size and height has also not been lost on education administrators. It has taken our schools over fifty years to discover these simple truths about soccer; but in typical American fashion, once we see our mistakes we set about rectifying them rapidly, and few can fail to be impressed by the speed with which soccer has become accepted by American schools in the last five years.

The success of American soccer domestically—in the schools and colleges and in rising NASL standards—has yet to be duplicated on the international front. But despite our national team's being knocked out of the 1976 Olympics and the 1978 World Cup in the qualifying rounds, our prospects for the future look much rosier. As greater sums of money are derived by the USSF from pro soccer clubs, so more funds will be available for the national team's preparation—its coaching, training camps and players' expenses. Couple this with the higher caliber of players who are graduating from collegiate soccer and the splendid displays of the pro rookies in the NASL and it becomes more understandable why I expect to see the United States become a dominant force in world soccer within the next decade.

But there is an enormous amount of hard work ahead of us before we take our rightful place alongside our international brothers as equals in the worldwide arena of soccer. First, I think we have to get serious about the World Cup, the Olympics and the general area of "internationals." By this I mean the USSF, the NASL and other soccer administrations' sitting down together and agreeing to long-range commitments. Above all they must be willing to earmark—for the first time in American soccer history —large sums of money.

Perhaps we should follow the example of the East Germans, who in the late 1960s decided they would undertake a nationwide program to improve their swimming standards. It was a large undertaking, requiring a large amount of funding and administrative effort, but by the 1972 Olympics their swimmers had improved beyond recognition, and by 1976 they were the talk of the Montreal Olympics with their outstanding performances.

Obviously it took an extreme commitment and a great deal of money to achieve this high degree of success in international sport, and I would not expect the American soccer organizations with their limited resources to try to duplicate the lavish scale of the East Germans. But surely we should be able to afford a national training center such as those in other countries —an all-weather facility that could be used throughout the year. And the first thing I would do at the training center is to take 40 to 60 of our best American players at the end of the pro season and train them for a month to six weeks every fall. Out of this group would emerge 15 to 20 of the best players, who could then become the nucleus of the U.S. national team.

I would also like to see the USSF give ample notice of all national-team scheduling so that our players—none of whom is paid a full-time salary —can make appropriate plans in order to be available for training sessions and international games. For example, if Al Trost of St. Louis, a schoolteacher in the off season, knows in March that there is to be a six-week training camp in November he will have the opportunity to seek a leave of absence. This type of notice would go a long way toward convincing American players that the USSF has at last become capable of handling the enormous responsibility of maintaining a nationwide system of professional soccer.

The NASL could also help by contributing to a development fund— say, $5,000 per club—that would enable the USSF to hire on a full-time basis the 15 to 20 players selected for the squad of the national team. With this financial backing the players could stay together at least during the fall months and not have to worry about where the next week's food money would be coming from.

The question of funding, of course, reappears every time one talks about elevating the U.S. national team to a top-class side. In the past, American soccer has always been at a disadvantage in the international field because of its lack of financial backing. But that no longer need continue now that the general public is becoming interested in the game. Properly, the time has come for us to tap this new interest by inviting foreign teams to play fund-raising games against the U.S. national team, perhaps in conjunction with a charity so as to raise money for another good cause in addition to the national team.

In addition to the revenue they raised, these charitable games would go a long way toward providing the players with the invaluable experience of playing together as a team and being exposed to top-level international soccer, where the speed and creativity reach heights never duplicated in club games. Such games would also help our players devote more of their time to soccer. Most of our American pro players, including me, do not spend all the time they should on the game. Of course, we cannot expect to see a ten-month pro season such as there is in England, but we have to ensure that in the very near future there is off-season soccer for our promising players.

Our college and high school seasons are also much too short. Two months a year is simply not enough for soccer-hungry players. On the other hand, I do not join in with the many soccer enthusiasts who see our higher educational system as a barrier to producing top soccer talent. They prefer the way soccer players are trained abroad—in England, for example, where a promising player is through with school and signed by a pro club by the time he is 16 and proceeds to play with and learn from the pros while he is still in his teens. I feel it is actually a great advantage that most of our players can and do get a college education while playing soccer. Not simply because they obviously have a better opportunity to enter a good occupation when their soccer careers are over, but also because their additional intellectual capability must be an asset to them as soccer players when it is complemented after their college days with first-class professional coaching.

What I think is needed in college soccer, however, is the continuing raising of standards to the point at which it comes as close as possible to the level of professional soccer, so that there can be a very direct funneling of talent, in the same way the NFL derives its football talent from the college system. At present, our collegiate soccer players generally have to take a much larger step when moving up into the pro world than do the collegiate athletes going into pro basketball, football or baseball.

Then, of course, something has to be done about the small number of Americans currently playing on NASL teams. To be frank, the ASL, despite its major administrative problems, is doing a better job in this area, as it has a much higher percentage of Americans playing regularly. I would venture to say that if the ASL is able to stay afloat financially it will soon be supplying the bulk of talent for the U.S. national and Olympic teams.

It would be good for American soccer if the ASL and the NASL were to agree to compete against each other, not on an all-star basis, but by fielding the best Americans in the ASL against the best Americans in the NASL. Such games might well force both of the leagues to devote more of their energies to developing promising American players, and the indirect benefit would be that our Olympic and national teams would be represented by more experienced and, I would hope, better players.

I also think the NASL should have all four of its divisions field American all-star teams which could play exhibition games against the four or five clubs in each division. It this manner we would be ensuring that at least 60 American players would be able to play regularly against top-class opposition. The games could all be played on weeknights, and if, for example, Steve Pecher, Neil Cohen, Glenn Myernick and I were selected for the Southern Division American team, we could play against Dallas on a Wednesday night but still play for Dallas on the weekend. Not only would there be little inconvenience for our club, but Dallas would get the opportunity to use the game as a part of its practice schedule.

When our national soccer administrators begin their concerted effort to improve our Olympic and national team, I think it would be wise if they also considered what type of players we need to raise the level of American soccer so that the players can compete successfully against foreign teams. My personal view is that our greatest need is for more and better wingers. It does not matter what type of winger: it can be the Georgie Best type, who can take on defenders, dribble past them and take the ball inside to score; or the Stanley Matthews variety, who simply beats an opponent out on the touchline before passing the ball into the penalty area. The style is not important as long as we can find players with a high degree of skill who can attack defenders with the ball.

I would say the second-most-critical need is for creative midfielders who are capable of making accurate transitions from defense to attack. We have been able to produce strong defensive midfielders and many who can shoot accurately when in attacking positions, but few are able to stamp their personal mark on the midfield as our foreign colleagues do. We need more midfielders who can receive the ball in midfield, turn and protect it under pressure and make a penetrating pass into the opponent's defense.

Thirdly, we also have a need for strikers who can take advantage of any loose balls around the box (penalty area). I don't expect to see a Gerd Müller or a Johan Cruyff produced here in the near future, but I would like to think that soon we will have some skilled American strikers who can take half chances and cause problems with them even against the best defenses.

One other improvement I would like to see emerge from any national coaching scheme is more mobile center backs. We have some good central defenders in the NASL right now. Defensively, Steve Pecher, Alex Skotarek and Werner Roth are equal to any center back in the league, all being good, solid defensive players, but we do not yet have that type of mobile center back who can take the ball into the midfield and turn the midfield into the attacking zone the way Beckenbauer can. Most of our central defenders are quite content to play the ball from defense out to the wings for the backs to overlap. Seldom do we see a center back getting into a shooting position.

Whatever else we are able to do in the coming years to raise the standards of American soccer, I would think it is absolutely essential that the United States qualify for the 1982 World Cup, to be held in Spain. And I believe it can be done. To place among the last 16 in Spain, however, would require the USSF to spare no expense or effort to ensure that our national team prepares for the World Cup at least two years before the qualifying rounds begin. It should not be beyond the USSF's financial ability to get the team together for weeklong training sessions in 1979 and for a broad exhibition schedule in 1980 so that the team will be physically and psychologically prepared to face the Mexicans and the Canadians in 1980.

I am confident that with the right preparation, young players like Boris Bandov (Seattle), Sam Bick (Minnesota), Neil Cohen (Dallas), Eugene DuChateau (Connecticut), Arnold Mausser (Denver), Glenn Myernick (Dallas), John Mason (Los Angeles), Steve Pecher (Dallas), and Jim Pollihan (Rochester) and Rick Davis (Cosmos), along with established international veterans of the caliber of Dave D'Errico (Minnesota), Bob Rigby (Los Angeles), Alex Skotarek (Chicago), Bobby Smith (New York), Al Trost (St. Louis), Denny Vanninger (St. Louis), Julie Vee (San Jose) and Dennis Wit (Tampa Bay), will prove a match for all but the very best worldwide talent in 1982. I am also just as positive that this list will be incomplete as the next few years provide us with many more American stars of the future.

More important than success in the World Cup or the Olympics is the gratifying fact that American men, women, boys and girls are at last turning to soccer for exercise and entertainment. As new leagues continue to sprout up across the country, it is clearly justifiable to state that soccer will soon reach the stage predicted by Thomas Cahill in 1924: that it would become the number one sport in the country after baseball. I think I will go one better than the good Mr. Cahill and go out on a limb and prophesy that within the next ten years it will be *the* number one sport—at least as far as the number of people playing it on a team basis goes.

There is no doubt that the next ten years will be the most exciting decade in American soccer history. Soccer's continuing growth will require cooperation among the USSF, the state associations and the professional and semiprofessional leagues. There will be many challenges to be met, many problems to be solved and a need for greater participation on the local administrative level—at least another 40,000 referees and 10,000 administrators will have to be recruited during the decade. But whether you are interested in becoming an administrator, a player or solely a spectator, I know you will enjoy being a part of American soccer's fascinating future.

Who's Who in the NASL

In referring to this biographical section, please bear in mind that there is a constant movement of personnel among NASL clubs and that many of the players listed here will probably change clubs in the near future.

Agostinis, Reno (Tampa Bay). Defender—6'11"—165—born 4/4/53. Played for Simon Fraser University. Canadian.

Aguirre, Roberto (Fort Lauderdale). Midfielder—5'11"—178—born 2/10/46. Argentinian international and NASL all-star.

Alcock Terry (Portland). Defender—6'1"—175—born 12/9/46. Played for Blackpool and Port Vale. British.

Alon, Benny (Chicago). Midfielder—5'11"—170—born 9/13/50. Played for Hapoel Haifa. Israeli.

Alston, Adrian (Tampa Bay). Forward—6'0"—170—born 2/6/49. Played for Australian and English clubs including Luton Town. Australian international.

Anderson, Willie (Portland). Forward—5'8"—150—born 1/26/47. Played for Manchester United, Aston Villa and Cardiff. British.

Askew, John (Washington). Forward—6'0"—175—born 4/17/57. Played for Essex Community College in Baltimore. U.S. citizen.

Auguste, Arsène (Tampa Bay). Defender—6'2"—185—born 2/3/51. Played for New Jersey Brewers in the ASL. Haitian international.

Backos, Des (Los Angeles). Forward—5'7"—160—born 11/13/50. Played for Highlands Park and Hellenic in South Africa. South African.

Bailey, Mike (Minnesota). Midfielder—5'8"—155—born 2/27/42. Played for Wolverhampton Wanderers. English international.

Bandov, Boris (Seattle). Forward—5'10"—175—born 11/23/53. Played for San Jose. U.S. international.

Banks, Gordon (Ft. Lauderdale). Goalkeeper—5'11"—170—born 12/30/39. Played for Leicester and Stoke City. England's Footballer of the Year in 1972. English international.

Barnett, Geoff (Minnesota). Goalkeeper—6'0"—166—born 10/16/46. Played for Everton and Arsenal. British.

Baumann, Steve (Ft. Lauderdale). Midfielder—5'11"—160—born 9/16/52. Played for Los Angeles. All-American at Pennsylvania.

Beal, Phil (Los Angeles). Defender—5'10"—160—born 1/8/45. Played for Tottenham Hotspur and Brighton. English Under-21 international.

Beckenbauer, Franz (Cosmos). Defender—5'11"—165—born 9/11/45. Played for Bayern Munich. European Footballer of the Year 1972 and 1976. German international.

Bell, Bobby (Ft. Lauderdale). Defender—6'0"—165—born 9/26/50. Played for Ipswich, Blackburn, Crystal Palace. British.

Bellinger, Tony (Dallas). Midfielder—5'11"—165—born 12/8/57. Went to Dallas straight from J. F. Kennedy High School in Willingsboro. Played for U.S. National Junior team.

Bennett, Chris (Seattle). Midfielder—5'9"—165—born 1/15/52. Played for Vancouver. Canadian international.

Bennett, Peter (St. Louis). Midfielder—5'11"—172—born 6/24/46. Played for West Ham United and Orient. British.

Berrico, José (Team Hawaii). Defender—5'8"—155—born 11/19/47. Played for Monterrey of Mexico. Brazilian.

Best, Clyde (Portland). Forward—6'2"—195—born 2/24/51. Played for West Ham of England and Tampa Bay. Native of Bermuda.

Betts, Tony (Portland). Midfielder—5'11"—168—born 10/31/53. Played for Aston Villa and Port Vale in England. British.

Bick, Sam (Minnesota). Defender—5'11"—175—born 1/30/55. All-American at Quincy. U.S. international.

Bilecki, Zeljko (Toronto). Goalkeeper—6'1"—180—born 4/28/50. Canadian international.

Binney, Fred (St. Louis). Forward—5'10"—170—born 8/12/46. Played for Torquay, Exeter and Brighton. British.

Bokern, Jim (St. Louis). Forward—5'9"—155—born 4/16/52. Played for St. Louis University.

Bowery, Bert (Team Hawaii). Forward—6'1"—195—born 10/29/54. Played for Nottingham Forest and Boston. British.

Brine, Peter (Minnesota). Midfielder—5'10"—148—born 7/18/53. Played for Middlesbrough in England. British.

Brooks, Doug (Minnesota). Forward—5'11"—165—born 9/14/53. Played for Florissant Valley College.

Brown, Graham (Portland). Goalkeeper—6'0"—175—born 3/21/46. Played for Mansfield, Doncaster and Swansea. British.

Budd, Brian (Vancouver). Forward—6'1"—180—born 4/8/52. Played for University of British Columbia. Canadian.

Burnett, Dennis (St. Louis). Midfielder—5'11"—165—born 7/27/44. Played for West Ham United, Milwall and other English clubs. British.

Butler, David (Seattle). Forward—5'8"—152—born 3/30/53. Played for West Bromwich Albion in England. British.

Buttle, Steve (Seattle). Midfielder—5'7"—138—born 1/1/45. Played for Ipswich and Bournemouth. British.

Cacciatore, Steve (St. Louis). Forward—5'7"—131—born 5/1/44. Played for SIU and Los Angeles Skyhawks of the ASL. U.S. citizen.

Calloway, Laurie (San Jose). Defender—5'10"—170—born 6/17/45. Played for Los Angeles. NASL all-star.

Carenza, Chris (Team Hawaii). Defender—6'2"—185—born 3/3/52. Played for SIU and U.S. Olympic team.

Carenza, John (St. Louis). Forward or defender—6'4"—190—born 1/3/56. Like his brother Chris, John played for SIU and the U.S. Olympic team.

Carlyle, Hillary (Las Vegas). Forward—6'1"—186—born 8/20/54. Played for Finn Harps of Ireland. Irish.

Cassaretto, Enrique (Ft. Lauderdale). Forward—6'2"—160—born 4/29/45. Played for Sporting Cristal in Peru. Peruvian international.

Cave, Mickey (Seattle). Midfielder—5'8—155—born 1/28/49. Played for Bournemouth and York in England and the Los Angeles Skyhawks in the ASL. British.

Cawston, Mervyn (Chicago). Goalkeeper—6'2"—175—born 2/4/52. Played for Norwich City and Gillingham in England. British.

Ceballos, Sergio (Ft. Lauderdale). Forward—5'11"—170—born 2/15/51. Played for Cruz Azul and Club de Fútbol in Mexico. Mexican.

Chadwick, David (Ft. Lauderdale). Midfielder—5'7"—145—born 8/19/43. Played for Southampton, Middlesbrough and other English clubs. Also played for Dallas and Tacoma in the ASL. British.

Chandler, Peter (Connecticut). Defender—6'0"—160—born 3/19/53. Played for Springfield College, Mass., and U.S. National team.

Child, Paul (San Jose). Forward—5'10"—165—born 12/8/52. Played for Aston Villa in England. U.S. international.

Chinaglia, Giorgio (Cosmos). Forward—6'1"—190—born 1/24/47. Played for Lazio in Italy. Italian international.

Chursky, Tony (Seattle). Goalkeeper—5'10½"—165—born 6/1/53. Played for Vancouver Olympic Columbians in Canada. Canadian international.

Clarke, Joe (St. Louis). Defender—5'9"—160—born 11/27/53. Played for St. Louis University and U.S. Olympic team.

Clements, Dave (Cosmos). Midfielder—5'10"—155—born 9/16/45. Played for Everton and other top English clubs. International for Northern Ireland.

Cohen, Martin (Los Angeles). Midfielder—5'10"—170—born 3/2/52. Played for Highlands Park in South Africa. South African Player of the Year in 1975.

Cohen, Neil (Dallas). Defender—6'1"—175—born 9/12/55. All-American at high school. Captained U.S. Under-19 team. U.S. international.

Coker, Ade (Minnesota). Forward—5'9"—155—born 5/19/54. Played for West Ham United and Boston. Native of Nigeria.

Cole, Phil (Las Vegas). Forward—5'7"—150—born 9/19/56. Played for San Jose State and U.S. Olympic team.

Coleman, Keith (Team Hawaii). Defender—5'9"—155—born 5/24/51. Played for Sunderland, Arsenal and West Ham United. British.

Connell, Mike (Tampa Bay). Defender—6'0"—150—born 11/11/56. South African.

Cooke, Charlie (Los Angeles). Midfielder—5'9"—160—born 10/14/42. Played for Chelsea in England. Scottish international.

Cooper, Ken (Dallas). Goalkeeper—5'11"—187—born 2/2/46. Played for Blackburn Rovers of England. NASL all-star. British.

Counce, Dan (Team Hawaii). Forward—5'11"—179—born 10/22/51. Played for Boston and San Antonio. U.S. international.

Coyne, John (Connecticut). Forward—5'10"—166—born 7/18/51. Played for Tranmere Rovers in England. British.

Cross, Roger (Seattle). Forward—6'0"—175—born 10/24/48. Played for West Ham United, Fulham and Orient. British.

Crossley, Paul (Seattle). Forward—5'7"—150—born 7/14/48. Played for Chester in England. British.

Cukon, Mladen (Toronto). Defender—5'10"—165—born 3/21/46. Played for Rijeka of Yugoslavia. Yugoslavian.

Cummings, Stan (Minnesota). Forward—5'3"—140—born 6/12/58. Played for Middlesbrough. British.

Dangerfield, Chris (Las Vegas). Midfielder—5'11"—159—born 8/9/55. Played for Wolverhampton Wanderers and Coventry City. British.

Darrell, Gary (Washington). Forward—5'9"—155—born 1/10/47. Played for Montreal Olympiques. International for Bermuda.

David, Steve (Los Angeles). Forward—6'0"—155—born 11/3/50. Played for Miami. NASL all-star. International for Trinidad. Most Valuable Player of NASL in 1975.

Davies, Geoff (San Jose). Forward—6'1"—180—born 7/1/47. Played for Chester in England and Boston and Chicago in U.S. British.

Davies, Ron (Los Angeles). Forward—6'1"—180—born 5/25/42. Played for Manchester United, Southampton and other English clubs. Welsh international.

Day, Graham (Portland). Defender—6'1"—170—born 11/22/53. Played for Bristol Rovers in England. British.

D'Errico, David (Minnesota). Defender—5'11"—165—born 3/2/52. Played for Seattle. U.S. international.

DeLeon, Leroy (San Jose). Forward—5'9"—165—born 2/7/48. Played for New York Generals, Miami Toros and Washington. Native of Trinidad.

Demling, Buzz (San Jose). Defender—5'11"—180—born 9/21/48. All-American at Michigan State. U.S. international.

Demling, Mark (San Jose). Defender—6'0"—180—born 10/4/51. Played for St. Louis University when it won three consecutive NCAA titles.

Dillon, Mike (Cosmos). Defender—5'11"—175—born 9/29/52. Played for Tottenham Hotspur in England and Montreal Olympiques. NASL all-star.

Dimitrijević, Victor (Cosmos). Midfielder—5'10"—170—born 12/11/48. Played for Olimpia in Yugoslavia. Yugoslavia Under-23 international.

Donlič, Tony (Cosmos). Forward—6'2"—195—born 3/24/56. A native of Yugoslavia.

DuBose, Winston (Tampa Bay). Goalkeeper—6'2"—180—born 7/28/55. All-American at Florida Tech. U.S. citizen.

DuChateau, Eugene (Connecticut). Goalkeeper—6'2"—180—born 1/23/54. Played for Adelphi and U.S. Olympic team.

Eagen, Kevin (Tampa Bay). Defender—6'3"—175—born 12/30/54. Played for University of South Florida. U.S. citizen.

Eddy, Keith (Cosmos). Defender—5'11"—155—born 10/23/44. Played for Sheffield United in England. NASL all-star.

England, Mike (Seattle). Defender—6'2"—184—born 12/2/41. Played for Tottenham Hotspur and Blackburn Rovers. Welsh international. NASL all-star.

Eusebio (Las Vegas). Forward—6'0"—180—born 1/25/42. Played for Benfica in Portugal and Boston and Toronto in the NASL. NASL all-star. International for Portugal.

Evans, Ray (St. Louis). Defender—5'11"—174—born 9/20/49. Played for Tottenham Hotspur and Milwall. British.

Fagan, Bobby (Los Angeles). Defender—5'9"—155—born 1/29/49. Played for Sunderland and other English clubs as well as Seattle. British.

Field, Tony (Cosmos). Forward—5'7"—154—born 6/7/46. Played for Sheffield United in England. British.

Fink, Joe (Tampa Bay). Forward—6'0"—160—born 7/31/51. Played for New York University, New York Cosmos and U.S. national team.

Flater, Mike (Minnesota). Foward—5'9"—160—born 1/22/51. All-American at Colorado School of Mines. Played for Denver and San Jose. U.S. international.

Formoso, Santiago (Connecticut). Forward—5'10"—150—born 7/4/53. Played at the University of Pennsylvania and for the U.S. Olympic team.

Fox, Peter (Team Hawaii). Goalkeeper—5'11"—165—born 7/5/57. Played for Sheffield Wednesday and West Ham United. British.

Futcher, Paul (Minnesota). Defender—5'10"—160—born 9/26/56. Played for Luton Town and England's Under/23 team. British.

Futcher, Ron (Minnesota). Forward—5'10"—148—born 9/26/56. Twin brother of Paul. Also played for Luton Town. British.

Galati, Tom (Las Vegas). Defender—5'8"—185—born 11/17/51. Played for Philadelphia. U.S. international.

Gant, Brian (Vancouver). Midfielder—6'0"—155—born 4/23/52. Native of Canada.

Garbett, Terry (Cosmos). Midfielder—5'9"—166—born 9/9/45. Played for Sheffield United and other top clubs in England. British.

Garcia, Frederico (Dallas). Forward—5'8"—150—born 7/7/52. High school all-American and U.S. Olympic player.

Geimer, Gene (Chicago). Forward—5'10"—170—born 1/31/49. Played for Boston and St. Louis. U.S. international.

Gillett, Dave (Seattle). Defender—6'1"—175—born 4/2/51. Played for Crewe in England. British.

Green, Alan (Washington). Forward—5'10"—165—born 1/1/54. Played for Coventry City. British.

Griffiths, Clive (Chicago). Defender—5'10"—160—born 1/22/55. Played for Manchester United and Tranmere in England. British.

Hamlyn, Alan (Ft. Lauderdale). Defender—5'10"—170—born 1/5/47. Played for the Atlanta Apollos and U.S. national team.

Hammond, Paul (Tampa Bay). Goalkeeper—6'1"—190—born 7/26/53. Played for Crystal Palace. British.

Hendrie, Paul (Portland). Forward—5'6"—142—born 3/27/54. Played for Birmingham City. British.

Henry, Jim (Team Hawaii). Midfielder—5'11"—168—born 2/24/49. Played for Dundee and Aberdeen in Scotland and Baltimore Comets in NASL. British.

Hernandez, Mani (San Jose). Forward—5'3"—142—born 8/2/48. All-American at San Jose State. U.S. international.

Hill, Ken (Washington). Defender—6'0"—165—born 7/3/53. Played for Gillingham in England and Baltimore Comets in NASL. British.

Hinton, Alan (Dallas). Forward—5'11"—190—born 10/6/42. Played for Wolverhampton Wanderers, Nottingham Forest and Derby County. English international.

Hoban, Mike (Portland). Defender—5'10"—165—born 4/6/52. Played for Aston Villa in England and Denver Dynamos in NASL. U.S. international.

Hockey, Trevor (Las Vegas). Midfielder—5'7"—150—born 1/5/43. Played for Sheffield United and many other top English teams. Welsh international.

Holland, Pat (Team Hawaii). Midfielder—5'8"—158—born—9/13/50. Played for West Ham United. British.

Hope, Bob (Dallas). Midfielder—5'8"—155—born 9/28/43. Played for West Bromwich Albion. Scottish international.

Hudson, Bruce (St. Louis). Defender—6'0"—175—born 10/31/50. All-American at St. Louis University. Played for U.S. Olympic team.

Hudson, Ray (Ft. Lauderdale). Midfielder—5'11"—157—born 3/24/55. Played for Newcastle. British.

Iarusci, Robert (Cosmos). Defender—5'11"—170—born 11/8/54. Played for Toronto. Canadian international.

Irving, David (Ft. Lauderdale). Forward—5'9"—170—born 9/10/51. Played for Everton and Oldham. British.

Ivanow, Mike (Seattle). Goalkeeper—6'4"—200—born 1/9/48. All-American with University of San Francisco. U.S. international.

Jackson, John (St. Louis). Goalkeeper—6'2"—188—born 9/5/42. Played for Crystal Palace and Orient. British.

Jenkins, Tom (Seattle). Midfielder—5'9"—148—born 12/2/47. Played for Southampton and Swindon. British.

Jennings, Bill (Chicago). Forward—5'9"—150—born 2/20/52. Played for West Ham. British.

Johnson, Glen (Vancouver). Forward—5'9"—160—born 4/22/51. Canadian international.

Jokerst, Dave (St. Louis). Goalkeeper—6'2"—170—1/1/48. Played for St. Louis University.

Jordan, Kip (Rochester). Defender—6'0"—190—born 11/19/51. All-American at Cornell. Played for Miami.

Joy, Brian (Las Vegas). Defender—5'9"—160—born 2/26/51. Played for Exeter and five other English teams. British.

Jump, Stewart (Tampa Bay). Defender—5'10"—160—born 1/27/52. Played for Crystal Palace. British.

Kelly, Jimmy (Chicago). Midfielder—5'6"—145—born 5/2/57. Played for Manchester United and Scotland's youth team.

Kelly, Jimmy (Portland). Forward—5'6"—134—born 2/6/54. Played for Wolverhampton Wanderers. Native of Northern Ireland.

Kemp, Davie (San Jose). Defender—5'5"—145—born 8/5/50. A native of Scotland.

Kerr, John (Washington). Midfielder—5'6"—145—born 10/15/43. A veteran NASL player. Played for Detroit Cougars and New York Cosmos. Canadian international.

Kewley, Kevin (Dallas). Midfielder—5'9"—166—born 2/3/55. Played for Liverpool. British.

Kodelja, Victor (Team Hawaii). Forward—5'10"—165—born 11/26/51. Played for Vancouver. Canadian international.

Leeper, Curtis (Ft. Lauderdale). Forward—5'11"—160—born 12/28/55. Played for Florida International University. U.S. citizen.

Lenarduzzi, Bob (Vancouver). Defender—5'10"—185—born 5/1/55. Played for Reading in England. Canadian international.

Lenarduzzi, Silvano (Vancouver). Defender—5'10"—165—born 12/19/48. Brother of Bob, Silvano has represented Canada more than any other player in the history of Canadian soccer.

Lettieri, Tino (Minnesota). Goalkeeper—5'8"—165—born 9/27/57. Played for Quebec Selects and the Canadian Olympic team.

Ley, George (Dallas). Defender—5'10"—165—born 4/1/46. Played for Exeter, Portsmouth and other English clubs. British.

Lindsay, Mark (Tampa Bay). Midfielder—5'8"—155—born 4/8/54. Played for Crystal Palace. British.

Liotart, Hank (Portland). Midfielder—5'11"—176—born 11/15/43. Played for top Dutch and Mexican teams and the Seattle Sounders. U.S. international.

Litt, Steve (Minnesota). Defender—6'1"—182—born 5/21/54. Played for Luton Town and other top English teams. British.

Liveric, Mark (Washington). Forward—5'11"—175—born 8/16/53. Played for New York, San Jose and U.S. national team.

Lopez, José (Los Angeles). Midfielder—5'10"—150—born 4/25/51. Played for UCLA. U.S. citizen.

Mackay, Ike (Portland). Forward—6'2"—170—born 8/2/48. Played for Vancouver. Canadian international.

Mancini, Terry (Los Angeles). Defender—6'0"—170—born 10/4/44. Played for Queens Park Rangers and Arsenal. Irish international.

Marcantonio, Carmine (Toronto). Midfielder—5'8"—150—born 11/21/54. Played for Toronto Italia of the Canadian National Soccer League. Canadian.

Marsh, Rodney (Tampa Bay). Midfielder or forward—6'1"—185—born 10/11/44. Played for Manchester City and other English clubs. English international.

Martin, Eric (Washington). Goalkeeper—6'0"—175—born 3/31/46. Played for Southampton in England. British.

Martin, Ray (Portland). Defender—5'9"—155—born 1/23/45. Played for Birmingham City. British.

Mason, John (Los Angeles). Midfielder—5'8"—150—born 6/24/53. U.S. international.

Matteson, Bob (St. Louis). Defender—6'0"—170—born 6/2/52. All-American at St. Louis University.

Mayer, Alan (Las Vegas). Goalkeeper—6'0"—185—born 7/3/52. All-American at Madison College in Virginia.

McAlister, Don (Washington). Defender—5'10"—160—born 5/26/53. Played for Tottenham Hotspur and Bolton Wanderers. British.

McAndrew, Tony (Vancouver). Midfielder—5'10"—166—born 4/11/56. Played for Middlesbrough and Scottish national junior team.

McCully, Henry (Connecticut). Forward—6'0"—175—born 4/30/48. Played for Dumbarton in Scotland and U.S. national team.

McLeod, Wes (Tampa Bay). Midfielder—5'8"—149—born 10/24/57. Canadian international.

McMahon, Pat (Portland). Midfielder—5'11"—160—born 9/19/45. Played for Aston Villa in England. British.

Messing, Shep (Cosmos). Goalkeeper—6'1"—175—born 10/9/49. All-American at Harvard. Played for Boston and U.S. national team.

Miflín, Ramón (Cosmos). Midfielder—5'9"—160—born 4/5/47. Played for Santos in Brazil. Peruvian international.

Mijatovič, Nikola (Rochester). Defender—6'0"—180—born 9/18/47. Played for Sloboda in Yugoslavia. Yugoslavian national.

Minnock, John (Las Vegas). Midfielder—5'9"—162—born 11/12/49. Played for Athlone in Ireland. Played for Ireland's Under-23 team.

Mishalow, Bill (Los Angeles). Goalkeeper—5'11"—170—born 3/6/52. Played for University of Alabama. U.S. citizen.

Mishalow, Gene (Washington). Defender—5'8"—150—born 8/10/53. Brother of Bill. Played for SIU. U.S. citizen.

Mitchell, Charlie (Team Hawaii). Defender—5'10"—165—born 5/18/48. Played for Washington, Rochester and New York. NASL all-star.

Mitič, Ilija (San Jose). Midfielder—5'10"—165—born 7/19/40. Veteran NASL player. NASL all-star and leading goal scorer. Native of Yugoslavia.

Moffat, Bobby (Dallas). Defender—5'11"—165—born 10/7/45. Played for Portsmouth and Gillingham in England. British.

Molnar, Tibor (Rochester). Midfielder—6'0"—born 6/6/52. Played for Dallas. Native of Hungary.

Moore, Ron (Chicago). Forward—6'0"—176—born 1/29/53. Played for Tranmere. British.

Morais, Nelsi (Cosmos). Midfielder—5'9"—155—born 10/22/51. Played for Santos in Brazil. Native of Brazil.

Moran, Mark (Minnesota). Midfielder—5'11"—165—born 9/26/54. Played for SIU. U.S. citizen.

Morgan, Willie (Chicago). Forward—5'9"—160—born 10/2/44. Former captain of Manchester United. Scottish international.

Mulroy, Tommy (Ft. Lauderdale). Midfielder—6'0"—150—born 9/28/56. All-American at Ulster Junior College. U.S. citizen.

Myernick, Glenn (Dallas). Defender—5'11"—180—born 12/29/54. All-American at Hartwick. U.S. international.

Nanchoff, George (Ft. Lauderdale). Forward—5'11"—160—born 4/17/54. All-American at Akron University. U.S. citizen.

Neumann, Axel (Team Hawaii). Midfielder—6'1"—165—born 4/22/52. Played for Tennis Borussia in Germany and Boston in the NASL. Native of West Germany.

Nover, Peter (Team Hawaii). Defender—6'5"—180—born 7/18/49. Played for FC Saarbrücken in Germany and Boston in the NASL. Native of West Germany.

Ntsolengoe, "Ace" Patrick (Minnesota). Midfielder—5'8"—155—born 2/26/52. Played for the Kaiser Chiefs in South Africa. NASL all-star.

Oakley, Graham (Washington). Defender—5'6"—140—born 5/10/54. Played for Coventry City. British.

Odoi, Frank (Rochester). Forward—5'6"—155—born 11/22/45. Played for Washington Whips and on Ghana's international team.

O'Hare, John (Dallas). Forward—5'8"—180—born 9/24/46. Played for Derby, Sunderland and other top English clubs. Scottish international.

O'Leary, Bob (St. Louis). Midfielder—5'10"—160—born 1/3/52. All-American at Florissant Valley. U.S. citizen.

O'Neill, Hugh (Connecticut). Forward—5'10"—160—born 7/16/54. All-American at University of Bridgeport. U.S. citizen.

Ord, Tommy (Seattle). Forward—5'10"—165—born 10/15/52. Played for Chelsea in England and Vancouver, New York Cosmos and Rochester in the NASL. British.

Parson, Les (Vancouver). Midfielder—5'9"—160—born 12/16/50. Played for Simon Frazer University. Canadian international.

Pavlovič, Miroslav (San Jose). Defender—5'10"—165—born 10/15/42. Played for Red Star Belgrade. Yugoslavian international.

Pecher, Steve (Dallas). Defender—6'0"—194—born 2/13/56. Played for Florissant Valley. U.S. international.

Pedro, John (Rochester). Midfielder—5'9"—145—born 1/2/51. Played for CUF in Portugal. A native of Portugal.

Pike, Geoff (Connecticut). Midfielder—5'8"—155—born 9/28/56. Played for West Ham United. British.

Polak, Ted (Toronto). Midfielder—5'8"—174—born 11/17/44. Played for Wisla in Poland. A native of Poland.

Pringle, Alex (Washington). Defender—5'9"—160—born 11/8/48. Played for Dundee United and Tampa Bay. British.

Pringle, Paul (Chicago). Forward—5'10"—155—born 2/5/54. Played for Howard University and Jamaican Under-19 national team.

Proctor, David (Ft. Lauderdale). Forward—6'1"—165—born 12/26/51. Played for Fulham and Brentford in England. British.

Quaraishi, Farrukh (Tampa Bay). Defender—5'9"—145—born 11/13/51. All-American at Oneonta State College. British.

Ralbovsky, Steve (Chicago). Forward—5'8"—155—born 1/9/53. All-American at Brown. Played for Los Angeles Skyhawks of the ASL. U.S. international.

Redfern, Jim (Washington). Forward—5'9"—150—born 1/8/52. Played for Bolton Wanderers and Chester. British.

Redknapp, Harry (Seattle). Forward—5'10"—158—born 3/2/47. Played for West Ham and Bournemouth in England. British.

Redmond, Tom (Chicago). Defender—6'1"—170—born 8/2/54. All-American at Indiana University. U.S. citizen.

Reiter, Len (Washington). Defender—6'1"—175—born 11/6/54. Played at Yale. U.S. citizen.

Renery, Len (Las Vegas). Defender—5'10"—175—born 11/9/49. All-American at Columbia. Played for New York Cosmos and Baltimore Comets. U.S. citizen.

Rensing, Gary (St. Louis). Defender—5'10"—165—born 10/5/47. Played for St. Louis University. U.S. citizen.

Reynolds, Tom (Dallas). Goalkeeper—5'11"—180—born 9/6/55. Played for California State at Hayward. U.S. citizen.

Rigby, Bob (Los Angeles). Goalkeeper—6'0"—175—born 7/3/51. All-American at East Stroudsburg State. U.S. international.

Robertson, Jimmy (Seattle). Foward—5'8"—147—born 12/17/44. Played for Tottenham Hotspur, Arsenal and other top English clubs. Scottish international.

Robinson, Brian (Vancouver). Midfielder—5'8"—155—born 6/29/48. Canadian international.

Roboostoff, Archie (Portland). Forward—6'0"—175—born 10/9/51. All-American at University of San Francisco. Played for San Jose and San Diego. U.S. international.

Rosul, Roman (Ft. Lauderdale). Forward—6'0"—175—born 5/10/50. All-American at Cleveland State. U.S. citizen.

Rote, Kyle, Jr. (Dallas). Forward—6'0"—180—born 12/25/50. Played for Sewanee. Rookie of the Year 1973 in NASL. U.S. international.

Roth, Steve (Ft. Lauderdale). Defender—6'2"—180—born 10/12/54. Played for Club de Fútbol America and Universidad de Mexico. U.S. citizen.

Roth, Werner (Cosmos). Defender—6'1"—185—born 4/4/48. NASL all-star. U.S. international.

Rowan, Brian (Cosmos). Defender—5'9"—142—born 6/28/48. Played for Aston Villa and Watford in England. British.

Rowlands, John (San Jose). Defender—6'1"—175—born 2/7/47. Played for Seattle Sounders. NASL all-star. British.

Rudroff, Bruce (Seattle). Midfielder—6'0"—160—born 5/11/55. All-American at St. Louis University. Played for U.S. Olympic team.

Ryan, Jim (Dallas). Forward—5'9"—151—born 5/12/45. Played for Manchester United and Luton in England. British.

Salvage, Barry (St. Louis). Forward—5'10"—156—born 12/21/47. Played for Milwall, Fulham and other top English clubs. British.

Scullion, Stewart (Portland). Forward—5'7"—155—born 4/18/46. Played for Sheffield United and Watford in England and Tampa Bay in NASL. British.

Seerey, Mike (St. Louis). Forward—6'2"—172—born 10/23/50. All-American at St. Louis University. U.S. international.

Sharp, Ronnie (Ft. Lauderdale). Midfielder—5'10"—175—born 1/30/48. Played for Cowdenbeath in Scotland. NASL all-star. British.

Short, Peter (Minnesota). Forward—6'1"—170—born 10/27/44. Veteran NASL player with Philadelphia Spartans, Cleveland Stokers, Rochester Lancers and Dallas Tornado. British.

Sibbald, Bobby (Los Angeles). Defender—5'6"—150—born 1/25/49. Played for Leeds and Southport. British.

Silva, Ibraim (Rochester). Forward—6'0"—150—born 11/29/53. Played for Benfica and Guirmaraes in Portugal. Portuguese.

Silvester, Peter (Washington). Forward—6'0"—170—born 2/19/48. Played for Southend in England and Baltimore Comets, San Diego Jaws and Vancouver Whitecaps in NASL. British.

Simões, Antonio (San Jose). Midfielder—5'8"—158—born 12/14/43. Played for Benfica in Portugal and Boston in NASL. NASL all-star. Portuguese international.

Skotarek, Alex (Chicago). Defender—6'1"—175—born 4/2/49. Played at Michigan State and in Dutch and Belgian pro soccer. U.S. international.

Smethurst, Derek (Tampa Bay). Forward—6'1"—165—born 10/27/47. Played for Chelsea in England. NASL all-star.

Smith, Bobby (Cosmos). Defender—5'11"—165—born 7/23/51. Played for Philadelphia Atoms. U.S. international.

Solem, Jeff (Minnesota). Defender—6'1"—173—born 1/28/48. Played for the Denver Dynamos and Atlanta Apollos. U.S. international.

Sono, Jomo (Cosmos). Forward—5'8"—165—born 6/28/55. Played for Orlando in South Africa. South African.

Spavin, Alan (Washington). Midfielder—5'8"—160—born 2/20/42. Played for Preston North End. British.

Stahl, Dave (Las Vegas). Defender—6'0"—175—born 6/9/55. Played for California State University at Chico. U.S. citizen.

Stojanovič, Mike (Rochester). Forward—6'0"—175—born 1/26/47. Played for Radnicki Kragujevac in Yugoslavia. Native of Yugoslavia.

Stremlau, John (St. Louis). Midfielder—5'9"—150—born 11/23/53. All-American at SIU. Played for Dallas and U.S. Olympic team.

Strenicer, Gene (Toronto). Midfielder—5'6"—140—born 8/12/45. Played in Hungary for Spartacus Budapest. Hungarian.

Sühnholz, Wolfgang (Las Vegas). Midfielder—5'10"—170—born 9/14/46. Played for Bayern Munich and other European clubs. NASL all-star. German.

Szefer, Stefan (Chicago). Defender—6'0"—175—born 5/8/42. Played for Maastricht in Holland and other European clubs. Polish international.

Taylor, Roberto (Connecticut). Midfielder—6'3"—190—born 9/28/49. Played for the Connecticut Yankees of the ASL. A native of Mexico.

Thompson, Bobby (Connecticut). Defender—6'0"—170—born 12/5/53. Played for Wolverhampton Wanderers. English international.

Thompson, Gary (Vancouver). Forward—5'11"—160—born 9/28/45. Native of Canada.

Thompson, Max (Dallas). Defender—6'3"—178—born 12/31/56. Played for Liverpool. British.

Tinnion, Brian (Team Hawaii). Forward—5'9"—155—born 6/11/48. Played for Workington and Wrexham in England and New York Cosmos in the NASL. British.

Tinsley, Alan (Ft. Lauderdale). Midfielder—5'11"—155—born 1/1/51. Played for Preston North End and Bury. British.

Toedebusch, Len (St. Louis). Goalkeeper—6'4"—210—born 1/5/57. Played for SIU. U.S. citizen.

Topič Jadranko (Cosmos). Forward—5'11"—163—born 4/20/49. Played for Velez in Yugoslavia. Yugoslavian.

Trost, Al (St. Louis). Midfielder—6'2"—166—born 2/7/49. All-American at St. Louis University. NASL all-star. U.S. international.

Turner, Roy (Dallas). Midfielder—6'2"—166—born 10/30/43. Veteran NASL player with Philadelphia Spartans, Cleveland Stokers and Toronto Falcons. NASL all-star. U.S. citizen.

Twamley, Bruce (Cosmos). Defender—5'9"—150—born 5/23/52. Played for Ipswich in England and Vancouver in NASL. Canadian.

Twellman, Tim (Minnesota). Forward—5'11"—175—born 5/1/55. Played for SIU. U.S. citizen.

Vanninger, Dennis (St. Louis). Forward—6'2"—185—born 3/14/52. All-American at Florissant Valley. U.S. international.

Vee, Julie (San Jose). Midfielder—5'11"—180—born 2/22/50. Played for Los Angeles. U.S. international.

Velazquez, Sergio (Portland). Forward—5'7"—148—born 2/25/52. All-American at UCLA. U.S. citizen.

Verdi, Roger (St. Louis). Defender—5'7"—150—born 2/4/53. Played for Ipswich. British.

Villa, Greg (Minnesota). Forward—6'1"—190—born 12/15/56. Played for SIU. U.S. citizen.

Wall, Peter (St. Louis). Defender—5'11"—170—born 9/13/44. Played for Crystal Palace. British.

Wark, Doug (Las Vegas). Forward—5'10"—160—born 12/24/51. Played for Rochester, Tampa Bay and San Diego. U.S. citizen.

Webb, John (Chicago). Defender—5'10"—155—born 2/10/52. Played for Liverpool and Tranmere. British.

Weber, Greg (Vancouver). Goalkeeper—6'1"—175—born 4/25/50. Played for the University of British Columbia. Canadian international.

Webster, Adrian (Seattle). Defender—5'9"—155—born 11/6/51. A native of England.

Webster, Ron (Minnesota). Defender—5'9"—163—born 4/21/43. Played for Derby County in England. British.

Wegerle, Steve (Tampa Bay). Forward—5'10"—145—born 5/15/53. Played for Arcadia Shepherds in South Africa and was South African Player of the Year in 1974. South African.

Welch, Art (Washington). Midfielder—5'7"—155—born 4/16/44. Veteran NASL player with Baltimore Bays, Atlanta Chiefs, San Jose Earthquakes and Vancouver Whitecaps. Jamaican international.

Welsh, Kevin (Connecticut). Forward—5'10"—160—born 10/26/53. Played at University of Bridgeport and for the U.S. Olympic team.

West, Alan (Minnesota). Midfielder—5'8"—148—born 12/18/51. Played for Burnley and Luton Town. British.

Whelan, Tony (Ft. Lauderdale). Forward—6'1"—170—born 11/20/52. Played for Manchester City and other top English clubs. British.

Whittle, Maurice (Ft. Lauderdale). Defender—5'8"—150—born 7/15/48. Played for Blackburn Rovers and Oldham. British.

Willey, Alan (Minnesota). Forward—5'11"—178—born 10/18/56. Played for Middlesbrough in England. British.

Willner, Roy (Washington). Midfielder—5'7"—145—born 10/22/49. All-American at Catonsville College. Played for Baltimore Bays. U.S. citizen.

Wilson, Bruce (Vancouver). Defender—5'10"—160—born 6/20/51. Played for University of British Columbia. Canadian international.

Wilson, Les (Vancouver). Midfielder—5'9"—162—born 7/10/47. Played for Wolverhampton Wanderers and other top English clubs. Canadian.

Wit, Dennis (Tampa Bay). Midfielder—6'2"—165—born 7/25/51. Played for Baltimore Comets and U.S. national team.

Woof, Billy (Vancouver). Forward—5'10"—162—born 8/16/52. Played for Middlesbrough. British.

Wright, Ralph (Ft. Lauderdale). Defender—6'0"—180—born 8/3/47. Played for Bolton Wanderers and other top English clubs. British.

Yasin, Erol (Cosmos). Goalkeeper—6'1"—170—born 10/11/48. Played for Galatasaray in Turkey. Turkish international.

nASL Facts and Figures

TEAMS

Chicago Sting

First season in NASL: 1975
Manager: Jim Walker
Coach: Malcolm Musgrove
Stadium: Soldier Field
Mailing address: Suite 1525, 333 North Michigan Avenue, Chicago, Ill. 60601
Team colors: Yellow/Black
Division: Northern Division of the Atlantic Conference

Connecticut Bicentennials (formerly Hartford Bicentennials)

First season in NASL: 1975 as Hartford, 1977 as Connecticut
Manager: Rudi Schiffer
Coach: Bobby Thompson
Stadium: Yale Bowl
Team colors: Red/White/Blue
Mailing address: 965 Dixwell Avenue, Suite 200, Hamden, Conn. 06514
Division: Northern Division of the Atlantic Conference

Cosmos (formerly the New York Cosmos)

First season in NASL: 1971
Manager: Michael Martin
Coach: Eddie Firmani
Stadium: Giants Stadium
Mailing address: 75 Rockefeller Plaza, New York, N.Y. 10019
Team colors: Green/White
Division: Eastern Division of the Atlantic Conference

Dallas Tornado

First season in NASL: 1968 (in 1967 member of USA)
Manager: Fred Hoster
Coach: Al Miller
Stadium: Ownby Stadium
Mailing address: 6116 North Central Expressway, Suite 33, Dallas, Texas 75206
Team colors: Red/White/Blue
Division: Southern Division of the Pacific Conference

Fort Lauderdale Strikers (formerly Miami Toros and Miami Gatos)

First season in NASL: 1972 as Miami, 1977 as Fort Lauderdale
Manager: Krikor Yepremian
Coach: Ron Newman
Stadium: Lockhart Stadium
Mailing address: 5100 North Federal Highway, Fort Lauderdale, Fla. 33308
Team colors: Orange/Yellow/Black
Division: Eastern Division of the Atlantic Conference

Las Vegas Quicksilvers (formerly San Diego Jaws and Baltimore Comets)

First season in NASL: 1974 as Baltimore, 1976 as San Diego, 1977 as Las Vegas
Manager: Paul Deese
Coach: Jim Fryatt
Stadium: Las Vegas Stadium
Mailing address: 3121 South Maryland Parkway, Suite 106,
    Las Vegas, Nev. 98109
Team colors: Silver/Blue
Division: Southern Division of the Pacific Conference

Los Angeles Aztecs

First season in NASL: 1974
Manager: John Chaffetz
Coach: Terry Fisher
Stadium: Los Angeles Memorial Coliseum
Mailing address: 1700 South Pacific Coast Highway,
    Redondo Beach, Calif. 90277
Team colors: Tangerine/White
Division: Southern Division of the Pacific Conference

Minnesota Kicks (formerly Denver Dynamos)

First season in NASL: 1974 as Denver, 1976 as Minnesota
Manager: Freddie Goodwin
Coach: Freddie Goodwin
Stadium: Metropolitan Stadium
Mailing address: 7200 France Avenue South, Suite 128,
    Minneapolis, Minn. 55435
Team colors: Blue/Orange/White
Division: Western Division of the Pacific Conference

Portland Timbers

First season in NASL: 1975
Manager: Don Paul, Sr.
Coach: Brian Tiler
Stadium: Portland Civic Stadium

Mailing address: Suite 101D, 10151 S.W. Barbur Boulevard,
    Portland, Ore. 97219
Team colors: Timber Green/Old Gold/White
Division: Western Division of the Pacific Conference

Rochester Lancers

First season in NASL: 1970
Manager: Sal DeRosa
Coach: Don Popovic
Stadium: Holleder Stadium
Mailing address: 812 Wilder Building, Rochester, N.Y. 14614
Team colors: Blue/Gold/White
Division: Northern Division of the Atlantic Conference

St. Louis Stars

First season in NASL: 1968 (in 1967 member of NPSL)
Manager: Casey Frankiewicz
Coach: John Sewell
Stadium: Francis Field
Mailing address: 940 West Port Plaza, Suite 317, St. Louis, Mo. 63141
Team colors: Red/White/Blue
Division: Northern Division of the Atlantic Conference

San Jose Earthquakes

First season in NASL: 1974
Manager: Johnny Moore
Coach: Gabbo Gavric
Stadium: Spartan Stadium
Mailing address: Suite 272, 2025 Gateway Place, San Jose, Calif. 95110
Team colors: Red/White
Division: Southern Division of the Pacific Conference

Seattle Sounders

First season in NASL: 1974
Manager: Jack Daley
Coach: Jim Gabriel
Stadium: Kingdome
Mailing address: 203 Metropole Building, Seattle, Wash. 98104
Team colors: Green/Blue/White
Division: Western Division of the Pacific Conference

Tampa Bay Rowdies

First season in NASL: 1975
Manager: T. Beauclerc Rogers, IV

Coach: Gordon Jago
Stadium: Tampa Stadium
Mailing address: 1311 North Westshore Boulevard, Tampa, Fla. 33607
Team colors: Green/Yellow/White
Division: Eastern Division of the Atlantic Conference

Team Hawaii (formerly San Antonio Thunder)

First season in NASL: 1975 as San Antonio, 1977 as Team Hawaii
Manager: Don Paul
Coach: Charlie Mitchell
Stadium: Aloha Stadium
Mailing address: 745 Fort Street, Suite 602, Honolulu, Hawaii 96813
Team colors: Gold/Blue/Green
Division: Southern Division of the Pacific Conference

Toronto Metros-Croatia (formerly Toronto Metros)

First season in NASL: 1971 as Metros, 1975 as Metros-Croatia
Manager: George Simcic
Coach: Ivan Sangulin
Stadium: Varsity Stadium
Mailing address: 1678 Bloor Street West, Toronto, Ont. M6P 1A8, Canada
Team colors: Red/White/Blue
Division: Northern Division of the Atlantic Conference

Vancouver Whitecaps

First season in NASL: 1974
Manager: Denny Veitch
Coach: Tony Waiters
Stadium: Empire Stadium
Mailing address: 885 Dunsmuir Street, Vancouver, B.C. V6C 1N8, Canada
Team colors: Red/White
Division: Western Division of the Pacific Conference

Washington Diplomats

First season in NASL: 1974
Manager: John Carbray
Coach: Gordon Bradley
Stadium: Robert F. Kennedy
Mailing address: One Tysons Corner, Center Office Building, Suite LL-1,
    McLean, Va. 22151
Team colors: Red/White/Blue
Division: Eastern Division of the Atlantic Conference

NOTE: The NASL plans to expand to 24 teams for the 1978 season. New clubs will operate out of Boston, Denver, Detroit, Houston, Memphis and Philadelphia. In addition, four franchises will relocate: Connecticut to Oakland, Las Vegas to San Diego, Team Hawaii to Tulsa and St. Louis to Anaheim.

PREVIOUS NASL CLUBS

Atlanta Apollos (1973)
Atlanta Chiefs (member of NPSL in 1967, member of NASL 1968–72)
Boston Beacons (1968)
Boston Minutemen (1974–76)
Chicago Mustangs (member of USA in 1967, member of NASL in 1968)
Cleveland Stokers (member of USA in 1967, member of NASL in 1968)
Detroit Cougars (member of USA in 1967, member of NASL in 1968)
Houston Stars (member of USA in 1967, member of NASL in 1968)
Kansas City Spurs (member of NPSL in 1967 as the Chicago Spurs, member of NASL 1968–70)
Los Angeles Toros (member of USA in 1967, member of NASL as the San Diego Toros in 1968)
Montreal Olympiques (1971–73)
New York Generals (member of NPSL in 1967, member of NASL in 1968)
New York Skyliners (member of USA in 1967)
Philadelphia Atoms (1973–76)
Philadelphia Spartans (member of NPSL in 1967)
Pittsburgh Phantoms (member of NPSL in 1967)
San Francisco Golden Gate Gales (member of USA in 1967)
Toronto Falcons (member of NPSL in 1967, member of NASL in 1968)
Vancouver Royals (member of USA in 1967, member of NASL in 1968)
Washington Whips (member of USA in 1967, member of NASL in 1968)

NASL MOST VALUABLE PLAYER

1967   Ruben Navarro   Philadelphia Spartans
1968   John Kowalik   Chicago Mustangs
1969   Cirilo Fernández   Kansas City Spurs
1970   Carlos Metidieri   Rochester Lancers
1971   Carlos Metidieri   Rochester Lancers
1972   Randy Horton   New York Cosmos
1973   Warren Archibald   Miami Toros
1974   Peter Silvester   Baltimore Comets
1975   Steven David   Miami Toros
1976   Wolfgang Sühnholz   Toronto Metros-Croatia
1977   Franz Beckenbauer   Cosmos

NASL ROOKIE OF THE YEAR

1967   Willy Roy   Chicago Spurs
1968   Kaizer Motaung   Atlanta Chiefs
1969   Siegfried Stritzl   Baltimore Bays
1970   Jim Leeker   St. Louis Stars
1971   Randy Horton   New York Cosmos

1972   Mike Winter   St. Louis Stars
1973   Kyle Rote, Jr.   Dallas Tornado
1974   Douglas McMillan   Los Angeles Aztecs
1975   Chris Bahr   Philadelphia Atoms
1976   Steve Pecher   Dallas Tornado
1977   Jim McAllister   Seattle Sounders

NASL LEADING GOAL SCORER

		Games	Goals	Assists	Pts
1967	Yanko Daucik Toronto Falcons	17	20	8	48
1968	John Kowalik Chicago Mustangs	28	30	9	69
1969	Kaizer Motaung Atlanta Chiefs	15	16	4	36
1970	Kirk Apostolidis Dallas Tornado	19	16	3	35
	Carlos Metidieri Rochester Lancers	22	14	7	35
1971	Carlos Metidieri Rochester Lancers	24	19	8	46
1972	Randy Horton New York Cosmos	13	9	4	22
1973	Kyle Rote, Jr. Dallas Tornado	18	10	10	30
1974	Paul Child San Jose Earthquakes	20	15	6	36
1975	Steven David Miami Toros	21	23	6	52
1976	Giorgio Chinaglia New York Cosmos	19	19	11	49
1977	Steven David Los Angeles Aztecs	24	26	6	58

NASL ALL-TIME GOAL SCORERS

	Games	Goals	Assists	Pts
1. Ilija Mitič San Jose	147	96	34	226
2. Warren Archibald Rochester	162	58	39	155
3. Carlos Metidieri Boston	128	61	28	150
4. Paul Child San Jose	121	61	26	148
5. Leroy DeLeon San Jose	141	56	32	144
6. Steve David Los Angeles	77	63	12	138
7. Derek Smethurst Tampa Bay	67	57	12	126
8. Randy Horton Hartford	89	51	23	125
9. Kaiser Motaung Denver	105	50	18	118
10. Manfred Seissler Montreal	87	43	27	113

NASL ALL-TIME RECORDS

Most scoring points in one season: 69 by John Kowalik (Chicago Mustangs) in 1968.

Most scoring points in one game: 12 by Giorgio Chinaglia (Cosmos) against Miami Toros, 8/10/76.

Most goals in one season: 30 by Cirilo Fernández (San Diego) in 1968 and John Kowalik (Chicago Mustangs) in 1968.

Most goals in one game: 5 by Steven David (Miami Toros) against Washington Diplomats, 6/20/75, Giorgio Chinaglia (Cosmos) against Miami Toros, 8/10/76, and Ron Moore (Chicago Sting) against Vancouver Whitecaps, 6/26/77.

Most consecutive games scoring a goal: 10 by Steven David (Los Angeles) in 1977.

Most games won in one season: 19 by Oakland Clippers in 1967 and Fort Lauderdale in 1977.

Most games lost in one season: 26 by Dallas Tornado in 1968.

Most goals scored in one season: 71 by Oakland Clippers in 1968.

Highest average goals per game in one season: 3:3 by Kansas City Spurs in 1969.

Fewest goals scored in one season: 15 by Dallas Tornado in 1972.

Most goals scored in one game: 9 by Oakland Clippers vs. St. Louis Stars on 7/26/67 and by New York Cosmos vs. Washington Diplomats on 6/29/75.

Most goals scored by both teams in one game: 12—Toronto Falcons (8) vs. Chicago Mustangs (4) on 8/27/68.

Most goals allowed in one season: 109 by Dallas Tornado in 1968.

Highest average goals per game allowed in one season: 3:4 by Dallas in 1968.

Largest attendance at a regular-season game: 62,394—Cosmos vs. Tampa Bay Rowdies, Meadowlands (Giants Stadium) on 6/19/77.

Largest attendance at a play-off game: 77,691—Cosmos vs. Ft. Lauderdale Strikers, Meadowlands (Giants Stadium) 8/14/77.

Largest attendance at an exhibition game: 58,128—Seattle vs. New York Cosmos, Seattle (Kingdome).

Largest average attendance in one season: Cosmos—34,142 in 1977.

Other U. S. Tournaments and Leagues

AMERICAN SOCCER LEAGUE CHAMPIONS

1934	Kearny Irish	1957	New York Hakoah
1935	Philadelphia Germans	1958	New York Hakoah
1936	New York Americans	1959	New York Hakoah
1937	Kearny Scots	1960	Colombo
1938	Kearny Scots	1961	Ukrainian Nationals
1939	Kearny Scots	1962	Ukrainian Nationals
1940	Kearny Scots	1963	Ukrainian Nationals
1941	Kearny Scots	1964	Ukrainian Nationals
1942	Philadelphia Americans	1965	Hartford S.C.
1943	Brooklyn Hispanos	1966	Roma S.C.
1944	Philadelphia Americans	1967	Baltimore St. Gerard's
1945	New York Brookhattan	1968	Ukrainian Nationals
1946	Baltimore Americans	1969	Washington Darts
1947	Philadelphia Americans	1970	Ukrainian Nationals
1948	Philadelphia Americans	1971	New York Greeks
1949	Philadelphia Nationals	1972	Cincinnati Comets
1950	Philadelphia Nationals	1973	New York Apollo
1951	Philadelphia Nationals	1974	Rhode Island Oceaneers
1952	Philadelphia Americans	1975	Boston Astros/New York Apollo
1953	Philadelphia Nationals		
1954	New York Americans	1976	Los Angeles Skyhawks
1955	Uhrik Truckers	1977	New Jersey Americans
1956	Uhrik Truckers		

THE NATIONAL OPEN CHALLENGE CUP (open to professional and amateur teams belonging to the United States Soccer Federation)

1914	Brooklyn Field Club	1916	Bethlehem Steel
1915	Bethlehem Steel	1917	Fall River Rovers

1918	Bethlehem Steel	1948	Simpkins of St. Louis
1919	Bethlehem Steel	1949	Morgan, Pennsylvania
1920	Ben Millers	1950	Simpkins of St. Louis
1921	Robbins Dry Dock	1951	German Hungarian
1922	Scullin Steel	1952	Harmarville, Pennsylvania
1923	Patterson	1953	Falcons, Illinois
1924	Fall River	1954	New York Americans
1925	Shawsheen	1955	Eintracht, New York
1926	Bethlehem Steel	1956	Harmarville, Pennsylvania
1927	Fall River	1957	Kutis of St. Louis
1928	New York Nationals	1958	Los Angeles Kickers
1929	Hakoah All-Stars	1959	San Pedro Canvasbacks
1930	Fall River	1960	Philadelphia Ukrainian
1931	Fall River	1961	Philadelphia Ukrainian
1932	New Bedford	1962	New York Hungaria
1933	Stix, Baer & Fuller	1963	Philadelphia Ukrainian
1934	Stix, Baer & Fuller	1964	Los Angeles Kickers
1935	Central Breweries	1965	New York Ukrainian
1936	Philadelphia Americans	1966	Philadelphia Ukrainian
1937	New York Americans	1967	New York Greek-Americans
1938	Sparta of Chicago	1968	New York Greek-Americans
1939	St. Mary's Celtic of Brooklyn	1969	New York Greek-Americans
1940	Baltimore S.C.	1970	Elizabeth, New Jersey
1941	Pawtucket	1971	New York Hota
1942	Gallatin of Pennsylvania	1972	Elizabeth, New Jersey
1943	Brooklyn Hispano	1973	Los Angeles Maccabees
1944	Brooklyn Hispano	1974	New York Greek-Americans
1945	Brookhattan	1975	Los Angeles Maccabees
1946	Chicago Vikings	1976	San Francisco Athletic Club
1947	Ponta Delgada	1977	Los Angeles Maccabees

THE NATIONAL AMATEUR CUP (open to amateur teams belonging to the United States Soccer Federation)

1924	Fleisher Yarn	1934	German-American
1925	Toledo	1935	W. W. Riehl
1926	Defenders	1936	Brooklyn S.C.
1927	Heidelberg	1937	Trenton Highlander
1928	Swedish-Americans	1938	Ponta Delgada
1929	Heidelberg	1939	St. Michael
1930	Raffies	1940	Morgan Strasser
1931	Goodyear	1941	Fall River
1932	Cleveland Shamrock	1942	Fall River
1933	German-American	1943	Morgan Strasser

1944	Eintracht	1961	Kutis, St. Louis
1945	Eintracht	1962	Carpathia Kickers
1946	Ponta Delgada	1963	Italian-Americans
1947	Ponta Delgada	1964	Schwaben
1948	Ponta Delgada	1965	German-Hungarians,
1949	Elizabeth		Philadelphia
1950	Ponta Delgada	1966	Chicago Kickers
1951	German Hungarian	1967	Hartford Italians
1952	Raiders	1968	Chicago Kickers
1953	Ponta Delgada	1969	British Lions
1954	Beadling	1970	Chicago Kickers
1955	Heidelberg Tornados	1971	Kutis, St. Louis
1956	Kutis, St. Louis	1972	Busch, St. Louis
1957	Kutis, St. Louis	1973	Philadelphia Inter
1958	Kutis, St. Louis	1974	Philadelphia Inter
1959	Kutis, St. Louis	1975	Chicago Kickers
1960	Kutis, St. Louis	1976	Milwaukee Bavarians
		1977	Denver Kickers

THE NATIONAL COLLEGIATE ATHLETIC ASSOCIATION CHAMPIONSHIPS

NCAA Division One

1959	St. Louis	1969	St. Louis
1960	St. Louis	1970	St. Louis
1961	West Chester State	1971	Howard (vacated for using
1962	St. Louis		ineligible players)
1963	St. Louis	1972	St. Louis
1964	Navy	1973	St. Louis
1965	St. Louis	1974	Howard
1966	San Francisco	1975	San Francisco
1967	Michigan State and St. Louis	1976	San Francisco
1968	Maryland and Michigan State	1977	Hartwick

NCAA Division Two

1972	Southern Illinois	1975	Baltimore
1973	Missouri, St. Louis	1976	Loyola, Baltimore
1974	Adelphi	1977	Alabama A and M

NCAA Division Three

1974	Brockport State	1976	Brandeis
1975	Babson College	1977	Lock Haven

THE NATIONAL ASSOCIATION FOR INTERCOLLEGIATE ATHLETICS CHAMPIONSHIP (NAIA)

1959	Pratt Institute	1968	Davis and Elkins
1960	Elizabethtown Newark College of Engineering	1969	Eastern Illinois
		1970	Davis and Elkins
1961	Howard	1971	Quincy
1962	East Stroudsburg State	1972	Westmont
1963	Earlham College and Castleton State	1973	Quincy
		1974	Quincy
1964	Trenton State	1975	Quincy
1965	Trenton State	1976	Simon Fraser
1966	Quincy	1977	Quincy
1967	Quincy		

International Soccer

The world organization of soccer, FIFA, is headquartered in Zurich, Switzerland. Its 142 members are divided into six continental confederations: Africa; North/Central America and the Caribbean; Asia; Europe; South America and Oceania.

AFRICA: THE AFRICAN FOOTBALL CONFEDERATION

Algeria: Fédération Algérienne de Football. Founded 1962.
Burundi: Fédération de Football du Burundi. Founded 1948.
Cameroon: Fédération Camerounaise de Football. Founded 1960.
Central African Republic: Fédération Centrafricaine de Football. Founded 1937.
Congo: Fédération Congolaise de Football. Founded 1962.
Dahomey: Fédération Dahoméenne de Football. Founded 1968.
Egypt: Egyptian Football Association. Founded 1921.
Ethiopia: Yeitiopia Football Federechin. Founded 1943.
Gabon: Fédération Gabonaise de Football. Founded 1962.
Gambia: Gambia Football Association. Founded 1952.
Ghana: Ghana Football Association. Founded 1957.
Guinea: Fédération Guinéenne de Football. Founded 1959.
Ivory Coast: Fédération Ivoirienne de Football. Founded 1960.
Kenya: Football Association of Kenya. Founded 1945.
Lesotho: Lesotho Sports Council. Founded 1932.
Liberia: The Liberia Football Association. Founded 1960.
Libya: Libyan General Football Federation. Founded 1963.
Madagascar: Fédération Malagasy de Football. Founded 1961.
Malawi: National Football Association of Malawi. Founded 1966.
Mali: Fédération Malienne de Football. Founded 1960.
Mauritania: Fédération de Football de la République Islamique de Mauritanie. Founded 1961.
Mauritius: Mauritius Sports Association. Founded 1952.
Morocco: Fédération Royale Marocaine de Football. Founded 1955.
Niger: Fédération Nigérienne de Football. Founded 1967.
Nigeria: Nigeria Football Association. Founded 1945.
Rhodesia: Football Association of Rhodesia. Founded 1965.
Senegal: Fédération Sénégalaise de Football. Founded 1960.
Sierra Leone: The Sierra Leone Amateur Football Association. Founded 1967.

Somalia: Federazione Somala Giuco Calcio. Founded 1951.
South Africa: The Football Association of South Africa. Founded 1892.
Sudan: Sudan Football Association. Founded 1936.
Tanzania: Football Association of Tanzania. Founded 1930.
Togo: Fédération Togolaise de Football. Founded 1960.
Tunisia: Fédération Tunisienne de Football. Found 1958.
Uganda: Federation of Uganda Football Association. Founded 1924.
Upper Volta: Fédération Voltaïque de Football. Founded 1960.
Zaïre: Fédération Zaïroise de Football Association. Founded 1919.

AMERICA: NORTH AND CENTRAL AMERICA AND THE CARIBBEAN
(Confederation of North and Central American and Caribbean Association Football, or CONCACAF)

Antigua: The Antigua Football Association. Founded 1967.
Bahamas: Bahamas Football Association. Founded 1967.
Barbados: Barbados Football Association. Founded 1910.
Bermuda: The Bermuda Football Association. Founded 1928.
Canada: The Canadian Soccer Association. Founded 1912.
Costa Rica: Federación Costarricense de Fútbol. Founded 1921.
Cuba: Asociación de Fútbol de Cuba. Founded 1924.
Dominican Republic: Federación Dominicana de Fútbol. Founded 1953.
El Salvador: Federación Salvadorena de Fútbol. Founded 1964.
Guatemala: Federación Nacional de Fútbol de Guatemala. Founded 1950.
Guyana: Guyana Football Association. Founded 1902.
Haiti: Fédération Haïtienne de Football. Founded 1912.
Honduras: Federación Nacional Deportiva Extraescolar de Honduras. Founded 1951.
Jamaica: The Jamaica Football Federation. Founded 1910.
Mexico: Federación Mexicana de Fútbol Asociación. Founded 1922.
Netherlands Antilles: Nederlands Antilliaanse Voetbal Unie. Founded 1921.
Nicaragua: Federación Nacional de Fútbol. Founded 1968.
Panama: Federación Nacional de Fútbol de Panama. Founded 1951.
Puerto Rico: Federación Puertorriqueña de Fútbol. Founded 1940.
Surinam: Surinaamse Voetbal Bond. Founded 1920.
Trinidad: Trinidad Football Association. Founded 1906.
U.S.A.: United States Soccer Federation. Founded 1913.

AMERICA: SOUTH AMERICA (Confederación Sudamerican de Fúbol, or CONMEBOL)

Argentina: Asociación del Fútbol Argentino. Founded 1893.
Bolivia: Federación Boliviana de Fútbol. Founded 1925.
Brazil: Confederação Brasileira de Desportos. Founded 1914.

Chile: Federación de Football de Chile. Founded 1895.
Colombia: Federación Colombiana de Fútbol. Founded 1925.
Ecuador: Asociación Ecuatoriana de Fútbol. Founded 1925.
Paraguay: Liga Paraguaya de Fútbol. Founded 1906.
Peru: Federación Peruana de Fútbol. Founded 1922.
Uruguay: Asociación Uruguaya de Fútbol. Founded 1900.
Venezuela: Federación Venezolana de Fútbol. Founded 1926.

ASIA: ASIAN FOOTBALL CONFEDERATION

Afghanistan: The Football Association of Afghanistan. Founded 1922.
Bahrain: Football Association of Bahrain. Founded 1951.
Brunei: Brunei State Amateur Football Association. Founded 1959.
Burma: Burma Football Association. Founded 1947.
China (Taiwan): Republic of China Football Association. Founded 1951.
Hong Kong: Hong Kong Football Association. Founded 1915.
India: All-India Football Federation. Founded 1937.
Indonesia: All-Indonesia Football Federation. Founded 1930.
Iran: Iranian Football Federation. Founded 1920.
Iraq: Iraq Football Association. Founded 1948.
Israel: Israel Football Association. Founded 1928.
Japan: The Football Association of Japan. Founded 1921.
Jordan: Jordan Football Association. Founded 1949.
Khmer (Cambodia): Fédération Khmère de Football Association. Founded 1933.
Korea (DPR): Football Association of the Democratic People's Republic of
    Korea. Founded 1945.
Korea (Republic of South Korea): Korea Football Association. Founded 1928.
Kuwait: Kuwait Football Association. Founded 1952.
Laos: Fédération Lao de Football. Founded 1951.
Lebanon: Fédération Libanaise de Football Association. Founded 1933.
Malaysia: Football Association of Malaysia. Founded 1933.
Nepal: All-Nepal Football Association. Founded 1951.
Pakistan: Pakistan Football Federation. Founded 1948.
Philippines: Philippine Football Association. Founded 1907.
Qatar: Qatar Football Association. Founded 1960.
Saudi Arabia: Saudi Arabian Football Association. Founded 1959.
Singapore: Football Association of Singapore. Founded 1892.
Sri Lanka: The Football Association of Sri Lanka. Founded 1939.
Syria: Fédération Arabe Syrienne de Foot-Ball. Founded 1936.
Thailand: The Football Association of Thailand. Founded 1916.
Vietnam: Association de Football de la République Démocratique de Viet-nam.
    Founded 1962.
Yemen (PDR): People's Democratic Republic of Yemen Football Association.
    Founded 1940.

EUROPE: UNION OF EUROPEAN FOOTBALL ASSOCIATIONS (NEFA)

Albania: Fédération Albanaise de Football. Founded 1932.

Austria: Oesterreichischer Fussball-Bund. Founded 1904.

Belgium: Union Royale Belge des Sociétés de Football-Association. Founded 1895.

Bulgaria: Fédération Bulgare de Football. Founded 1923.

Cyprus: Cyprus Football Association. Founded 1934.

Czechoslovakia: Československý Fotbalový Svaz. Founded 1901.

Denmark: Dansk Boldspil-Union. Founded 1889.

England: The Football Association. Founded 1863.

Finland: Suomen Palloliitto—Finlands Bollforbund. Founded 1907.

France: Fédération Française de Football. Founded 1919.

German Democratic Republic (East Germany): Deutscher Fussball-Verband der DDR. Founded 1948.

German Federal Republic (West Germany): Deutscher Fussball-Bund. Founded 1900.

Greece: Elliniki Podesfairiki Omospondia. Founded 1926.

Hungary: Magyar Labdarugok Szovetsege. Founded 1901.

Iceland: Knattspyrnusamband Islands. Founded 1947.

Ireland, Northern: Irish Football Association, Ltd. Founded 1880.

Ireland, Republic of (Eire): The Football Association of Ireland. Founded 1921.

Italy: Federazione Italiana Giuoco Calcio. Founded 1898.

Luxembourg: Fédération Luxembourgeoise de Football. Founded 1908.

Malta: Malta Football Association. Founded 1900.

Netherlands: Koninklijke Nederlandsche Voetbalbond. Founded 1889.

Norway: Norges Fotballforbund. Founded 1902.

Poland: Fédération Polonaise de Football. Founded 1919.

Portugal: Federação Portuguesa de Futebol. Founded 1914.

Rumania: Federatia Romana de Fotbal. Founded 1908.

Scotland: The Scottish Football Association, Ltd. Founded 1873.

Spain: Real Federación Española de Fútbol. Founded 1913.

Sweden: Svenska Fotbollforbundet. Founded 1904.

Switzerland: Association Suisse de Football. Founded 1895.

Turkey: Türkiye Futbol Federasyonu. Founded 1923.

U.S.S.R.: U.S.S.R. Football Federation. Founded 1912.

Wales: The Football Association of Wales, Ltd. Founded 1876.

Yugoslavia: Fudbaiski Savez Jugoslavije. Founded 1919.

OCEANIA: OCEANIA FOOTBALL CONFEDERATION (OFC)

Australia: Australia Soccer Federation. Founded 1961.

Fiji: Fiji Football Association. Founded 1936.

New Zealand: New Zealand Football Association, Inc. Founded 1891.

Papua–New Guinea: Papua–New Guinea Football Association. Founded 1962.

INTERNATIONAL TOURNAMENTS

The World Cup

1930   Uruguay 4, Argentina 2
Uruguay: Ballesteros (g.), Nasazzi (r.b.), Mascheroni (l.b.), Andrade (r.h.), Fernández (c.h.), Gestido (l.h.), Dorado (o.r.), Scarone (i.r.), Castro (c.f.), Cea (i.l.), Iriarte (o.l.).
Argentina: Botasso (g.), Della Toree (r.b.), Paternoster (l.b.), Evaristo, J. (r.h.), Monti (c.h.), Suarez (l.h.), Peucelle (o.r.), Varallo (i.r.), Stabile (c.f.), Ferreira (i.l.), Evaristo, M. (o.l.).

1934   Italy 2, Czechoslovakia 1
Italy: Combi (g.), Monzeglio (r.b.), Allemandi (l.b.), Ferraris (r.h.), Monti (c.h.), Bertolini (l.h.), Guaita (o.r.), Meazza (i.r.), Schiavio (c.f.), Ferrari (i.l.), Orsi (o.l.).
Czechoslovakia: Planicka (g.), Zenisek (r.b.), Čtyroky (l.b.), Kostalek (r.h.), Cambal (c.h.), Krčil (l.h.), Junek (o.r.), Svoboda (i.r.), Sobotka (c.f.), Nejedlý (i.l.), Puc (o.l.).

1938   Italy 4, Hungary 2
Italy: Olivieri (g.), Foni (r.b.), Rava (l.b.), Serantoni (r.h.), Andreolo (c.h.), Locatelli (l.h.), Biavati (o.r.), Meazza (i.r.), Piola (c.f.), Ferrari (i.l.), Colaussi (o.l.).
Hungary: Szabó (g.), Polgár (r.b.), Bíró (l.b.), Szalay (r.h.), Szucs (c.h.), Lazar (l.h.), Sas (o.r.), Vincze (i.r.), Sarosi (c.f.), Szengellér (i.l.), Titkos (o.l.).

1950   Uruguay 2, Brazil 1 (deciding game in final pool)
Uruguay: Maspoli (g.), Gonzáles (r.b.), Tejera (l.b.), Gambetta (r.h.), Varela (c.h.), Andrade (l.h.), Ghiggia (o.r.), Pérez (i.l.), Miguez (c.f.), Schiaffino (i.l.), Moran (o.l.).
Brazil: Barbosa (g.), Augusto (r.b.), Juvenal (l.h.), Bauer (r.h.), Danilo (c.h.), Bigode (l.h.), Friaca (o.r.), Zizinho (i.r.), Ademir (c.f.), Jair (i.l.), Chico (o.l.).

1954   West Germany 3, Hungary 2
West Germany: Turek (g.), Posipal (r.b.), Kohlmeyer (l.b.), Eckel (r.h.), Liebrich (c.h.), Mai (l.h.), Rahn (o.r.), Morlock (i.r.), Walter, O. (c.f.), Walter, F. (i.l.), Schaefer (o.l.).
Hungary: Grosics (g.), Buzansky (r.b.), Lantos (l.b.), Bozsik (r.h.), Lorant (c.h.), Zakariás (l.h.), Czibor (o.r.), Kocsis (i.r.), Hidégkuti (c.f.), Puskás (i.l.), Toth (o.l.).

1958   Brazil 5, Sweden 2
Brazil: Gylmar (g.), Santos, D. (def.), Bellini (def.), Orlando (def.), Santos, N. (def.), Zito (mid.), Didí (mid.), Garrincha (for.), Vavá (for.), Pelé (for.), Zagalo (for.).

Sweden: Svensson (g.), Bergmark (r.b.), Axbom (l.b.), Boerjesson (r.h.), Gustavsson (c.h.), Parling (l.h.), Hamrin (o.r.), Gren (i.r.), Simonsson (c.f.), Liedholm (i.l.), Sköglund (o.l.).

1962   Brazil 3, Czechoslovakia 1
Brazil: Gylmar (g.), Santos, D. (def.), Mauro (def.), Zozimo (def.), Santos, N. (def.), Zito (mid.), Didí (mid.), Garrincha (for.), Vavá (for.), Amarildo (for.), Zagalo (for.).
Czechoslovakia: Schroiff (g.), Tichý (def.), Pluskal (def.), Popluhar (def.), Novák (def.), Masopust (mid.), Kvasniak (mid.), Pospíchal (for.), Scherer (for.), Kadraba (for.), Jelinek (for.).

1966   England 4, West Germany 2
England: Banks (g.), Cohen (def.), Charlton, J. (def.), Moore (def.), Wilson (def.), Stiles (mid.), Charlton, R. (mid.), Peters (mid.), Ball (for.), Hurst (for.), Hunt (for.).
West Germany: Tilkowski (g.), Hottges (def.), Schulz (def.), Weber (def.), Schnellinger (def.), Beckenbauer (mid.), Overath (mid.), Held (for.), Haller (for.), Seeler (for.), Emmerich (for.).

1970   Brazil 4, Italy 1
Brazil: Felix (g.), Carlos Alberto (def.), Brito (def.), Wilson Piazza (def.), Everaldo (def.), Clodoaldo (mid.), Gerson (mid.), Jairzinho (for.), Tostão (for.), Pelé (for.), Rivelino (for.).
Italy: Albertosi (g.), Burgnich (def.), Cera (def.), Rosato (def.), Facchetti (def.), Bertini (mid.), Mazzola (mid.), De Sisti (mid.), Domenghini (for.), Boninsegna (for.), Riva (for.). Substitutes: Juliano (mid.) and Rivera (for.).

1974   West Germany 2, Netherlands (Holland) 1
West Germany: Maier (g.), Vogts (def.), Schwarzenbeck (def.), Beckenbauer (def.), Breitner (def.), Bonhof (mid.), Hoeness (mid.), Overath (mid.), Grabowski (for.), Müller (for.), Hölzenbein (for.).
Netherlands: Jongbloed (g.), Suurbier (def.), Rijsbergen (def.), Haan (def.), Krol (def.), Jansen (mid.), Van Hanegem (mid.), Neeskens (mid.), Rep (for.), Cruyff (for.), Rensenbrink (for.). Substitutes: De Jong (def.) and Van der Kerkhof (for.).

Olympic Soccer (became officially a part of the Olympics in 1908)
1908   Great Britain (United Kingdom) 2, Denmark 0
1912   Great Britain (United Kingdom) 4, Denmark 2
1920   Belgium 2, Czechoslovakia 0
1924   Uruguay 3, Switzerland 0
1928   Uruguay 2, Argentina 1
1932   No competition

1936   Italy 2, Austria 1
1948   Sweden 3, Yugoslavia 1
1952   Hungary 2, Yugoslavia 0
1956   Russia 1, Yugoslavia 0
1960   Yugoslavia 3, Denmark 1
1964   Hungary 2, Czechoslovakia 1
1968   Hungary 4, Bulgaria 1
1972   Poland 2, Hungary 1
1976   East Germany 3, Poland 1

The European Champions Cup (The European Cup. Open to all national champions of Europe)

1956   Real Madrid 4, Stade de Rheims 3
1957   Real Madrid 2, Fiorentina 0
1958   Real Madrid 3, AC Milan 2
1959   Real Madrid 2, Stade de Rheims 0
1960   Real Madrid 7, Eintracht Frankfurt 3
1961   Benfica 3, Barcelona 2
1962   Benfica 5, Real Madrid 3
1963   AC Milan 2, Benfica 1
1964   Internazionale Milan 3, Real Madrid 1
1965   Internazionale Milan 1, Benfica 0
1966   Real Madrid 2, Partizan (Belgrade) 1
1967   Celtic (Glasgow) 2, Internazionale Milan 1
1968   Manchester United 4, Benfica 1
1969   AC Milan 4, Ajax (Amsterdam) 1
1970   Feyenoord (Rotterdam) 2, Celtic (Glasgow) 1
1971   Ajax (Amsterdam) 2, Panathinaikos 0
1972   Ajax (Amsterdam) 2, Internazionale Milan 0
1973   Ajax (Amsterdam) 1, Juventus 0
1974   Bayern Munich 4, Atlético Madrid 0 (after first game was tied at 1–1)
1975   Bayern Munich 2, Leeds 0
1976   Bayern Munich 1, St.-Étienne 0
1977   Liverpool 3, Borussia Mönchengladbach 1

The European Cup Winners Cup (open to all European cup winners)

1961   Fiorentina 4, Rangers (Glasgow) 1
1962   Atlético Madrid 3, Fiorentina 0
1963   Tottenham Hotspur 5, Atlético Madrid 1
1964   Sporting Lisbon 1, MTK Budapest 0
1965   West Ham United 2, Munich 1860 0
1966   Borussia Dortmund 2, Liverpool 1
1967   Bayern Munich 1, Rangers (Glasgow) 0
1968   AC Milan 2, Hamburg 0

1969   Slovan Bratislava 3, Barcelona 2
1970   Manchester City 2, Gornik (Poland) 1
1971   Chelsea 2, Real Madrid 1
1972   Rangers (Glasgow) 3, Dynamo (Moscow) 2
1973   AC Milan 1, Leeds 0
1974   FC Magdeburg (East Germany) 2, AC Milan 0
1975   Dynamo Kiev 3, Ferencvaros (Hungary) 0
1976   Anderlecht (Belgium) 4, West Ham United 2
1977   Hamburg SV 2, Anderlecht 0

The UEFA Cup (This competition was formerly called the Fairs Cup and was open to teams from all European cities that held annual industrial fairs. It became the UEFA Cup in 1972, and entry to the tournament is open to one or more top teams from any European country that have failed to qualify for either the European Cup or the Cup Winners Cup. A special committee from the UEFA selects the entrants.)

1958   Barcelona 6, London (represented by Chelsea) 0
       London 2, Barcelona 0
1959   No competition
1960   Birmingham City 0, Barcelona 0
       Barcelona 4, Birmingham City 1
1961   AS Roma 2, Birmingham City 0
       Birmingham City 2, AS Roma 2
1962   Barcelona 1, Valencia 1
       Valencia 6, Barcelona 2
1963   Dynamo Zagreb 2, Valencia 1
       Valencia 2, Dynamo Zagreb 0
1964   Real Zaragoza 2, Valencia 1 (only one game played)
1965   Ferencváros 1, Juventus 0 (only one game played)
1966   Barcelona 1, Real Zaragoza 0
       Real Zaragoza 4, Barcelona 2 (Barcelona won on "away goal" rule under which goals scored away from home are weighted as 2 goals instead of the usual 1.)
1967   Dynamo Zagreb 2, Leeds 0
       Leeds 0, Dynamo Zagreb 0
1968   Ferencváros 0, Leeds 0
       Leeds 1, Ferencváros 0
1969   Newcastle United 3, Újpest Dosza (Hungary) 0
       Újpest Dosza 2, Newcastle 3
1970   Anderlecht 3, Arsenal 1
       Arsenal 3, Anderlecht 0
1971   Juventus 2, Leeds 2
       Leeds 1, Juventus 1 (Leeds won on "away goal" rule.)
1972   Wolverhampton Wanderers 1, Tottenham Hotspur 2

Tottenham Hotspur 1, Wolverhampton Wanderers 1
1973   Liverpool 3, Borussia Mönchengladbach (West Germany) 0
Borussia Mönchengladbach 2, Liverpool 0
1974   Tottenham Hotspur 2, Feyenoord 2
Feyenoord 2, Tottenham Hotspur 0
1975   Borussia Mönchengladbach 2, Twente Enschede (Holland) 0
Twente Enschede 1, Borussia Mönchengladbach 5
1976   Liverpool 3, FC Bruges (Belgium) 2
FC Bruges 1, Liverpool 1
1977   Juventus 1, Atlético Bilbao 0
Atlético Bilbao 2, Juventus 1 (Juventus won on "away goal" rule.)

The European Football Championship (formerly the European Nations Cup. Open to all European nations belonging to UEFA)

1960   U.S.S.R. 2, Yugoslavia 1
1964   Spain 2, U.S.S.R. 1
1968   Italy 2, Yugoslavia 0 (after a 1–1 tie game)
1972   West Germany 3, U.S.S.R. 0
1976   Czechoslovakia 2, West Germany 2 (Czechoslovakia won on penalties after overtime).

South American Football Championship (Campeonato Sudamericano de Fútbol)

1917	Uruguay	1926	Uruguay	1953	Paraguay
1919	Brazil	1927	Argentina	1955	Argentina
1920	Uruguay	1937	Argentina	1957	Argentina
1921	Argentina	1939	Peru	1959	Argentina
1922	Brazil	1942	Uruguay	1963	Bolivia
1923	Uruguay	1947	Argentina	1967	Uruguay
1924	Uruguay	1949	Brazil	1975	Peru
1925	Argentina				

The Liberators Cup (Copa de los Libertadores. Open to champion and runner-up from member countries of CONMEBOL)

1960	Peñarol (Argentina)	1969	Estudiantes
1961	Peñarol	1970	Estudiantes
1962	Santos (Brazil)	1971	Nacional (Uruguay)
1963	Santos	1972	Independiente
1964	Independiente (Argentina)	1973	Independiente
1965	Independiente	1974	Independiente
1966	Peñarol	1975	Independiente
1967	Racing Club (Argentina)	1976	Cruzeiro (Brazil)
1968	Estudiantes (Argentina)	1977	Boca Juniors (Argentina)

CONCACAF Champions Tournament (open to all champions from North and Central America and the Caribbean)

1963	Guadalajara (Mexico)	1970	Cruz Azul, Saprissa (Costa
1964	Guadalajara		Rica) and Transval (Surinam)
1965	Guadalajara		shared the trophy.
1966	Racing (Haiti)	1971	Cruz Azul
1967	Alianza (El Salvador)	1972	Olimpia (Honduras)
1968	Toluca (Mexico)	1973	Municipal (Guatemala)
1969	Cruz Azul (Mexico)	1974	Transval
		1975	Atlético Español (Mexico)

The Inter-American Cup (Copa Interamericana is contested by the winner of the CONCACAF Championship and the winner of the Liberator Cup.)

1969	Estudiantes (Argentina)	1974	Independiente
1972	Nacional (Uruguay)	1975	Independiente
1973	Independiente (Argentina)	1976	Independiente

World Club Championship (Copa Intercontinentale. Contested by the winner of the European Cup and the South American Liberators Cup.)

1960	Real Madrid (Spain)	1969	AC Milan (Italy)
1961	Peñarol (Uruguay)	1970	Feyenoord (Holland)
1962	Santos (Brazil)	1971	Nacional (Uruguay)
1963	Santos	1972	Ajax (Holland)
1964	Internazionale Milan (Italy)	1973	Independiente (Argentina)
1965	Internazionale Milan	1974	Atlético Madrid (Spain)
1966	Peñarol	1975	Not played
1967	Racing (Argentina)	1976	Bayern Munich
1968	Estudiantes (Argentina)		(West Germany)

African Cup (open to national champions of Africa)

1964	Oryz Douala (Cameroon)	1970	Asante Kotoko (Ghana)
1965	No competition	1971	Canon Yaounde (Cameroon)
1966	Stade d'Abidjan (Ivory Coast)	1972	Hafia (Guinea)
1967	Engelbert Lumumbashi	1973	Vita (Zaïre)
	(now called Mazembe—of Zaïre)	1974	Cara (Congo)
1968	Engelbert Lumumbashi	1975	Hafia
1969	Ismail (Egypt)	1976	Mouloudia Chalia (Algeria)
		1977	Hafia

SOME NATIONAL CHAMPIONS OF THE MODERN SOCCER ERA

Argentina (Metropolitan League)

1958	Racing	1960	Independiente
1959	San Lorenzo	1961	Racing

Argentina *(continued)*

1962	Boca Juniors		1970	Independiente
1963	Independiente		1971	Independiente
1964	Boca Juniors		1972	San Lorenzo
1965	Boca Juniors		1973	Huracán
1966	Racing		1974	Newells Old Boys
1967	Estudiantes		1975	River Plate
1968	San Lorenzo		1976	Boca Juniors
1969	Chacarita Juniors		1977	River Plate

Austria

1958	Wiener SK		1968	Rapid Vienna
1959	Wiener SK		1969	FK Austria
1960	Rapid		1970	FK Austria
1961	FK Austria		1971	Wacker Innsbruck
1962	FK Austria		1972	Tirol-Svarowski
1963	FK Austria		1973	Tirol-Svarowski
1964	Rapid Vienna		1974	Voest Linz
1965	Linz ASK		1975	Tirol-Svarowski
1966	Admira-Energie		1976	Austria/WAC
1967	Rapid Vienna		1977	SW Innsbruck

Belgium

1958	Standard Liège		1968	Anderlecht
1959	Anderlecht		1969	Standard Liège
1960	Lierse SK		1970	Standard Liège
1961	Standard Liège		1971	Standard Liège
1962	Anderlecht		1972	Anderlecht
1963	Standard Liège		1973	Bruges
1964	Anderlecht		1974	Anderlecht
1965	Anderlecht		1975	Molenbeek
1966	Anderlecht		1976	Bruges
1967	Anderlecht		1977	Bruges

Brazil (National Championship)

1971	Atlético Mineiro		1974	Vasco da Gama
1972	Palmeiras		1975	Internacional
1973	Palmeiras		1976	Internacional

Brazil (Rio League)

1958	Vasco da Gama		1961	Botafogo
1959	Fluminense		1962	Botafogo
1960	America		1963	Flamengo

1964	Fluminense	1971	Fluminense
1965	Flamengo	1972	Flamengo
1966	Bangu	1973	Fluminense
1967	Botafogo	1974	Flamengo
1968	Botafogo	1975	Fluminense
1969	Fluminense	1976	Fluminense
1970	Vasco da Gama	1977	Vasco da Gama

Brazil (São Paulo League)

1958	Santos	1969	Santos
1959	Santos	1970	São Paulo
1960	Santos	1971	São Paulo
1961	Santos	1972	Palmeiras
1962	Santos	1973	Santos, Portuguesa and
1963	Palmeiras		Palmeiras, co-champions
1964	Santos	1974	Palmeiras
1965	Santos	1975	São Paulo
1966	Palmeiras	1976	Palmerias
1967	Santos	1977	Corinthians
1968	Santos		

Chile

1958	Santiago Wanderers	1968	Wanderers Valparaiso
1959	Universidad de Chile	1969	Universidad de Chile
1960	Colo-Colo	1970	Colo-Colo
1961	Universidad Católica	1971	Union San Felipe
1962	Universidad Católica	1972	Colo-Colo
1963	Colo-Colo	1973	Union Española
1964	Universidad de Chile	1974	Huachipato
1965	Universidad de Chile	1975	Union Española
1966	Universidad Católica	1976	Everton
1967	Universidad de Chile		

Czechoslovakia

1958	Dukla Prague	1968	Spartak Trnava
1959	Red Star Bratislava	1969	Spartak Trnava
1960	Spartak Hradec Kralove	1970	Slovan Bratislava
1961	Dukla Prague	1971	Spartak Trnava
1962	Dukla Prague	1972	Spartak Trnava
1963	Dukla Prague	1973	Spartak Trnava
1964	Dukla Prague	1974	Slovan Bratislava
1965	Sparta Prague	1975	Slovan Bratislava
1966	Dukla Prague	1976	Banik Ostrava
1967	Sparta Prague	1977	Dukla Prague

England

1958	Wolverhampton Wanderers	1968	Manchester City
1959	Wolverhampton Wanderers	1969	Leeds United
1960	Burnley	1970	Everton
1961	Tottenham Hotspur	1971	Arsenal
1962	Ipswich Town	1972	Derby County
1963	Everton	1973	Liverpool
1964	Liverpool	1974	Leeds United
1965	Manchester United	1975	Derby County
1966	Liverpool	1976	Liverpool
1967	Manchester United	1977	Liverpool

Holland

1958	DOS Utrecht	1968	Ajax
1959	Sparta	1969	Feyenoord
1960	Ajax	1970	Ajax
1961	Feyenoord	1971	Feyenoord
1962	Feyenoord	1972	Ajax
1963	PSV Eindhoven	1973	Ajax
1964	DWS Amsterdam	1974	Feyenoord
1965	Feyenoord	1975	PSV Eindhoven
1966	Ajax	1976	PSV Eindhoven
1967	Ajax	1977	Ajax

Hungary

1958	MTK	1968	Ferencváros
1959	Csepel	1969	Újpest Dozsa
1960	Újpest Dozsa	1970	Újpest Dozsa
1961	Vasas Budapest	1971	Újpest Dozsa
1962	Vasas Budapest	1972	Újpest Dozsa
1963	Ferencváros	1973	Újpest Dozsa
1964	Ferencváros	1974	Újpest Dozsa
1965	Vasas Budapest	1975	Újpest Dozsa
1966	Vasas Budapest	1976	Ferencváros
1967	Ferencváros	1977	Vasas Budapest

Italy

1958	Juventus	1965	Internazionale Milan
1959	AC Milan	1966	Internazionale Milan
1960	Juventus	1967	Juventus
1961	Juventus	1968	AC Milan
1962	AC Milan	1969	Fiorentina
1963	Internazionale Milan	1970	Cagliari
1964	Bologna	1971	Internazionale Milan

1972	Juventus	1975	Juventus
1973	Juventus	1976	Torino
1974	Lazio	1977	Juventus

Poland

1958	LKS Lodz	1968	Ruch Chorzow
1959	Gornik Zabrze	1969	Legia Warsaw
1960	Ruch Chorzow	1970	Legia Warsaw
1961	Gornik Zabrze	1971	Gornik Zabrze
1962	Polonia Bytom	1972	Gornik Zabrze
1963	Gornik Zabrze	1973	Stal Mielec
1964	Gornik Zabrze	1974	Ruch Chorzow
1965	Gornik Zabrze	1975	Ruch Chorzow
1966	Gornik Zabrze	1976	Stal Mielec
1967	Gornik Zabrze	1977	Slask Wroclaw

Portugal

1958	Sporting	1968	Benfica
1959	FC Porto	1969	Benfica
1960	Benfica	1970	Sporting
1961	Benfica	1971	Benfica
1962	Sporting	1972	Benfica
1963	Benfica	1973	Benfica
1964	Benfica	1974	Sporting
1965	Benfica	1975	Benfica
1966	Sporting	1976	Benfica
1967	Benfica	1977	Benfica

Scotland

1958	Hearts	1968	Celtic
1959	Rangers	1969	Celtic
1960	Hearts	1970	Celtic
1961	Rangers	1971	Celtic
1962	Dundee	1972	Celtic
1963	Rangers	1973	Celtic
1964	Rangers	1974	Celtic
1965	Kilmarnock	1975	Rangers
1966	Celtic	1976	Rangers
1967	Celtic	1977	Celtic

Spain

1958	Real Madrid	1961	Real Madrid
1959	Barcelona	1962	Real Madrid
1960	Barcelona	1963	Real Madrid

Spain (continued)

1964	Real Madrid	1971	Valencia
1965	Real Madrid	1972	Real Madrid
1966	Atlético Madrid	1973	Atlético Madrid
1967	Real Madrid	1974	Barcelona
1968	Real Madrid	1975	Real Madrid
1969	Real Madrid	1976	Real Madrid
1970	Atlético Madrid	1977	Atlético Madrid

Sweden

1958	IFK Gothenburg	1968	Oester Vaexjoe
1959	Djurgaarden	1969	IFK Gothenburg
1960	IFK Norrköping	1970	Malmö
1961	IF Elfsborg	1971	Malmö
1962	IFK Norrköping	1972	Atvidaberg
1963	IFK Norrköping	1973	Atvidaberg
1964	Djurgaarden	1974	Malmö
1965	Malmö	1975	Malmö
1966	Djurgaarden	1976	IFK Halmstad
1967	Malmö	1977	Malmö

West Germany

1958	FC Shalke	1968	Nuremberg
1959	Eintracht Frankfurt	1969	Bayern Munich
1960	Hamburg	1970	Borussia Mönchengladbach
1961	Nuremberg	1971	Borussia Mönchengladbach
1962	Cologne	1972	Bayern Munich
1963	Borussia Dortmund	1973	Bayern Munich
1964	Cologne	1974	Bayern Munich
1965	Werder Bremen	1975	Borussia Mönchengladbach
1966	Munich 1860	1976	Borussia Mönchengladbach
1967	Eintracht Brunswick	1977	Borussia Mönchengladbach

Uruguay

1958	Peñarol	1968	Peñarol
1959	Peñarol	1969	Nacional
1960	Peñarol	1970	Nacional
1961	Peñarol	1971	Nacional
1962	Peñarol	1972	Nacional
1963	Nacional	1973	Peñarol
1964	Peñarol	1974	Peñarol
1965	Peñarol	1975	Peñarol
1966	Nacional	1976	Nacional
1967	Peñarol		

U.S.S.R.

1958	Spartak Moscow	1968	Dynamo Kiev
1959	Dynamo Moscow	1969	Spartak Moscow
1960	Torpedo Moscow	1970	CSKA Moscow
1961	Dynamo Kiev	1971	Dynamo Kiev
1962	Spartak Moscow	1972	Saria Voroshilovgrad
1963	Dynamo Moscow	1973	Ararat Erevan
1964	Dynamo Tbilisi	1974	Dynamo Kiev
1965	Torpedo Moscow	1975	Dynamo Kiev
1966	Dynamo Kiev	1976	Torpedo Moscow
1967	Dynamo Kiev	1977	Dynamo Kiev

Yugoslavia

1958	Dynamo Zagreb	1968	Red Star Belgrade
1959	Red Star Belgrade	1969	Red Star Belgrade
1960	Red Star Belgrade	1970	Red Star Belgrade
1961	Red Star Belgrade	1971	Hajduk Split
1962	Red Star Belgrade	1972	Zeljeznicar
1963	Red Star Belgrade	1973	Red Star Belgrade
1964	Red Star Belgrade	1974	Hajduk Split
1965	Partizan Belgrade	1975	Hajduk Split
1966	Vojvodina Novi Sad	1976	Partizan Belgrade
1967	Sarajevo	1977	Red Star Belgrade

U.S. NATIONAL TEAM RECORD

Date	Opponent	Result	Venue
Nov. 25, 1885	Canada	W 3–2	Newark
Nov. 28, 1885	Canada	L 0–1	Newark
Aug. 20, 1916	Sweden	W 3–2	Stockholm
Sept. 3, 1916	Norway	T 1–1	Oslo
June 10, 1924	Poland	W 3–2	Warsaw
June 16, 1924	Erie	L 1–3	Dublin
June 27, 1925	Canada	L 0–1	Montreal
Nov. 8, 1925	Canada	W 6–1	Brooklyn
Nov. 6, 1926	Canada	W 6–2	Brooklyn
June 10, 1928	Poland	T 3–3	Warsaw
July 13, 1930	Belgium	W 3–0	Montevideo
July 17, 1930	Paraguay	W 3–0	Montevideo
July 26, 1930	Argentina	L 1–6	Montevideo
Aug. 17, 1930	Brazil	L 3–4	Rio de Janeiro
May 24, 1934	Mexico	W 4–2	Rome
May 27, 1934	Italy	L 1–7	Rome

Date	Opponent	Result	Venue
July 13, 1947	Mexico	L 0–5	Havana
July 20, 1947	Cuba	L 2–5	Havana
Aug. 6, 1948	Norway	L 0–11	Oslo
Aug. 11, 1948	N. Ireland	L 0–5	Belfast
Sept. 4, 1949	Mexico	L 0–6	Mexico City
Sept. 14, 1949	Cuba	T 1–1	Mexico City
Sept. 18, 1949	Mexico	L 2–6	Mexico City
Sept. 21, 1949	Cuba	W 5–2	Mexico City
June 25, 1950	Spain	L 1–3	Curitiba, Brazil
June 29, 1950	England	W 1–0	Belo Horizonte
July 2, 1950	Chile	L 2–5	Recife, Brazil
April 30, 1952	Scotland	L 0–6	Glasgow
June 8, 1953	England	L 3–6	New York
Jan. 10, 1954	Mexico	L 0–4	Mexico City
Jan. 14, 1954	Mexico	L 1–3	Mexico City
April 3, 1954	Haiti	W 3–2	Port-au-Prince
April 4, 1954	Haiti	W 3–0	Port-au-Prince
Aug. 25, 1955	Iceland	L 2–3	Reykjavik
April 7, 1957	Mexico	L 0–6	Mexico City
April 28, 1957	Mexico	L 2–7	Long Beach
June 22, 1957	Canada	L 1–5	Toronto
July 6, 1957	Canada	L 2–3	St. Louis
May 28, 1959	England	L 1–8	Los Angeles
Nov. 6, 1960	Mexico	T 3–3	Los Angeles
Nov. 13, 1960	Mexico	L 0–3	Mexico City
May 27, 1964	England	L 0–10	New York
March 7, 1965	Mexico	T 2–2	Los Angeles
March 12, 1965	Mexico	L 0–2	Mexico City
March 17, 1965	Honduras	W 1–0	San Pedro Sula
March 21, 1965	Honduras	T 1–1	Tegucigalpa
Sept. 15, 1968	Israel	T 3–3	New York
Sept. 25, 1968	Israel	L 0–4	Philadelphia
Oct. 17, 1968	Canada	L 2–4	Toronto
Oct. 20, 1968	Haiti	W 6–3	Port-au-Prince
Oct. 21, 1968	Haiti	L 2–5	Port-au-Prince
Oct. 23, 1968	Haiti	W 1–0	Port-au-Prince
Oct. 27, 1968	Canada	W 1–0	Atlanta
Nov. 2, 1968	Bermuda	W 6–2	Kansas City
Nov. 10, 1968	Bermuda	W 2–0	Hamilton, Ber.
April 20, 1969	Haiti	L 0–2	Port-au-Prince
May 11, 1969	Haiti	L 0–1	San Diego
Aug. 20, 1972	Canada	L 2–3	St. John's
Aug. 29, 1972	Canada	T 2–2	Baltimore

Date	Opponent	Result	Venue
Sept. 3, 1972	Mexico	L 1–3	Mexico City
Sept. 10, 1972	Mexico	L 1–2	Los Angeles
March 17, 1973	Bermuda	L 0–4	Hamilton, Ber.
March 20, 1973	Poland	L 0–4	Lodz
Aug. 3, 1973	Poland	L 0–1	Chicago
Aug. 5, 1973	Canada	W 2–0	Windsor
Aug. 10, 1973	Poland	L 0–4	San Francisco
Aug. 12, 1973	Poland	W 1–0	New Britain
Sept. 9, 1973	Bermuda	W 1–0	Hartford
Oct. 16, 1973	Mexico	L 0–2	Puebla
Nov. 3, 1973	Haiti	L 0–1	Port-au-Prince
Nov. 5, 1973	Haiti	L 0–1	Port-au-Prince
Nov. 13, 1973	Israel	L 1–3	Tel Aviv
Nov. 15, 1973	Israel	L 0–2	Beersheba
Sept. 5, 1974	Mexico	L 1–3	Monterrey
Sept. 8, 1974	Mexico	L 0–1	Dallas
March 26, 1975	Poland	L 0–7	Poznan
April 4, 1975	Italy	L 0–10	Rome
June 24, 1975	Poland	L 0–4	Seattle
Aug. 19, 1975	Costa Rica	L 1–3	Mexico City
Aug. 21, 1975	Argentina	L 0–6	Mexico City
Aug. 24, 1975	Mexico	L 0–2	Mexico City
Sept. 24, 1976	Canada	T 1–1	Vancouver
Oct. 3, 1976	Mexico	T 0–0	Los Angeles
Oct. 15, 1976	Mexico	W 3–0	Puebla
Oct. 20, 1976	Canada	W 2–0	Seattle
Dec. 22, 1976	Canada	L 0–3	Port-au-Prince

FAMOUS PLAYERS FROM AROUND THE WORLD

European Footballer of the Year (organized by *France Football,* Europe's leading soccer magazine)

1956	Stanley Matthews (England)	Second: Alfredo di Stéfano (Spain)
1957	Alfredo di Stéfano	Second: Billy Wright (England)
1958	Raymond Kopa (France)	Second: Helmut Rahn (W. Germany)
1959	Alfredo di Stéfano	Second: Raymond Kopa
1960	Luis Suárez (Spain)	Second: Ferenc Puskás (Spain)
1961	Omar Sivori (Italy)	Second: Luis Suárez
1962	Josef Masopust (Czechoslovakia)	Second: Eusebio (Portugal)
1963	Lev Yashin (U.S.S.R.)	Second: Gianni Rivera (Italy)
1964	Denis Law (Scotland)	Second: Luis Suárez

1965	Eusebio	Second: Giacinto Facchetti (Italy)
1966	Bobby Charlton (England)	Second: Eusebio
1967	Florian Albert (Hungary)	Second: Bobby Charlton
1968	George Best (N. Ireland)	Second: Bobby Charlton
1969	Gianni Rivera	Second: Luigi Riva (Italy)
1970	Gerd Müller (W. Germany)	Second: Bobby Moore (England)
1971	Johan Cruyff	Second: Sandro Mazzola (Italy)
1972	Franz Beckenbauer (W. Germany)	Second: Gerd Müller
1973	Johan Cruyff	Second: Dino Zoff (Italy)
1974	Johan Cruyff	Second: Franz Beckenbauer
1975	Oleg Blokhin (U.S.S.R.)	Second: Franz Beckenbauer
1976	Franz Beckenbauer	Second: Rob Rensenbrink (Holland)
1977	Allan Simonsen (Denmark)	Second: Kevin Keegan (England)

South American Player of the Year (for Central and South American players. Organized by *El Mundo* of Venezuela)

1971	Tostão (Brazil)	1974	Elías Figueroa (Chile)
1972	Teófilo Cubillas (Peru)	1975	Elías Figueroa
1973	Pelé (Brazil)	1976	Elías Figueroa

40 Other World-famous Players of the 1970s

Norberto Alonso, River Plate (Argentina)
Roberto Bettega, Juventus (Italy)
Ricardo Bochini, Independiente (Argentina)
Rainer Bonhoff, Borussia Mönchengladbach (West Germany)
Paul Breitner, Eintracht Brunswick (West Germany)
Martin Buchan, Manchester United (England)
Mike Channon, Manchester City (England)
Ray Clemence, Liverpool (England)
Jurgen Croy, Swickau (East Germany)
Yvan Curkovic, St.-Étienne (France)
Kazimierz Deyna, Legia (Poland)
Ralf Edstrom, FIFK Gothenburg (Sweden)
Rudi Geels, Ajax (Holland)
Gil, Fluminense (Brazil)
Francesco Graziani, Torino (Italy)
Uli Hoeness, Bayern Munich (West Germany)
Pat Jennings, Arsenal (England)
Josip Katalinski, Nice (France)
Kevin Keegan, Hamburg SV (West Germany)
Victor Kolotov, Dynamo Kiev (Russia)
Ruud Kroll, Ajax (Holland)
Raoul Lambert, FC Bruges (Holland)

Grzegory Lato, Stal Mielec (Poland)
Mario Marinho, Fluminense (Brazil)
Fernando Morena, Peñarol (Uruguay)
Dieter Muller, Cologne (West Germany)
Johan Neeskens, Barcelona (Spain)
Nelinho, Cruzeiro (Brazil)
Anton Ondrus, Slovan Bratislava (Czechoslovakia)
Antonin Panenka, Bohemians (Czechoslovakia)
Luis Pereira, Atlético Madrid (Spain)
Jan Peters, AZ '67 Alkmaar (Holland)
Oswaldo Piazza, St.-Étienne (France)
Michael Platini, Nancy (France)
Paolino Pulici, Torino (Italy)
Dominique Rocheteau, St.-Étienne (France)
Hugo Sotil, Barcelona (Spain)
Wim Suurbier, Ajax (Holland)
Bertie Vogts, Borussia Mönchengladbach (West Germany)
Zico, Flamengo (Brazil)

Advice to Young Players

In this section I would like to share with my younger readers who are perhaps contemplating a career in professional soccer some of my thoughts and impressions on what it really means to be a serious athlete. In passing along these personal observations I am in no way suggesting that young athletes should strive for a career in pro soccer—or in any other sport, for that matter—since I can think of hundreds of equally fascinating and rewarding vocations to enter. But if you are endowed with athletic abilities and potential, and you are willing to face many years of repetitive practices, the physical agony of two-a-day training sessions, endless road trips and early nights, while at the same time you look forward to sharing the excitement and comradeship of professional soccer, then by all means read on.

I suppose the one outstanding trait common to all successful athletes is a fierce dedication to their chosen sport. A desire for self-improvement is the most important element of this dedication and can best be exemplified by the endless hours top athletes devote to training on their own.

Probably nothing demands more dedication than the lonely business of training on one's own, but I believe that all young athletes, regardless of their sport, must learn to adapt to it. Not only does it ensure that you will improve at least as fast as others of your age and experience, but it also enables you to experiment with new techniques that might well be embarrassing to try out in front of others.

This urge to train alone pervades all sports. Pete Rose, John Havlicek, Muhammad Ali and Jimmy Connors have all spent a good part of their lifetimes practicing alone. In soccer we need look no further than the young Pelé, who was unable to afford a ball in his native Brazil and juggled with a grapefruit for hours at a time, or Stanley Matthew, who worked alone each day on his dribbling skills even when he was in his late 40s, or the 13-year-old Tommy Lawton, who headed a tennis ball against a brick wall every day after school. Despite their abundance of natural talent, I think it is fair to ask whether any of them would have attained world acclaim without that special effort that went into their individual practice sessions.

When on my own, I spend as much time as I can on juggling and dribbling and, of course, on running with and without the ball. I also find that this private practice is the best time to experiment with new kicking ideas: perhaps an attempt to improve my chip shot or to find new ways to bend the ball.

232

It is important when you're on your own to devise various challenges for yourself. For example, you might decide to head the ball consecutively twenty times without its touching any other part of your body or the ground. In this situation, if the ball hits the ground after the eighteenth header you would have to start all over again. The same approach would work if you are practicing shooting against a wall or a wooden kickboard. There are endless challenges you can set yourself, and all of them will help you to take your practice sessions seriously as well as make them more enjoyable.

Another reason why I consider this form of training so important is that even when you want to practice with others, quite often no one is available, particularly during the off-season. This was almost always the case for me when I was doing my Superstar training. Many of my workouts were after midnight, and naturally few athletes are around at that time (and rightly so, since sleep, as I will note later, is a most precious necessity for athletes). I have always enjoyed practicing alone, so this has never bothered me. I am not going to say the reason is spiritual, but I do think people who are comfortable on their own have a much better chance of improving themselves.

One drawback to working out alone, as opposed to team practice under the watchful eye of coach, is that quite often an athlete will begin his practice without adequately warming up. The first thing you should do whenever you commence training is flexibility exercises; you should then run a number of laps around the field, with or without the ball, so that your muscles become warm enough to handle the stress that will result from your activity.

In addition to training and self-improvement, three other factors that must be of prime importance to any budding athlete are diet, avoidance of harmful substances and rest; and as is true with training, the responsibility for them has to lie with no one but the athlete himself.

In recent years research has shown that some athletes, such as marathon runners and soccer players who are playing a grueling season, need a special diet or a special supplement to their diet. I think for the normal athlete, however, all that is needed is three well-balanced meals a day containing, whenever possible, one item from each of the four basic food groups. A protein-rich dish, a grain-based item, a dairy product and a leafy vegetable make up such a well-balanced meal. I try to follow this regimen throughout the year.

One important development in recent years has been the findings of British and American scientists that whole-grain breads are vital to our well-being. If you are still eating white bread, I urge you to switch to whole-wheat or rye, neither of which is made with starchy, nutritionless white flour. White sugar is another food substance that should be avoided. If you cannot shake the sugar habit, try raw unfiltered honey.

Athletes should also try to keep away from overcooked foods, for they have lost most of their vitamin content. Try a steady diet of raw vegetables and fruits instead. And while you are improving your dietary habits, cut out those "junk food" snacks and replace them with raw carrots, celery, apples, bananas or even plain old lettuce. It will be one of the best habits you will ever form.

The two most common substances damaging to an athlete's body are, of course, tobacco and alcohol. I am convinced that if all smokers were forced to view a lung-draining operation when liquid tar is suctioned out of a heavy smoker's lung, few would smoke again. Thankfully, few pro soccer players smoke, and those who do smoke infrequently. The pros know only all too well that it is impossible to develop what we term "oxygen uptake levels," which are necessary during a game, if the lungs are clogged up with tar.

As for alcohol, there is very little that can be said in its favor. Besides its debilitating effect, it also destroys brain cells every time it is consumed. Studies have shown that one ounce of alcohol can kill many millions of brain cells, and even more shocking is the scientific evidence that none of these brain cells can ever be replaced. Each brain cell has a special function, and so it is not surprising that alcoholics suffer blackouts and loss of memory.

In addition to the physical damage of alcohol, there is the social damage—what it does to your relationships with other people. The normal lack of control that comes with heavy alcoholic consumption is a devastating force that can destroy both friendships and home life.

I would like to make it quite clear that I see nothing wrong with the occasional drink. I always enjoy a beer on a warm afternoon, and I certainly never hesitate to join in with my teammates at social events when they are drinking beer. Most American soccer players are fond of beer—many of us like to justify our imbibing by reminding others that there are enough carbohydrates in beer to make it an effective part of a training regimen—but even with its low alcoholic content, too much of it can also be dangerous. All too often after drinking too many beers soccer players have found themselves saying things to coaches, managers and teammates that later upon sober reflections they wished they had not.

The third area, rest, is, of course, vitally important to young athletes who are still growing. It is even more important during periods of hard training. If, for instance, you are doing two-a-day high-stress workouts, eight hours' sleep a night and perhaps a one-hour nap in the afternoon would seem to be a minimum. Most youngsters, for varying reasons, seem to resent being sent to bed for a nap. If you are one of those who finds naps distasteful, at least go to bed at the same time every night so that your body can develop a rhythm. This body rhythm, often called biorhythm, enables your body to optimize its digestive and excretory functioning and facilitates the transfer of energy to your muscular system.

To maintain a vibrant biorhythm, it is far better to go to bed every night at eleven o'clock and get only seven hours sleep than to sleep eight hours per night but to get to bed at such varying times as nine o'clock one night and midnight the next.

When you do retire for the night, it is important that you eliminate as many of the surrounding noises as possible to help your body and mind enjoy complete rest. When I was in high school I had the habit of falling asleep with the radio on. This was clearly a mistake, since my subconscious mind was responding to what was happening on the radio. If you find it difficult to fall asleep at night, don't rely upon the radio or TV to relax you; try reading a book instead.

Another area of more than passing interest to young athletes is the question of how to accept failure and success. Whether you hope to play soccer at college or your goals are set even higher and you hope for a tryout with a pro team, I think you might benefit from some of my personal beliefs on this subject.

I define failure in athletes as a temporary loss. I also define a loser as a person who takes failure as final. There is no doubt in my mind that there are many ways to be a winner but there is really only one way to be a loser and that is to fail and not look beyond the failure.

Everyone fails at one time or another, and this has been so throughout history. There is no doubt that King David failed when he committed adultery and murder. Even the disciples of Christ failed in their inability to understand fully or to respond to His teachings. And yet would anyone who has studied the Bible really consider the disciples or King David "failures"? I doubt it. But I do believe all of them learned from their bad experiences and reacted positively to their failures.

Success or failure, after all, must be measured against the standards we set ourselves. All one has to do is take a look at the standards set for acceptance into law and medical schools to see how difficult it is to judge success or failure. Those entering these professional schools are students who for most of their lives have been academically successful—probably all in the top 25 percent of their class in high school and college. Now, before they attend the first day of law or medical classes, they know that all the way through law or medical school, half of their classmates will statistically be in the bottom half of the class. This does not mean the standards at these schools are not proper; it just simply means the standard is different and that we must be careful always to look at the measuring stick with which we judge ourselves. Some of us measure ourselves too harshly; others let themselves off far too easily.

I believe the fairest way to set standards for measuring ourselves for everything is by determining the number of opportunities afforded us and the quantity of natural abilities we are blessed with. In my case, for example, I know I must try to be a good athlete because the good Lord has blessed me generously with natural ability and it is my responsibility to compete at the highest level I think I can attain.

Just as important, we must always be certain to make our successes balance our failures. By success here I am not referring to the late Vince Lombardi's well-known axiom, "Winning is the only thing"; rather, I am speaking of fulfillment of a self-determined standard. For instance, if I play basketball with a 14-year-old neighbor, on the "Winning is the only thing" principle my responsibility ends if I can beat him in a game; but my responsibility should not end there. I should ask myself, Have I done all that I possibly can to improve myself? Have I used all the natural talents I possess? In this way a challenge is faced when you are playing either a weaker or a better player. You are obviously trying to compete against your particular opponent, but judging whether the day has been a success or a failure does not hinge on whether you have won or lost but rather on how nearly you approached your own best performance.

Another question I would like to discuss is the problem of humility, a quality most of our better athletes retain throughout their careers. I can remember that in my younger days when I had succeeded in some event or game and someone would compliment me I would invariably reply, "Oh, it was nothing." I think I was dishonest, making little of true accomplishment, particularly those which required a great deal of energy and time to execute. I believe now that true humility is admitting the achievement and saying, "Yes, it really was a good accomplishment," and then adding that the reason for it was the help received from teammates, coaches and others and that you have been blessed with some abilities.

I also believe that not only should one thank one's teammates: one should also thank one's opponents. Indeed, I would like to take this one step further and add that not only do I love my teammates but I love my opponents too. They, after all, are going to bring out the best in me, which is the very reason why I am an athlete in the first place. Some of you younger readers will be surprised to hear talk about loving opponents, or even teammates, for that matter; but I can tell you that despite the fierce competitiveness of the NASL and the rough physical play in most of the games, deep friendships do exist between many players from opposing teams.

If you are able to play professional soccer, I do hope you will bear in mind the special influence pro athletes have on youngsters who watch them. A heavy responsibility comes with this influence, for the impressionable youngster is always ready to emulate his sporting heroes. And it is not only the big stars who share this responsibility. To a 10-year-old fan any professional athlete, no matter how low his skill level, is a superman, and an obscene remark or an unsportsmanlike act by him will have the same deleterious effect as any willfully harmful action or remark by a superstar.

In closing, let me reiterate once again that the true importance of soccer— or any other competitive sport, for that matter—is not that it gives an athlete a chance to help win a game or demonstrate that he is the best player on the field; rather, it is that it gives a healthy athlete a chance to compete and perform to his optimum level so that he may earn the respect not only of his teammates and opponents but of his inner self as well.

Glossary

ADVANTAGE RULE: Law 5 states that the referee must refrain from awarding a free kick whenever he believes that by doing so he would be giving the offending team an advantage. For instance, if the player in possession is unfairly charged but continues to keep possession, the referee will in all probability wave play on.

BACK (Fullback): Any defender. Formerly the term referred to right and left backs only.

CAUTION: An official warning by the referee for a foul or unsportsmanlike conduct. The referee now shows the offending player a yellow card so that despite any language difficulties there can be no doubt that it is an official caution.

CENTERING (Center): Kicking a ball from the wing into the goal mouth. Also described as crossing the ball.

CHARGING: Using the shoulder to attempt to knock an opponent off the ball or to unbalance him. It is the only legal charge in soccer.

CHIP: A ball kicked so that it will rise rapidly, usually to go over an opponent's head.

CLEARANCE (Clear): Kicking or heading the ball away from the goal mouth or penalty area. A goalkeeper may, of course, throw as well as kick a clearance.

CORNER AREA: A small arc 1 yard in radius located at each of the four corners of the field. When corner kicks are taken, the ball must be within the arc.

CORNER KICK (Corner): A direct free kick which is awarded whenever a defender last touches the ball before it goes completely over the goal line.

CROSSING (Cross): See Centering.

DANGEROUS PLAY: Any action on the field considered by the referee to constitute a danger to the players. The most common is kicking a shoulder-high ball when an opponent is attempting to head it.

DEAD BALL: The name given the ball when the referee stops play or the ball has gone completely over the goal lines or the touchlines.

DRIBBLING: Maneuvering the ball past opponents with the feet.

DROP BALL: A method of restarting the game when the referee has stopped play other than for an infringement of the laws. He restarts the game by dropping the ball between two opposing players, who must wait for the ball to bounce before playing it.

EJECTION (Sending off): Dismissal of a player from a game by a referee for any flagrant violation of the laws. At such time the referee will show the player a red card and then write his name into his notebook. In most soccer leagues, being ejected from a game usually means suspension for the player in one or more future games.

FAR POST: The goalpost farther from the man who has the ball.

FIRST-TIME (One-touch): Kicking or heading the ball without stopping it first.

FOUL: Any infraction of the laws.

FREE KICK: The kick awarded against the offending team whenever the referee sees an infringement of the laws. The kick is taken from the place where the infringement occurred. There are two types of free kicks: the direct, for the more serious infringements, and the indirect, for lesser violations. All members of the offending team must stand 10 yards from the ball when the kick is taken.

GOAL: The score made whenever the ball passes completely over the goal line between the two upright posts and under the crossbar. The term is also used to describe the posts and the netting that constitute the goal structure, which measures 8 feet high and 8 yards wide.

GOAL AREA: The area immediately in front of the goal, measuring 20 yards in width and 6 yards in depth.

GOAL KICK: The kick awarded the defending team whenever the ball goes over the goal line and is last touched by a member of the attacking team. The kick must be taken from inside the goal area.

GOAL LINE: The boundary line that runs along each of the shorter ends of the field.

HALF VOLLEY: The act of kicking the ball just as it rebounds off the ground, usually no higher than 1 or 2 inches.

HALFWAY LINE: The dividing line that runs across the width of the field at the midpoint.

HANDBALL (Hands): Intentionally playing the ball with the hands or arms (except by the goalkeeper, who may use any part of his body while inside his own penalty area).

HAT TRICK: The act by a single player of scoring three goals in a game.

HEADING (Header): Using the head to propel the ball.

HOLDING: Using the hands to obstruct or hinder an opponent's movements.

INSWINGER: A corner kick that curves or swings into the goal.

INTERCEPTION: Moving to the ball to cut it off before it reaches an opponent.

INTERNATIONAL: A player who has been selected to play for his country's national team.

KICK-OFF: A kick from the center spot on the halfway line used to start the game at the beginning of the first and second halves and to restart the game after a goal has been scored.

LATERAL PASS (Square pass): A ball that is kicked across the field.

LINESMEN: The two officials stationed on the touchlines who assist the referee. Their main responsibilities are deciding which team will receive the throw-ins and helping the referee to spot offsides.

MAN-TO-MAN DEFENSE: A defensive system in which each defender guards, or marks, a specific opponent.

MARKING: Guarding an opponent.

MATCH: A game.

MIDFIELDMEN (Linkmen): The players who are the link between the defensive players and the offensive players.

NEAR POST: The goalpost nearer to the player with the ball.

OBSTRUCTION: Any attempt to impede or prevent an opponent's progress with or without the ball.

OFFSIDE: Any player who is nearer his opponent's goal line than the ball is when the ball is played to him is offside unless:

1. There are two or more opponents nearer the goal line than he is.
2. He is in his own half of the field.
3. The ball was last touched or played by an opponent.
4. He receives the ball directly from a corner kick, goal kick or throw-in or a drop-ball situation.

OFF THE BALL: A term used to denote movement of players without the ball.

OUTSWINGER: A corner kick that curves or swings away from the goal.

OVERHEAD KICK: Kicking the ball over one's head.

OVERLAPPING (Overlap): A defender or midfielder's moving down the touch-line to assist the forwards.

OWN GOAL: A goal scored by a player against his own team.

PASS: The movement of the ball from one teammate to another.

PENALTY ARC: An arc drawn 10 yards from the penalty spot to ensure that all players are 10 yards from the ball at the moment a penalty kick is taken.

PENALTY AREA: The 44-by-18-yard box in front of the goal.

PENALTY KICK: Any direct free kick awarded to the attacking team in the penalty area. The penalty kick is taken from the penalty spot, 12 yards from the goal, and only the kicker and goalkeeper may remain in the penalty area when the kick is taken. The goalkeeper may not move until the player has kicked the ball.

PENALTY SPOT: The designated place 12 yards from goal from which penalty kicks are taken.

PITCH: A British term for field.

PUNT: A kick used by goalkeepers. The ball is dropped by the hand and kicked on the volley.

RETREATING (funnel) DEFENSE: A defensive tactic in which the defenders and midfielders withdraw deep inside their own half before engaging the advancing opponents.

SAVE: Any successful attempt by the goalkeeper or other players to stop the ball from going into the net.

SCISSORS KICK: An overhead volley kick performed while both legs are in the air.

SCREENING: Attempting to shield the ball from an opponent by keeping one's body between the ball and the opponent.

SHOT: Any kick at goal with the intention of scoring.

SHOULDER CHARGE: See Charging.

SIDELINES: See Touchline.

STRIKER: An offensive player.

SWEEPER: A defender who plays behind his defensive line in order to deal with any attacking player or ball that penetrates it.

TACKLE: The attempt to dispossess an opponent of the ball by using the feet.

THROW-IN: The method of restarting the game whenever the ball has crossed the touchlines. The ball must be thrown with both hands over the head, and the thrower must keep both feet on the ground.

TOUCHLINE (Sideline): The boundary line that runs along each of the longer ends of the field.

TRAPPING: The act of stopping a moving ball with either the foot, thigh, chest or, less frequently, the head.

VOLLEY: The act of kicking the ball while it is still in the air.

WALL PASS (Give-and-go): Interpassing between two teammates, with one player acting as a rebounding wall so as to bypass an opponent.

WING: The area along the touchline.

WORK RATE: A term used to describe the amount of running on and off the ball by either a player or a team.

ZONE DEFENSE: A defensive system in which each defender is given a specific area to guard.

Laws of the Game

The Laws of the Game, 1977 edition, are reprinted here with the kind permission of FIFA. Line drawings by Wendy Frost.

LAW I. – THE FIELD OF PLAY

The Field of Play and appurtenances shall be as shown in the following plan:

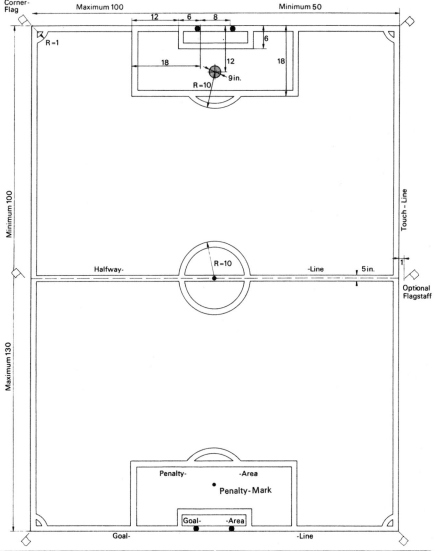

(N.B. All measurements not marked are in yards)

| *Laws of the Game* | *Decisions of the International Board* |

LAW I *(continued)*

(1) Dimensions. The field of play shall be rectangular, its length being not more than 130 yards nor less than 100 yards and its breadth not more than 100 yards nor less than 50 yards. (In International Matches the length shall be not more than 120 yards nor less than 110 yards and the breadth not more than 80 yards nor less than 70 yards.) The length shall in all cases exceed the breadth.

(2) Marking. The field of play shall be marked with distinctive lines, not more than 5 inches in width, not by a V-shaped rut, in accordance with the plan, the longer boundary lines being called the touch-lines and the shorter the goal-lines. A flag on a post not less than 5 ft. high and having a non-pointed top, shall be placed at each corner; a similar flag-post may be placed opposite the half-way line on each side of the field of play, not less than 1 yard outside the touch-line. A halfway-line shall be marked out across the field of play. The centre of the field of play shall be indicated by a suitable mark and a circle with a 10 yards radius shall be marked round it.

(3) The Goal-Area. At each end of the field of play two lines shall be drawn at right-angles to the goal-line, 6 yards from each goal-post. These shall extend into the field of play for a distance of 6 yards and shall be joined by a line drawn parallel with the goal-line. Each of the spaces enclosed by these lines and the goal-line shall be called a goal-area.

(4) The Penalty-Area. At each end of the field of play two lines shall be drawn at right-angles to the goal-line, 18 yards from each goal-post. These shall extend into the field of play for a distance of 18 yards and shall be joined by a line drawn parallel with the goal-line. Each of the spaces enclosed by these lines and the goal-line shall be called a penalty-area. A suitable mark shall be made within each penalty-area, 12 yards from the mid-point of the goal-line, measured along an undrawn line at right-angles thereto. These shall be the penalty-kick marks. From each penalty-kick mark an arc of a circle, having a radius of 10 yards, shall be drawn outside the penalty-area.

(1) In International matches the dimensions of the field of play shall be: maximum 110 x 75 metres; minimum 100 x 64 metres.

(2) National Associations must adhere strictly to these dimensions. Each National Association organising an International Match must advise the visiting Association, before the match, of the place and the dimensions of the field of play.

(3) The Board has approved this table of measurements for the Laws of the Game:

130 yards	.....	120 Metres
120 yards	.....	110
110 yards	.....	100
100 yards	.....	90
80 yards	.....	75
70 yards	.....	64
50 yards	.....	45
18 yards	.....	16.50
12 yards	.....	11
10 yards	.....	9.15
8 yards	.....	7.32
6 yards	.....	5.50
1 yard	.....	1
8 feet	.....	2.44
5 feet	.....	1.50
28 inches	.....	0.71
27 inches	.....	0.68
9 inches	.....	0.22
5 inches	.....	0.12
3/4 inch	.....	0.019
1/2 inch	.....	0.0127
3/8 inch	.....	0.010
14 ounces	.....	396 grams
16 ounces	.....	453 grams
15 lb./sq.in.	.....	1 kg/cm^2

(4) The goal-line shall be marked the same width as the depth of the goal-posts and the cross-bar, so that the goal-line and goal-posts will conform to the same interior and exterior edges.

(5) The 6 yards (for the outline of the goal-area) and the 18 yards (for the outline of the penalty-area) which have to be measured along the goal-line, must start from the inner sides of the goal-posts.

(6) The space within the inside areas of the field of play includes the width of the lines marking these areas.

(7) All Associations shall provide standard equipment, particularly in International Matches, when the Laws of the Game must be complied with in every respect and especially with regard to the size of the ball and other equipment which must conform to the regu-

Laws of the Game	*Decisions of the International Board*

LAW 1 *(continued)*

(5) **The Corner-Area.** From each corner-flag post a quarter circle, having a radius of 1 yard, shall be drawn inside the field of play.

(6) **The Goals.** The goals shall be placed on the centre of each goal-line and shall consist of two upright posts, equidistant from the corner-flags and 8 yards apart (inside measurement), joined by a horizontal cross-bar the lower edge of which shall be 8 ft. from the ground. The width and depth of the goal-posts and the width and depth of the cross-bars shall not exceed 5 inches (12 cm). The goal-posts and the cross-bars shall have the same width.

Nets may be attached to the posts, cross-bars and ground behind the goals. They should be appropriately supported and be so placed as to allow the goal-keeper ample room.

lations. All cases of failure to provide standard equipment must be reported to F.I.F.A.

(8) In a match played under the Rules of a Competition if the cross-bar becomes displaced or broken play shall be stopped and the match abandoned unless the cross-bar has been repaired and replaced in position or a new one provided without such being a danger to the players. A rope is not considered to be a satisfactory substitute for a cross-bar.

In a Friendly Match, by mutual consent, play may be resumed without the cross-bar provided it has been removed and no longer constitutes a danger to the players. In these circumstances, a rope may be used as a substitute for a cross-bar. If a rope is not used and the ball crosses the goal-line at a point which in the opinion of the Referee is below where the cross-bar should have been he shall award a goal.

The game shall be restarted by the Referee dropping the ball at the place where it was when play was stopped.

(9) National Associations may specify such maximum and minimum dimensions for the cross-bars and goal-posts, within the limits laid down in Law I, as they consider appropriate.

(10) Goal-posts and cross-bars must be made of wood, metal or other approved material as decided from time to time by the International F.A. Board. They may be square, rectangular, round, half-round or elliptical in shape Goal-posts and cross-bars made of other materials and in other shapes are not permitted.

(11) 'Curtain-raisers' to International matches should only be played following agreement on the day of the match, and taking into account the condition of the field of play, between representatives of the two Associations and the Referee (of the International Match).

(12) National Associations, particularly in International Matches, should
- restrict the number of photographers around the field of play,
- have a line ("photographers' line") marked behind the goal-lines at least two metres from the corner flag going through a point situated at least 3.5 metres behind the intersection of the goal-line with the line marking the goal area to a point

Footnote:

Goal nets. The use of nets made of hemp, jute or nylon is permitted. The nylon strings may, however, not be thinner than those made of hemp or jute.

Laws of the Game	*Decisions of the International Board*
	situated at least six metres behind the goal-posts,
	— prohibit photographers from passing over these lines,
	— forbid the use of artificial lighting in the form of "flashlights".

LAW II. – THE BALL

The ball shall be spherical; the outer casing shall be of leather or other approved materials. No material shall be used in its construction which might prove dangerous to the players.

The circumference of the ball shall not be more than 28 in. and not less than 27 in. The weight of the ball at the start of the game shall not be more than 16 oz. nor less than 14 oz. The pressure shall be equal to 0.6-0.7 atmosphere, which equals 9.0-10.5 lb./sq.in. (= 600-700 gr/cm^2) at sea level. The ball shall not be changed during the game unless authorised by the Referee.

(1) The ball used in any match shall be considered the property of the Association or Club on whose ground the match is played, and at the close of play it must be returned to the Referee.

(2) The International Board, from time to time, shall decide what constitutes approved materials. Any approved material shall be certified as such by the International Board.

(3) The Board has approved these equivalents of the weights specified in the Law: 14 to 16 ounces = 396 to 453 grammes.

(4) If the ball bursts or becomes deflated during the course of a match, the game shall be stopped and restarted by dropping the new ball at the place where the first ball became defective.

(5) If this happens during a stoppage of the game (place-kick, goal-kick, corner-kick, free-kick, penalty-kick or throw-in) the game shall be restarted accordingly.

Laws of the Game	*Decisions of the International Board*

LAW III. – NUMBER OF PLAYERS

(1) A match shall be played by two teams, each consisting of not more than eleven players, one of whom shall be the goalkeeper.

(2) Substitutes may be used in any match played under the rules of an official competition at FIFA, Confederation or National Association level, subject to the following conditions:

(a) that the authority of the international association(s) or national association(s) concerned, has been obtained,

(b) that, subject to the restriction contained in the following paragraph (c) the rules of a competition shall state how many, if any, substitutes may be used, and

(c) that a team shall not be permitted to use more than two substitutes in any match.

(3) Substitutes may be used in any other match, provided that the two teams concerned reach agreement on a maximum number, not exceeding five, and that the terms of such agreement are intimated to the Referee, before the match. If the Referee is not informed, or if the teams fail to reach agreement, no more than two substitutes shall be permitted.

(4) Any of the other players may change places with the goalkeeper, provided that the Referee is informed before the change is made, and provided also, that the change is made during a stoppage in the game.

(5) When a goalkeeper or any other player is to be replaced by a substitute, the following conditions shall be observed:

(a) the Referee shall be informed of the proposed substitution, before it is made,

(b) the substitute shall not enter the field of play until the player he is replacing has left, and then only after having received a signal from the Referee,

(c) he shall enter the field during a stoppage in the game, and at the half-way line.

Punishment:

(a) Play shall not be stopped for an infringement of paragraph 4. The players concerned shall be cautioned immediately the ball goes out of play.

(b) For any other infringement of this law, the player concerned shall be cautioned, and if the game is stopped by the Referee, to administer the caution, it shall be re-started by an indirect free-kick, to be taken by a player of the opposing team, from the place where the ball was, when play was stopped.

(1) The minimum number of players in a team is left to the discretion of National Associations.

(2) The Board is of the opinion that a match should not be considered valid if there are fewer than seven players in either of the teams.

(3) A competition may require that the referee shall be informed, before the start of the match, of the names of not more than five players, from whom the substitutes (if any) must be chosen.

(4) A player who has been ordered off before play begins may only be replaced by one of the named substitutes. The kick-off must not be delayed to allow the substitute to join his team.

A player who has been ordered off after play has started may not be replaced.

A named substitute who has been ordered off, either before or after play has started, may not be replaced (this decision only relates to players who are ordered off under Law XII. It does not apply to players who have infringed Law IV.)

(5) A player who has been replaced shall not take any further part in the game.

(6) A substitute shall be deemed to be a player and shall be subject to the authority and jurisdiction of the Referee whether called upon to play or not. For any offence committed on the field of play a substitute shall be subject to the same punishment as any other player whether called upon or not.

| *Laws of the Game* | *Decisions of the International Board* |

LAW IV. – PLAYERS' EQUIPMENT

(1) A player shall not wear anything which is dangerous to another player.

(2) Footwear (boots or shoes) must conform to the following standard:

(a) Bars shall be made of leather or rubber and shall be transverse and flat, not less than half an inch in width and shall extend the total width of the sole and be rounded at the corners.

(b) Studs which are independently mounted on the sole and are replaceable shall be made of leather, rubber, aluminium, plastic or similar material and shall be solid. With the exception of that part of the stud forming the base, which shall not protrude from the sole more than one quarter of an inch, studs shall be round in plan and not less than half an inch in diameter. Where studs are tapered, the minimum diameter of any section of the stud must not be less than half an inch. Where metal seating for the screw type is used, this seating must be embedded in the sole of the footwear and any atachment screw shall be part of the stud. Other than the metal seating for the screw type of stud, no metal plates even though covered with leather or rubber shall be worn, neither studs which are threaded to allow them to be screwed on to a base screw that is fixed by nails or otherwise to the soles of footwear, nor studs which, apart from the base, have any form of protruding edge rim or relief marking or ornament, should be allowed.

(c) Studs which are moulded as an integral part of the sole and are not replaceable shall be made of rubber, plastic, polyurethene or similar soft materials. Provided that there are no fewer than ten studs on the sole, they shall have a minimum diameter of three eights of an inch (10 mm.). Additional supporting material to stabilise studs of soft materials, and ridges which shall not protrude more than 5 mm. from the sole and moulded to strengthen it, shall be permitted provided that they are in no way dangerous to other players. In all other respects they shall conform to the general requirements of this Law.

(d) Combined bars and studs may be worn, provided the whole conforms to the general requirements of this Law. Neither bars nor studs on the soles shall project more

(1) The usual equipment of a player is a jersey or shirt, shorts, stockings and footwear. In a match played under the rules of a competition, players need not wear boots or shoes, but shall wear jersey or shirt, shorts, or track suit or similar trousers, and stockings.

(2) The Law does not insist that boots or shoes must be worn. However, in competition matches Referees should not allow one or a few players to play without footwear when all the other players are so equipped.

(3) In International Matches, International Competitions, International Club Competitions and friendly matches between clubs of different National Associations, the Referee, prior to the start of the game, shall inspect the players' footwear, and prevent any player whose footwear does not conform to the requirements of this Law from playing until such time as it does comply.

The rules of any competition may include a similar provision.

(4) If the Referee finds that a player is wearing articles not permitted by the Laws and which may constitute a danger to other players, he shall order him to take them off. If he fails to carry out the Referee's instruction, the player shall not take part in the match.

(5) A player who has been prevented from taking part in the game or a player who has been sent off the field for infringing Law IV must report to the Referee during a stoppage of the game and may not enter or re-enter the field of play unless and until the Referee has satisfied himself that the player is no longer infringing Law IV.

(6) A player who has been prevented from taking part in a game or who has been sent off because of an infringement of Law IV, and who enters or re-enters the field of play to join or re-join his team, in breach of the conditions of Law XII, shall be cautioned. If the Referee stops the game to administer the caution, the game shall be restarted by an indirect free-kick, taken by a player of the opposing side, from the place where the ball was when the Referee stopped the game.

Laws of the Game	*Decisions of the International Board*

LAW IV *(continued)*

than three-quarters of an inch. If nails are used they shall be driven in flush with the surface.

(3) The goalkeeper shall wear colours which distinguish him from the other players and from the referee.

Punishment: For any infringement of this Law, the player at fault shall be sent off the field of play to adjust his equipment and he shall not return without first reporting to the Referee, who shall satisfy himself that the player's equipment is in order; the player shall only re-enter the game at a moment when the ball has ceased to be in play.

Laws of the Game	*Decisions of the International Board*

LAW V. – REFEREES

A Referee shall be appointed to officiate in each game. His authority and the exercise of the powers granted to him by the Laws of the Game commence as soon as he enters the field of play.

His power of penalising shall extend to offences committed when play has been temporarily suspended, or when the ball is out of play. His decision on points of fact connected with the play shall be final, so far as the result of the game is concerned. He shall:

(a) Enforce the Laws.

(b) Refrain from penalising in cases where he is satisfied that, by doing so, he would be giving an advantage to the offending team.

(c) Keep a record of the game; act as timekeeper and allow the full or agreed time, adding thereto all time lost through accident or other cause.

(d) Have discretionary power to stop the game for any infringement of the Laws and to suspend or terminate the game whenever, by reason of the elements, interference by spectators, or other cause, he deems such stoppage necessary. In such a case he shall submit a detailed report to the competent authority, within the stipulated time, and in accordance with the provisions set up by the National Association under whose jurisdiction the match was played. Reports will be deemed to be made when received in the ordinary course of post.

(e) From the time he enters the field of play, caution any player guilty of misconduct or ungentlemanly behaviour and, if he persists, suspend him from further participation in the game. In such cases the Referee shall send the name of the offender to the competent authority, within the stipulated time, and in accordance with the provisions set up by the National Association under whose jurisdiction the match was played. Reports will be deemed to be made when received in the ordinary course of post.

(f) Allow no person other than the players and linesmen to enter the field of play without his permission.

(g) Stop the game if, in his opinion, a player has been seriously injured; have the player removed as soon as possible from the

(1) Referees in International Matches shall wear a blazer or blouse the colour of which is distinct from the colours worn by the contesting teams.

(2) Referees for International Matches will be selected from a neutral country unless the countries concerned agree to appoint their own officials.

(3) The Referee must be chosen from the official list of International Referees. This need not apply to Amateur and Youth International Matches.

(4) The Referee shall report to the appropriate authority misconduct or any misdemeanour on the part of spectators, officials, players, named substitutes or other persons which take place either on the field of play or in its vicinity at any time prior to, during, or after the match in question so that appropriate action can be taken by the Authority concerned.

(5) Linesmen are assistants of the Referee. In no case shall the Referee consider the intervention of a Linesman if he himself has seen the incident and from his position on the field, is better able to judge. With this reserve, and the Linesman neutral, the Referee can consider the intervention and if the information of the Linesman applies to that phase of the game immediately before the scoring of a goal, the Referee may act thereon and cancel the goal.

(6) The Referee, however, can only reverse his first decision so long as the game has not been restarted.

(7) If the Referee has decided to apply the advantage clause and to let the game proceed, he cannot revoke his decision if the presumed advantage has not been realised, even though he has not, by any gesture, indicated his decision. This does not exempt the offending player from being dealt with by the Referee.

(8) The Laws of the Game are intended to provide that games should be played with as little interference as possible, and in this view it is the duty of Referees to penalise only deliberate breaches of the Law. Constant whistling for trifling and doubtful breaches produces bad feeling and loss of temper on the part of the players and spoils the pleasure of spectators.

(9) By para. (d) of Law V the Referee is

Laws of the Game	*Decisions of the International Board*

LAW V *(continued)*

field of play, and immediately resume the game. If a player is slightly injured, the game shall not be stopped until the ball has ceased to be in play. A player who is able to go to the touch or goal-line for attention of any kind, shall not be treated on the field of play.

(h) Send off the field of play, any player who, in his opinion, is guilty of violent conduct, serious foul play, or the use of foul or abusive language.

(i) Signal for recommencement of the game after all stoppages.

(j) Decide that the ball provided for a match meets with the requirements of Law II.

empowered to terminate a match in the event of grave disorder, but he has no power or right to decide, in such event, that either team is disqualified and thereby the loser of the match. He must send a detailed report to the proper authority who alone has power to deal further with this matter.

(10) If a player commits two infringements of a different nature at the same time, the Referee shall punish the more serious offence.

(11) It is the duty of the Referee to act upon the information of neutral Linesmen with regard to incidents that do not come under the personal notice of the Referee.

(12) The Referee shall not allow any person to enter the field until play has stopped, and only then, if he has given him a signal to do so, nor shall he allow coaching from the boundary lines.

Laws of the Game	*Decisions of the International Board*

LAW VI. – LINESMEN

Two Linesmen shall be appointed, whose duty (subject to the decision of the Referee) shall be to indicate when the ball is out of play and which side is entitled to the corner-kick, goal-kick or throw-in. They shall also assist the Referee to control the game in accordance with the Laws. In the event of undue interference or improper conduct by a Linesman, the Referee shall dispense with his services and arrange for a substitute to be appointed. (The matter shall be reported by the Referee to the competent authority.) The Linesmen should be equipped with flags by the Club on whose ground the match is played.

(1) Linesmen, where neutral, shall draw the Referee's attention to any breach of the Laws of the Game of which they become aware if they consider that the Referee may not have seen it, but the Referee shall always be the judge of the decision to be taken.

(2) National Associations are advised to appoint official Referees of neutral nationality to act as Linesmen in International Matches.

(3) In International Matches Linesmen's flags shall be of a vivid colour, bright reds and yellows. Such flags are recommended for use in all other matches.

(4) A Linesman may be subjéct to disciplinary action only upon a report of the Referee for unjustified interference or insufficient assistance.

LAW VII. – DURATION OF THE GAME

The duration of the game shall be two equal periods of 45 minutes, unless otherwise mutually agreed upon, subject to the following: (a) Allowance shall be made in either period for all time lost through accident or other cause, the amount of which shall be a matter for the discretion of the Referee; (b) Time shall be extended to permit a penalty-kick being taken at or after the expiration of the normal period in either half.

At half-time the interval shall not exceed five minutes except by consent of the Referee.

(1) If a match has been stopped by the Referee, before the completion of the time specified in the rules, for any reason stated in Law V it must be replayed in full unless the rules of the competition concerned provide for the result of the match at the time of such stoppage to stand.

(2) Players have a right to an interval at half-time.

Laws of the Game	*Decisions of the International Board*

LAW VIII. – THE START OF PLAY

(a) **At the beginning of the game,** choice of ends and the kick-off shall be decided by the toss of a coin. The team winning the toss shall have the option of choice of ends or the kick-off. The Referee having given a signal, the game shall be started by a player taking a place-kick (i.e., a kick at the ball while it is stationary on the ground in the centre of the field of play) into his opponents' half of the field of play. Every player shall be in his own half of the field and every player of the team opposing that of the kicker shall remain not less than 10 yards from the ball until it is kicked-off; it shall not be deemed in play until it has travelled the distance of its own circumference. The kicker shall not play the ball a second time until it has been touched or played by another player.

(b) **After a goal has scored,** the game shall be restarted in like manner by a player of the team losing the goal.

(c) **After half-time;** when restarting after half-time, ends shall be changed and the kick-off shall be taken by a player of the opposite team to that of the player who started the game.

Punishment. For any infringement of this Law, the kick-off shall be retaken, except in the case of the kicker playing the ball again before it has been touched or played by another player; for this offence, an indirect free-kick shall be taken by a player of the opposing team from the place where the infringement occurred. A goal shall not be scored direct from a kick-off.

(d) **After any other temporary suspension;** when restarting the game after a temporary suspension of play from any cause not mentioned elsewhere in these Laws, provided that immediately prior to the suspension the ball has not passed over the touch or goal-lines, the Referee shall drop the ball at the place where it was when play was suspended and it shall be deemed in play when it has touched the ground; if, however, it goes over the touch or goal-lines after it has been dropped by the Referee, but before it is touched by a player, the Referee shall again drop it. A player shall not play the ball until it has touched the ground. If this section of the Law is not complied with the Referee shall again drop the ball.

(1) If, when the Referee drops the ball, a player infringes any of the Laws before the ball has touched the ground, the player concerned shall be cautioned or sent off the field according to the seriousness of the offence, but a free-kick cannot be awarded to the opposing team because the ball was not in play at the time of the offence. The ball shall therefore be again dropped by the Referee.

(2) Kicking-off by persons other than the players competing in a match is prohibited.

Laws of the Game	*Decisions of the International Board*
LAW IX. – BALL IN AND OUT OF PLAY The ball is out of play: (a) When it has wholly crossed the goal-line or touch-line, whether on the ground or in the air. (b) When the game has been stopped by the Referee. The ball is in play at all other times from the start of the match to the finish including: (a) If it rebounds from a goal-post, cross-bar or corner-flag post into the field of play. (b) If it rebounds off either the Referee or Linesmen when they are in the field of play. (c) In the event of a supposed infringement of the Laws, until a decision is given.	(1) The lines belong to the areas of which they are the boundaries. In consequence, the touch-lines and the goal-lines belong to the field of play.

Laws of the Game	*Decisions of the International Board*

LAW X. – METHOD OF SCORING

Except as otherwise provided by these Laws, a goal is scored when the whole of the ball has passed over the goal-line, between the goal-posts and under the cross-bar, provided it has not been thrown, carried or intentionally propelled by hand or arm, by a player of the attacking side, except in the case of a goalkeeper, who is within his own penalty-area.

The team scoring the greater number of goals during a game shall be the winner; if no goals, or an equal number of goals are scored, the game shall be termed a "draw".

(1) Law X defines the only method according to which a match is won or drawn; no variation whatsoever can be authorised.

(2) A goal cannot in any case be allowed if the ball has been prevented by some outside agent from passing over the goal-line. If this happens in the normal course of play, other than at the taking of a penalty-kick: the game must be stopped and restarted by the Referee dropping the ball at the place where the ball came into contact with the interference.

(3) If, when the ball is going into goal, a spectator enters the field before it passes wholly over the goal-line, and tries to prevent a score, a goal shall be allowed if the ball goes into goal unless the spectator has made contact with the ball or has interfered with play, in which case the Referee shall stop the game and restart it by dropping the ball at the place where the contact or interference occurred.

Laws of the Game	*Decisions of the International Board*

LAW XI. – OFF-SIDE

A player is off-side if he is nearer his opponents' goal-line than the ball **at the moment the ball is played unless:**

(a) He is in his own half of the field of play.

(b) There are two of his opponents nearer to their own goal-line than he is.

(c) The ball last touched an opponent or was last played by him.

(d) He receives the ball direct from a goal-kick, a corner-kick, a throw-in, or when it was dropped by the Referee.

Punishment. For an infringement of this Law, an indirect free-kick shall be taken by a player of the opposing team from the place where the infringement occurred.

A player in an off-side position shall not be penalised unless, in the opinion of the Referee, he is interfering with the play or with an opponent, or is seeking to gain an advantage by being in an offside position.

(1) Off-side shall not be judged at the moment the player in question receives the ball, but at the moment when the ball is passed to him by one of his own side. A player who is not in an off-side position when one of his colleagues passes the ball to him or takes a free-kick, does not therefore become off-side if he goes forward during the flight of the ball.

Laws of the Game	*Decisions of the International Board*

LAW XII. – FOULS AND MISCONDUCT

A player who intentionally commits any of the following nine offences:

(a) Kicks or attempts to kick an opponent;

(b) Trips an opponent, i.e., throwing or attempting to throw him by the use of the legs or by stooping in front of or behind him;

(c) Jumps at an opponent;

(d) Charges an opponent in a violent or dangerous manner;

(e) Charges an opponent from behind unless the latter be obstructing;

(f) Strikes or attempts to strike an opponent;

(g) Holds an opponent;

(h) Pushes an opponent;

(i) Handles the ball, i.e., carries, strikes or propels the ball with his hand or arm. (This does not apply to the goalkeeper within his own penalty-area);

shall be penalised by the award of a **direct free-kick** to be taken by the opposing side from the place where the offence occurred.

Should a player of the defending side intentionally commit one of the above nine offences within the penalty-area he shall be penalised by a **penalty-kick**.

A penalty-kick can be awarded irrespective of the position of the ball, if in play, at the time an offence within the penalty-area is committed.

A player committing any of the five following offences:

1. Playing in a manner considered by the Referee to be dangerous, e.g., attempting to kick the ball while held by the goalkeeper;

2. Charging fairly, i.e., with the shoulder, when the ball is not within playing distance of the players concerned and they are definitely not trying to play it;

3. When not playing the ball, intentionally obstructing an opponent, i.e., running between the opponent and the ball, or interposing the body so as to form an obstacle to an opponent;

4. Charging the goalkeeper except when he

    (a) is holding the ball;

    (b) is obstructing an opponent;

(1) If the goalkeeper either intentionally strikes an opponent by throwing the ball vigorously at him or pushes him with the ball while holding it, the Referee shall award a penalty-kick, if the offence took place within the penalty-area.

(2) If a player deliberately turns his back to an opponent when he is about to be tackled, he may be charged but not in a dangerous manner.

(3) In case of body-contact in the goal-area between an attacking player and the opposing goalkeeper not in possession of the ball, the Referee, as sole judge of intention, shall stop the game if, in his opinion, the action of the attacking player was intentional, and award an indirect free-kick.

(4) If a player leans on the shoulders of another player of his own team in order to head the ball, the Referee shall stop the game, caution the player for ungentlemanly conduct and award an indirect free-kick to the opposing side.

(5) A player's obligation when joining or rejoining his team after the start of the match to 'report to the Referee' must be interpreted as meaning 'to draw the attention of the Referee from the touch-line'. The signal from the Referee shall be made by a definite gesture which makes the player understand the he may come into the field of play; it is not necessary for the Referee to wait until the game is stopped (this does not apply in respect of an infringement of Law IV), but the Referee is the sole judge of the moment in which he gives his signal of acknowledgement.

(6) The letter and spirit of Law XII do not oblige the Referee to stop a game to administer a caution. He may, if he chooses, apply the advantage. If he does apply the advantage, he shall caution the player when play stops.

(7) If a player covers up the ball without touching it in an endeavour not to have it played by an opponent, he obstructs but does not infringe Law XII para. 3 because he is already in possession of the ball and covers it for tactical reasons whilst the ball remains within playing distance. In fact, he is actually playing the ball and does not commit an infringement; in this case, the

Laws of the Game	*Decisions of the International Board*

LAW XII *(continued)*
(c) has passed outside his goal-area;
5. When playing as goalkeeper,
   (a) takes more than 4 steps whilst holding, bouncing or throwing the ball in the air and catching it again without releasing it so that it is played by another player, or
   (b) indulges in tactics which, in the opinion of the Referee, are designed merely to hold up the game and thus waste time and so give an unfair advantage to his own team

shall be penalised by the award of an **indirect free-kick** to be taken by the opposing side from the place where the infringement occurred.

A player shall be **cautioned** if:
(j) he enters or re-enters the field of play to join or rejoin his team after the game has commenced, or leaves the field of play during the progress of the game (except through accident) without, in either case, first having received a signal from the Referee showing him that he may do so. If the Referee stops the game to administer the caution the game shall be restarted by an indirect free-kick taken by a player of the opposing team from the place where the ball was when the referee stopped the game. If, however, the offending player has committed a more serious offence he shall be penalised according to that section of the law he infringed;
(k) he persistently infringes the Laws of the Game;
(l) he shows by word or action, dissent from any decision given by the Referee;
(m) he is guilty of ungentlemanly conduct.

For any of these last three offences, in addition to the caution, an **indirect free-kick** shall also be awarded to the opposing side from the place where the offence occurred unless a more serious infringement of the Laws of the Game was committed.

A player shall be **sent off** the field of play, if:
(n) in the opinion of the Referee he is guilty of violent conduct or serious foul play;
(o) he uses foul or abusive language
(p) he persists in misconduct after having received a caution.

player may be charged because he is in fact playing the ball.
(8) If a player intentionally stretches his arms to obstruct an opponent and steps from one side to the other, moving his arms up and down to delay his opponent, forcing him to change course, but does not make "bodily contact" the Referee shall caution the player for ungentlemanly conduct and award an indirect free-kick.
(9) If a player intentionally obstructs the opposing goalkeeper, in an attempt to prevent him from putting the ball into play in accordance with Law XII, 5(a), the referee shall award an indirect free-kick.
(10) If after a Referee has awarded a free-kick a player protests violently by using abusive or foul language and is sent off the field, the free-kick should not be taken until the player has left the field.
(11) Any player, whether he is within or outside the field of play, whose conduct is ungentlemanly or violent, whether or not it is directed towards an opponent, a colleague, the Referee, a linesman or other person, or who uses foul or abusive language, is guilty of an offence, and shall be dealt with according to the nature of the offence committed.
(12) If, in the opinion of the Referee a goalkeeper intentionally lies on the ball longer than is necessary, he shall be penalised for ungentlemanly conduct and
(a) be cautioned and an indirect free-kick awarded to the opposing team;
(b) in case of repetition of the offence, be sent off the field.
(13) The offence of spitting at opponents, officials or other persons, or similar unseemly behaviour shall be considered as violent conduct within the meaning of section (n) of Law XII.
(14) If, when a Referee is about to caution a player, and before he has done so, the player commits another offence which merits a caution, the player shall be sent off the field of play.

Laws of the Game	*Decisions of the International Board*
LAW XII *(continued)* If play be stopped by reason of a player being ordered from the field for an offence without a separate breach of the Law having been committed, the game shall be resumed by an **indirect free-kick** awarded to the opposing side from the place where the infringement occurred.	

Laws of the Game	*Decisions of the International Board*

LAW XIII. – FREE-KICK

Free-kicks shall be classified under two headings: "Direct" (from which a goal can be scored direct against the offending side), and "Indirect" (from which a goal cannot be scored unless the ball has been played or touched by a player other than the kicker before passing through the goal).

When a player is taking a direct or an indirect free-kick inside his own penalty-area, all of the opposing players shall remain outside the area, and shall be at least ten yards from the ball whilst the kick is being taken. The ball shall be in play immediately it has travelled the distance of its own circumference and is beyond the penalty-area. The goalkeeper shall not receive the ball into his hands, in order that he may thereafter kick it into play. If the ball is not kicked direct into play, beyond the penalty-area, the kick shall be retaken.

When a player is taking a direct or an indirect free-kick outside his own penalty-area, all of the opposing players shall be at least ten yards from the ball, until it is in play, unless they are standing on their own goal-line, between the goal-posts. The ball shall be in play when it has travelled the distance of its own circumference.

If a player of the opposing side encroaches into the penalty-area, or within ten yards of the ball, as the case may be, before a free-kick is taken, the Referee shall delay the taking of the kick, until the Law is complied with.

The ball must be stationary when a free-kick is taken, and the kicker shall not play the ball a second time, until it has been touched or played by another player.

Punishment. If the kicker, after taking the free-kick, plays the ball a second time before it has been touched or played by another player an indirect free-kick shall be taken by a player of the opposing team from the spot where the infringement occurred.

(1) In order to distinguish between a direct and an indirect free-kick, the Referee, when he awards an indirect free-kick, shall indicate accordingly by raising an arm above his head. He shall keep his arm in that position until the kick has been taken.

(2) Players who do not retire to the proper distance when a free-kick is taken must be cautioned and on any repetition be ordered off. It is particularly requested of Referees that attempts to delay the taking of a free-kick by encroaching should be treated as serious misconduct.

(3) If, when a free-kick is being taken, any of the players dance about or gesticulate in a way calculated to distract their opponents, it shall be deemed ungentlemanly conduct for which the offender(s) shall be cautioned.

| *Laws of the Game* | *Decisions of the International Board* |

LAW XIV. – PENALTY-KICK

A penalty-kick shall be taken from the penalty-mark and, when it is being taken, all players with the exception of the player taking the kick, and the opposing goalkeeper, shall be within the field of play but outside the penalty-area, and at least 10 yards from the penalty-mark. The opposing goalkeeper must stand (without moving his feet) on his own goal-line, between the goalposts, until the ball is kicked. The player taking the kick must kick the ball forward; he shall not play the ball a second time until it has been touched or played by another player. The ball shall be deemed in play directly it is kicked, i.e., when it has travelled the distance of its circumference, and a goal may be scored direct from such a penalty-kick. If the ball touches the goalkeeper before passing between the posts, when a penalty-kick is being taken at or after the expiration of half-time or full-time, it does not nullify a goal. If necessary, time of play shall be extended at half-time or full-time to allow a penalty-kick to be taken.

Punishment:

For any infringement of this Law:

(a) by the defending team, the kick shall be retaken if a goal has not resulted.

(b) by the attacking team other than by the player taking the kick, if a goal is scored it shall be disallowed and the kick retaken.

(c) by the player taking the penalty-kick, committed after the ball is in play, a player of the opposing team shall take an indirect free-kick from the spot where the infringement occurred.

(1) When the Referee has awarded a penalty-kick, he shall not signal for it to be taken, until the players have taken up position in accordance with the Law.

(2) (a) If, after the kick has been taken, the ball is stopped in its course towards goal, by an outside agent, the kick shall be retaken.

(b) If, after the kick has been taken, the ball rebounds into play, from the goalkeeper, the cross-bar or a goal-post, and is then stopped in its course by an outside agent, the Referee shall stop play and restart it by dropping the ball at the place where it came into contact with the outside agent.

(3) (a) If, after having given the signal for a penalty-kick to be taken, the Referee sees that the goalkeeper is not in his right place on the goal-line, he shall, nevertheless, allow the kick to proceed. It shall be retaken, if a goal is not scored.

(b) If, after the Referee has given the signal for a penalty-kick to be taken, and before the ball has been kicked, the goalkeeper moves his feet, the Referee shall, nevertheless, allow the kick to proceed. It shall be retaken, if a goal is not scored.

(c) If, after the Referee has given the signal for a penalty-kick to be taken, and before the ball is in play, a player of the defending team encroaches into the penalty-area, or within ten yards of the penalty-mark, the Referee shall, nevertheless, allow the kick to proceed. It shall be retaken, if a goal is not scored.

The player concerned shall be cautioned.

(4) (a) If, when a penalty-kick is being taken, the player taking the kick is guilty of ungentlemanly conduct, the kick, if already taken, shall be retaken, if a goal is scored.

The player concerned shall be cautioned.

(b) If, after the referee has given the signal for a penalty-kick to be taken, and before the ball is in play, a colleague of the player taking the kick encroaches into the penalty-area or within ten yards of the penalty-mark, the Referee shall, nevertheless, allow the kick to proceed. If a goal is scored, it shall be disallowed, and the kick retaken.

The player concerned shall be cautioned.

(c) If, in the circumstances described in the foregoing paragraph, the ball rebounds into play from the goalkeeper, the cross-bar or a goal-post, the Referee shall stop

Laws of the Game	*Decisions of the International Board*
	the game, caution the player and award an indirect free-kick to the opposing team from the place where the infringement occurred.

Decisions of the International Board (continued)

(5) (a) If, after the referee has given the signal for a penalty-kick to be taken, and before the ball is in play, the goalkeeper moves from his position on the goal-line, or moves his feet, and a colleague of the kicker encroaches into the penalty-area or within 10 yards of the penalty-mark, the kick, if taken, shall be retaken.

The colleague of the kicker shall be cautioned.

(b) If, after the Referee has given the signal for a penalty-kick to be taken, and before the ball is in play, a player of each team encroaches into the penalty-area, or within 10 yards of the penalty-mark, the kick, if taken, shall be retaken.

The players concerned shall be cautioned.

(6) When a match is extended, at half-time or full-time, to allow a penalty-kick to be taken or retaken, the extension shall last until the moment that the penalty-kick has been completed, i.e. until the Referee has decided whether or not a goal is scored.

A goal is scored when the ball passes wholly over the goal-line.

(a) direct from the penalty-kick,

(b) having rebounded from either goal-post or the cross-bar, or

(c) having touched or been played by the goalkeeper.

The game shall terminate immediately the Referee has made his decision.

(7) When a penalty-kick is being taken in extended time:

(a) the provisions of all of the foregoing paragraphs, except paragraphs (2) (b) and (4) (c) shall apply in the usual way, and

(b) in the circumstances described in paragraphs (2) (b) and (4) (c) the game shall terminate immediately the ball rebounds from the goalkeeper, the cross-bar or the goal-post.

Laws of the Game	*Decisions of the International Board*

LAW XV. – THROW-IN

When the whole of the ball passes over a touch-line, either on the ground or in the air, it shall be thrown in from the point where it crossed the line, in any direction, by a player of the team opposite to that of the player who last touched it. The thrower at the moment of delivering the ball must face the field of play and part of each foot shall be either on the touch-line or on the ground outside the touch-line. The thrower shall use both hands and shall deliver the ball from behind and over his head. The ball shall be in play immediately it enters the field of play, but the thrower shall not again play the ball until it has been touched or played by another player. A goal shall not be scored direct from a throw-in.

Punishment:

(a) If the ball is improperly thrown in the throw-in shall be taken by a player of the opposing team.

(b) If the thrower plays the ball a second time before it has been touched or played by another player, an indirect free-kick shall be taken by a player of the opposing team from the place where the infringement occurred.

(1) If a player taking a throw-in, plays the ball a second time by handling it within the field of play before it has been touched or played by another player, the Referee shall award a direct free-kick.

(2) A player taking a throw-in must face the field of play with some part of his body.

(3) If, when a throw-in is being taken, any of the opposing players dance about or gesticulate in a way calculated to distract or impede the thrower, it shall be deemed ungentlemanly conduct, for which the offender(s) shall be cautioned.

Laws of the Game	*Decisions of the International Board*

LAW XVI. – GOAL-KICK

When the whole of the ball passes over the goal-line excluding that portion between the goal-posts, either in the air or on the ground, having last been played by one of the attacking team, it shall be kicked direct into play beyond the penalty-area from a point within that half of the goal-area nearest to where it crossed the line, by a player of the defending team. A goalkeeper shall not receive the ball into his hands from a goal-kick in order that he may thereafter kick it into play. If the ball is not kicked beyond the penalty-area, i.e., direct into play, the kick shall be retaken. The kicker shall not play the ball a second time until it has touched – or been played by – another player. A goal shall not be scored direct from such a kick. Players of the team opposing that of the player taking the goal-kick shall remain outside the penalty-area whilst the kick is being taken.

Punishment: If a player taking a goal-kick plays the ball a second time after it has passed beyond the penalty-area, but before it has touched or been played by another player, an indirect free-kick shall be awarded to the opposing team, to be taken from the place where the infringement occurred.

(1) When a goal-kick has been taken and the player who has kicked the ball touches it again before it has left the penalty-area, the kick has not been taken in accordance with the Law and must be retaken.

Laws of the Game	*Decisions of the International Board*

LAW XVII. – CORNER-KICK

When the whole of the ball passes over the goal-line, excluding that portion between the goal-posts, either in the air or on the ground, having last been played by one of the defending team, a member of the attacking team shall take a corner-kick, i.e., the whole of the ball shall be placed within the quarter circle at the nearest corner-flag-post, which must not be moved, and it shall be kicked from that position. A goal may be scored direct from such a kick. Players of the team opposing that of the player taking the corner-kick shall not approach within 10 yards of the ball until it is in play, i.e., it has travelled the distance of its own circumference, nor shall the kicker play the ball a second time until it has been touched or played by another player.

Punishment:

(a) If the player who takes the kick plays the ball a second time before it has been touched or played by another player, the Referee shall award an indirect free-kick to the opposing team, to be taken from the place where the infringement occurred.

(b) For any other infringement the kick shall be retaken.

QUESTIONS AND ANSWERS

The following questions have from time to time
been submitted to the FIFA by National Associations

The answers given have been approved by
The International F.A. Board

Law I

1. Q. If the cross-bar becomes displaced through breakage or faulty construction in a competitive match and there are no available means of repairing and replacing it, should the match be abandoned ?
   A. *Yes. The cross-bar may not be substituted by a rope in order to finish the match.*

2. Q. Is it necessary for flags to be placed at the half-way line ?
   A. *No.*

Law III

1. Q. If a player passes accidentally over one of the boundary-lines of the field of play, is he considered to have left the field of play without the permission of the Referee ?
   A. *No.*

2. Q. If a player in possession of the ball passes over the touch-line or the goal-line without the ball in order to beat an opponent, should the Referee penalise him for leaving the field of play without permission ?
   A. *No. Going outside the field of play may be considered as part of a playing movement, but players are expected, as a general rule, to remain within the playing-area.*

3. Q. Is it permissible for a goalkeeper to take a throw-in ?
   A. *Yes.*

Law IV

1. Q. If a player, following doctor's orders, protects his elbow or any similar part of his body with a plaster bandage to prevent further injury, has the Referee power to decide if the bandage constitutes a danger to to other players ?
   A. *Yes.*

2. Q. Should a player be permitted to take part in a game when he is wearing ordinary kind of boots instead of the normal football boots ?
   A. *The Laws of the Game do not specify that a player should wear any particular type of boot; if, however, they are equipped with bars or studs, the bars or studs must conform with Law IV.*

Law V

1. Q. If a Referee is struck in the face by the ball which then enters the goal while he is temporarily incapacitated, should a goal be allowed although he has not seen it scored ?
   A. *Yes, if in the opinion of a neutral Linesman nearer to the incident the goal was properly scored.*

2. Q. A Linesman signals that the ball has passed over the touch-line, but before the Referee has given the ball out of play, a defending player inside the penalty-area strikes an attacking player. What action should the Referee take ?
   A. *After having taken the appropriate action in relation to the offence the Referee should re-start the game with a throw-in because the ball was out of play when the offence occurred.*

3. Q. What action should a Referee take against a player who lights a cigarette during the game ?
   A. *Caution him for ungentlemanly conduct.*

4. Q. Can a captain send off one of his own team for serious misconduct ?
   A. *No. Only a Referee can send a player off the field.*

5. Q. What should the Referee do if two Captains agree to forego the half-time interval and one of the players insists on his right to 5 minutes' rest ?
   A. *Players have a right to 5 minutes' interval and the Referee must grant it.*

Law VI

1. Q. May a Referee ask a neutral Linesman to give an opinion as to whether or not the ball crossed the goal-line between the posts ?
   A. *Yes.*

Law VIII

1. Q. May a game be started by a person, other than one of the players taking part in the match, kicking-off ?
   A. *No. But if, in certain matches (e.g. charity or exhibition matches) a ceremony is arranged for a person not taking part in the game to kick the ball, it must be brought back to the centre of the field and kicked off in accordance with the Law.*

2. Q. When extra time is played, which team kicks off ?
   A. *The Captains toss for the choice of ends or kick-off for the extra time period.*

3. Q. If the ball is kicked straight into the opponents' goal from the kick-off, what decision does the Referee give ?
   A. *Goal-kick to the opposing team.*

Law IX

1. Q. Is the ball out of play if any part of the ball overlaps either the goal-line or the touch-line ?
   A. *No, the whole of the ball must cross the line.*

2. Q. A player asks to leave the field and as he is walking off the ball comes towards him and he shoots a goal. What action should the Referee take ?
   A. *The player shall be cautioned. The game shall be re-started by an indirect free-kick, taken by a player of the opposing team, from the place where infringement occurred.*

Law X

1. Q. If a Referee signals a goal before the ball has passed wholly over the goal-line and he immediately realises his error, is the goal valid ?
   A. *No. The game should be re-started by dropping the ball at the place where it was when the Referee inadvertently stopped play.*

Law XI

1. Q. Does a player infringe the Law if he is in an off-side position and moves a little way beyond the boundary of the field of play to show clearly to the Referee that he is not interfering with play ?
   A. *No, but if the Referee considers that such a movement has a tactical aim or is in any way a feint, and the player takes part in the game immediately after, the Referee should blow his whistle for off-side.*

2. Q. Is a team-mate allowed to stand in an off-side position at the taking of a penalty-kick ?
   A. *Yes, but he would be given off-side if the kicker failed to score directly and the player attempted to interfere with the game. The player would not be off-side if the goalkeeper had parried the ball and the ball went to him.*

Law XII

1. Q. Should a penalty be awarded, if while the ball is in play, a player intentionally trips or strikes an opponent who is in an off-side position in the penalty-area, but who is not attempting to play the ball nor interfere with play in any way ?
   A. *Yes.*

2. Q. What is the decision if a player, after receiving the approval of the Referee to leave the field of play because of slight injury or other cause, places himself near the touch-line and puts his foot into the field causing an opponent to fall ?
   A. *The player should be cautioned and the game re-started by a direct free-kick because the offence occurred within the field of play.*

3. Q. Should the Referee award a penalty-kick when a defending player is ordered off the field for kicking or striking an opponent within the penalty-area ?
   A. *Yes, provided the ball was in play at the moment when the offence was committed.*

4. Q. If a player intentionally lies on the ball for an unreasonable length of time, is he guilty of ungentlemanly conduct ?
   A. *Yes. He must be cautioned, and an indirect free-kick awarded to the opposing team. In case of repetition of the offence, he must be sent off the field.*

5. Q. How should the game be re-started if, when the ball is about to be dropped within the penalty-area, a defending player strikes an opponent before the ball touched the ground ?
   A. *After having taken the appropriate action in relation to the offence the Referee should drop the ball. If the misconduct took place inside the penalty-area he must not award a penalty-kick because the ball was not in play at the time the offence was committed.*

6. Q. What action should the Referee take if a player of the defending team, other than the goalkeeper, standing outside the penalty-area, intentionally handles the ball within the penalty-area ?
   A. *He should penalise the player by awarding a penalty-kick because the offence took place within the penalty-area.*

7. Q. What action should the Referee take if two players of the same team commit ungentlemanly or violent conduct towards each other on the field of play ?
   A. *The Referee should caution them or dismiss them from the field of play and re-start the game by an indirect free-kick.*

8. Q. If a player who enters or returns to the field of play without receiving a signal from the Referee to do so, and who, apart from this, commits another more serious infringement, e.g. handles the ball or strikes an opponent, how should he be penalised ?
   A. *1. The Referee shall caution the player for entering or returning to the field of play without having received a signal from the Referee.*
   2. The Referee shall furthermore punish the more serious infringement.

9. Q. If a Referee cautions a player who in turn apologises for his misconduct, can the Referee omit to report the incident ?
   A. *No, all cautions must be reported.*

Law XIII

1. Q. If a player takes a free-kick and then intentionally handles the ball before it has been played by another player, should the Referee punish the more serious offence and if so, how ?
   A. *Yes, by a direct free-kick or by a penalty-kick if the offence took place in the penalty-area.*

2. Q. May a free-kick be passed backwards ?

   A. *Yes. The provisions of Law XIII must, however, be observed in respect of free-kicks taken by the defending side from within its own penalty-area.*

3. Q. A player is awarded a free-kick in his own half of the field of play and he passes it back to his own goalkeeper who misses it completely and the ball enters the net. Is it a goal or corner-kick ?

   A. *The Referee should award a corner-kick provided that, in the case of the free-kick in the penalty-area, the ball has already gone into play, otherwise the free-kick inside the penalty-area must be retaken.*

4. Q. If the ball from an indirect free-kick touches another player and enters the net, should a goal be awarded ?

   A. *Yes.*

Law XIV

1. Q. If a player intentionally goes beyond the boundary of the field of play at the taking of a penalty-kick, should the Referee caution him and if he repeats the offence, send him off ?

   A. *Yes.*

2. Q. If a penalty-kick is re-taken because the goalkeeper moved his leg, must the same player take the kick again or could another player do so ?

   A. *Another player could re-take the penalty-kick.*

3. Q. If a player taking a penalty-kick back-heels the ball to a colleague, who scores, should the goal be allowed ?

   A. *No. The goal should be disallowed and the penalty-kick re-taken.*

4. Q. Can a player taking a penalty-kick push the ball forward for a colleague to run to it and score ?

   A. *Yes, provided –*
   (a) all of the players, with the exception of the player taking the penalty-kick and the opposing goalkeeper, are outside the penalty-area and not within 10 yards of the penalty-mark, at the time the kick is taken.
   (b) the colleague to whom the ball is passed is not in an off-side position when it is kicked, and
   (c) the penalty-kick is taken in normal time and the requirements of the Law are satisfied.

5. Q. If a defender, whilst standing in his own penalty-area, strikes an opponent while the ball is in play in the opponents' penalty-area, should the Referee award a penalty-kick ?

   A. *Yes.*

6. Q. Is a player taking a penalty-kick allowed to place the ball elsewhere than on the penalty-spot owing to the water-logged state of the pitch ?
   A. *No.*

7. Q. What action does the Referee take if, at the taking of a penalty-kick, the ball strikes the goal-post and/or cross-bar and bursts ?
   A. (i) *He asks for another ball and re-starts the game by dropping the ball.*
      (ii) *If the penalty-kick is being taken in extended time (see Universal Guide – Law XIV, decision 8) and the ball strikes the goal-post and/or cross-bar and bursts, the game ends.*

8. Q. What are the decisions of the Referee if, the signal having been given, but before the ball is kicked, a colleague of the player taking the kick encroaches into the penalty-area and the Referee notices the offence but allows the kick to be taken and the ball rebounds from the goalkeeper, cross-bar or goal-posts to the player who has encroached and this player sends the ball into goal ?
   A. *The Referee shall disallow the goal, caution the player at fault for ungentlemanly conduct and re-start the game by an indirect free-kick.*

Law XV

1. Q. The ball is in touch, but before it is thrown in, a player deliberately kicks an opponent, what action should the Referee take ?
   A. *He should caution the player or order him off the field and re-start the game by a throw-in.*

2. Q. If a player taking a throw-in, throws the ball so that it does not enter the field of play but passes outside the touch-line, what action should be taken ?
   A. *Throw should be re-taken.*

Law XVI

1. Q. If a player who has taken a goal-kick properly, intentionally plays the ball with the hand when the ball has left the penalty-area but before it has been touched by another player, what is the decision ?
   A. *A direct free-kick should be awarded to the opposite side.*

2. Q. Should the Referee award a penalty-kick if a player other than the goalkeeper takes a goal-kick and the ball passes out of the penalty-area into play but is blown back by a strong wind without any other player having touched it, and a player of the defending side other than the goalkeeper plays the ball with his hand within the penalty-area ?
   A. *Yes. If, in similar circumstances, the goalkeeper takes the goal-kick and he tries to stop the ball entering the goal and just touches the ball with his hand*

but fails to prevent it passing into goal, the Referee shall award an indirect free-kick.

3. Q. If, at a goal-kick, when the ball has travelled the distance of its circumference towards leaving the penalty-area, an opponent then enters the penalty-area and is intentionally fouled by a defending player, can a penalty-kick be awarded ?

   A. *No, because the ball was not in play at the time the offence was committed. The offending player shall be cautioned or ordered off, according to the nature of the offence, and the goal-kick retaken. If the ball has passed outside the penalty-area before the game is stopped, a goal-kick should still be re-taken as the player of the attacking side has entered the penalty-area before the ball was in play.*

4. Q. If a player is intentionally tripped before the ball passes out of the penalty-area at the taking of a goal-kick, should a free-kick be awarded ?

   A. *No, the ball is not in play until it has been out of the penalty-area. The offender should be cautioned or sent off and the goal-kick retaken.*

DIAGRAMS
ILLUSTRATING POINTS
IN CONNECTION WITH
OFF-SIDE

Diagram 1.—OFF-SIDE

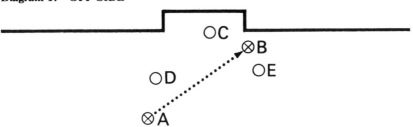

Clear pass to one of same side

A has run the ball up, and having **D** in front passes to **B**. **B** is off-side because he is in front of **A** and there are not two opponents between him and the goal-line when the ball is passed by **A**.

If **B** waits for **E** to fall back before he shoots, this will not put him on-side, because it does not alter his position with relation to **A** at the moment the ball was passed by **A**.

Diagram 2.—NOT OFF-SIDE

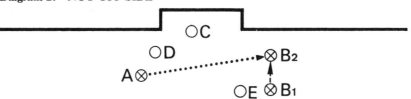

Clear pass to one of same side *(continued)*

A has run the ball up, and having **D** in front passes across the field. **B** runs from position **1** to position **2**. **B** is not off-side because at the moment the ball was passed by **A** he was not in front of the ball, and had two opponents between him and the goal-line.

Diagram 3.—OFF-SIDE

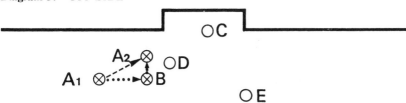

Clear pass to one of same side *(continued)*

A and **B** make a passing run up the wing. **A** passes the ball to **B** who cannot shoot because he has **D** in front. **A** then runs from position **1** to position **2** where he receives the ball from **B**. **A** is off-side because he is in front of the ball and he had not two opponents between him and the goal-line when the ball was played by **B**.

Diagram 4.—OFF-SIDE

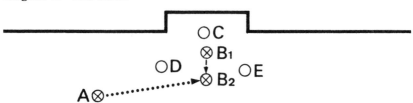

Running back for the ball

A centres the ball. **B** runs back from position **1** to position **2**, and then dribbles between **D** and **E** and scores. **B** is off-side because he is in front of the ball and he had not
two opponents between him and the goal-line at the moment the ball was played by **A**.

Diagram 5.—OFF-SIDE

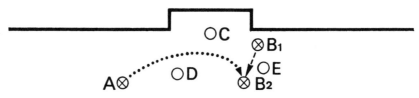

Running back for ball *(continued)*

A makes a high shot at goal, and the wind and screw carry the ball back. **B** runs
from position **1** to position **2** and scores. **B** is off-side because he is in front of the ball
and he had not two opponents between him and the goal-line at the moment the ball
was played by **A**.

Diagram 6.—OFF-SIDE

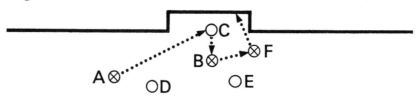

Shot at goal returned by goalkeeper C

A shoots at goal. The ball is played by **C** and **B** obtains possession, but slips and
passes the ball to **F** who scores. **F** is off-side because he is in front of **B**, and when the ball
was passed by **B** he had not two opponents between him and the goal-line.

Diagram 7.—NOT OFF-SIDE

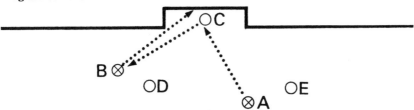

Shot at goal returned by goalkeeper *(continued)*

A shoots at goal. The ball is played out by **C** but **B** obtains possession and scores. **B** was in front of the ball and did not have two opponents between him and the goal-line when the ball was played by **A**, but he is not off-side because the ball has been last played by an opponent, **C**.

Diagram 8.—OFF-SIDE

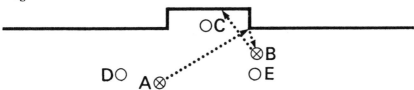

Ball rebounding from goal-posts or cross-bar

A shoots for goal and the ball rebounds from the goal-post into play. **B** secures the ball and scores. **B** is off-side because the ball is last played by **A**, a player of his own side, and when **A** played it **B** was in front of the ball and did not have two opponents between him and the goal-line.

Diagram 9.—OFF-SIDE

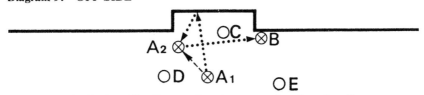

Ball rebounding from goal-posts or cross-bar *(continued)*

A shoots for goal and the ball rebounds from the cross-bar into play. **A** follows up from position **1** to position **2**, and then passes to **B** who has run up on the other side. **B** is off-side because the ball is last played by **A**, a player of his own side, and when **A** played it **B** was in front of the ball and did not have two opponents between him and the goal-line. If **A** had scored himself at the second attempt, instead of passing to **B**, it would have been a goal.

Diagram 10.—NOT OFF-SIDE

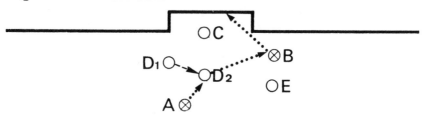

Ball touching an opponent

A shoots at goal. **D** runs from position **1** to position **2** to intercept the ball, but it glances off his foot to **B** who scores. **B** is not off-side because, although he is in front of the ball and has not two opponents between him and the goal-line the ball was last played by an opponent, **D**.

Diagram 11.—OFF-SIDE

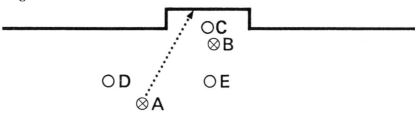

Obstructing the goalkeeper

A shoots for goal and scores. **B**, however, obstructs **C** so that he cannot get at the ball. The goal must be disallowed, because **B** is in an off-side position and may not touch the ball himself, nor in any way whatever interfere with an opponent.

Diagram 12.—OFF-SIDE

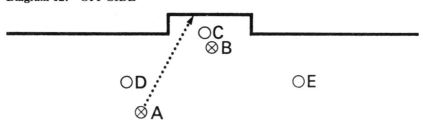

Obstructing the goalkeeper *(continued)*

A shoots for goal. **B** runs in while the ball is in transit and prevents **C** playing it properly. **B** is off-side because he is in front of **A** and has not two opponents between him and the goal-line when **A** plays the ball. When in this position **B** may not touch the ball himself, nor in any way whatever interfere with an opponent.

Diagram 13.—OFF-SIDE

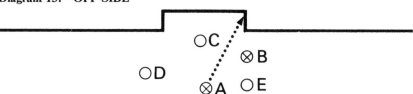

Obstructing an opponent other than the goalkeeper

A shoots for goal. **B** prevents **E** running in to intercept the ball. **B** is off-side because he is in front of **A** and has not two opponents between him and the goal-line when **A** plays the ball. When in this position **B** may not touch the ball himself, nor in any way whatever interfere with an opponent.

Diagram 14.—OFF-SIDE

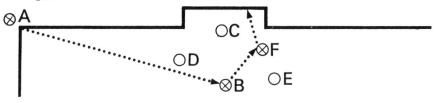

After a corner-kick

A takes a corner-kick and the ball goes to **B**. **B** shoots for goal and as the ball is passing through, **F** touches it. **F** is off-side because after the corner-kick has been taken the ball is last played by **B**, a player of his own side, and when **B** played it **F** was in front of the ball and had not two opponents between him and the goal-line.

Diagram 15.—NOT OFF-SIDE

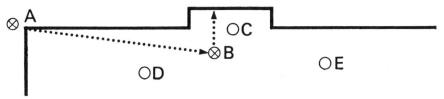

After a corner-kick *(continued)*

A takes a corner-kick and the ball goes to **B**, who puts it through goal. **B** has only one opponent between him and the goal-line, but he is not off-side because a player cannot be off-side from a corner-kick.

Diagram 16.—NOT OFF-SIDE

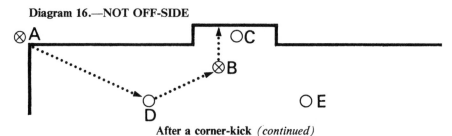

After a corner-kick *(continued)*

A takes a corner-kick and the ball glances off **D** and goes to **B**, who puts it through goal. **B** is not off-side because the ball was last played by an opponent, **D**.

Diagram 17.—OFF-SIDE

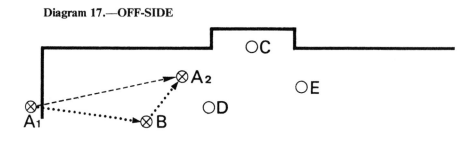

After a throw-in from the touch-line

A throws to **B** and then runs from touch-line to position **A2**. **B** passes the ball to **A** in position **2**. **A** is off-side because he is in front of the ball and has not two opponents between him and the goal-line when the ball is passed forward to him by **B**.

Diagram 18.—NOT OFF-SIDE

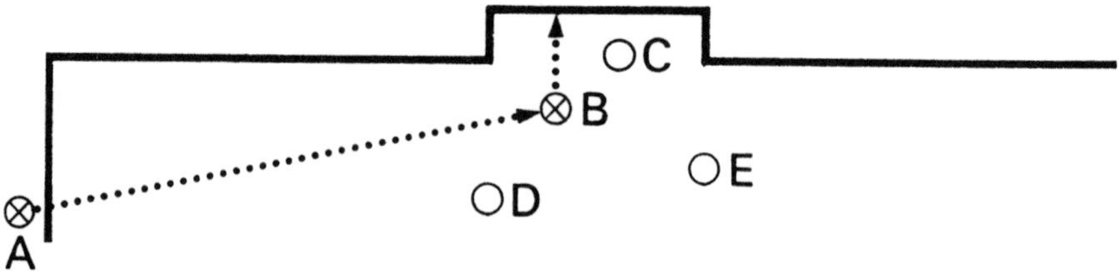

After a throw-in from the touch-line *(continued)*

A throws the ball to **B**. Although **B** is in front of the ball and has not two opponents between him and the goal line, he is not off-side because a player cannot be off-side from a throw-in.

Diagram 19.—OFF-SIDE   **Diagram 20.—NOT OFF-SIDE**

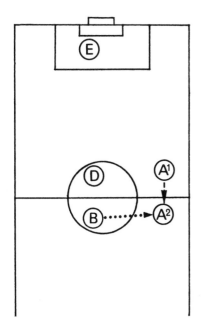 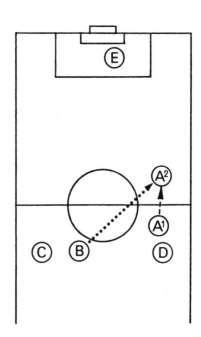

A player cannot put himself on-side by running back into his own half of the field of play

If **A** is in his opponents' half of the field of play, and is off-side in position when **B** last played the ball, he cannot put himself on-side by moving back into his own half of the field of play.

A player within his own half of the field of play is not off-side when he enters his opponents' half of the field of play

If **A** is in his own half of the field of play he is on-side, although he is in front of the ball and there are not two opponents nearer their own goal-line when **B** last played the ball. **A** is therefore not off-side when he enters his opponents' half of the field of play.

Signals by
Referee and Linesmen

Instructions prepared by the FIFA Referees' Committee and approved by the International Football Association Board

The signals illustrated in this Memorandum are the only official signals approved by the International F.A. Board and no other signals should be used by registered Referees of affiliated National Associations.

Comments and Instructions

The referee has no need of signals beyond those few already universally in use and well understood. (Illustrations concerning Signals by the Referee see pages 57-60.)

The duties of the referee and linesmen are set out briefly but clearly in the Laws of the Game, Laws V and VI.

There is further exposition of co-operation between the referee and linesmen in the memorandum explaining the universally adopted system of "diagonal control".

The proper use of the whistle, approved hand signals by the referee and the flags by the linesmen is all that is needed to make decisions clear.

It is not the duty of the referee nor is it a useful function to explain his decisions to the players or spectators. Any attempt to do so can lead to confusion, uncertainty and delay.

All signals used by the referee should be simple, clear and instinctive. They are designed to control the game efficiently and to ensure continuous play as far as possible; they are intended to indicate what the next action in the game should be, not to justify that action.

An arm pointing to indicate a corner-kick, goal-kick or foul, and the direction in which it is to be taken is sufficient. The raised arm to indicate that a free-kick is indirect is clearly understood.

To go beyond these requirements invites argument, dissent or exaggeration. The only other signal required is one to indicate that play should continue when the "advantage" clause is being invoked.

Co-operation between Linesmen and Referee

When play has been stopped the linesman should assist the referee by signalling in the following manner for the following incidents:

1. Off-side. The linesman should lower his flag at full arm's length to the positions illustrated, and point across the field of play to indicate the spot from which the kick should be taken. The only exception would be where the referee has decided to position himself to judge off-side when play develops from a corner-kick, penalty-kick or free-kick close to goal.

2. Throw-in. When the ball goes out of play over the touch-line on his side of the field, the linesman should indicate the direction of the throw. He should also signal if the thrower's feet, at the moment of release of the ball, are incorrectly placed.

3. Corner and goal-kicks. When the whole of the ball goes out of play over the goal-line the linesman should indicate whether a corner-kick or goal-kick should be given.

4. Goal. When the referee indicates that a goal is scored the linesman should return quickly to his position towards the half-way line.

Law XII. If the linesman senses that the referee has not seen an infringement he should raise his flag high. If the referee stops play the linesman shall indicate the direction of the free-kick (direct or indirect), otherwise he shall lower his flag.

(Illustrations concerning Signals by the Linesmen see pages 61-64.)

SIGNALS BY THE REFEREE

Play On—Advantage
Where the referee sees an offense but uses the Advantage, he shall indicate that play shall continue.

Indirect Free Kick
This signal shall be maintained
until the kick has been taken.

Direct Free Kick
The hand and arm clearly indicate the direction.

Penalty Kick
The referee clearly indicates the penalty mark, but there is no need to run toward it.

Goal Kick

Corner Kick

Caution or Expulsion
With the card system in operation, the card shall be shown in the manner illustrated. The player's identity *must* be recorded at the time.

SIGNALS BY THE LINESMEN

Offside
Flag held upright to indicate Offside.

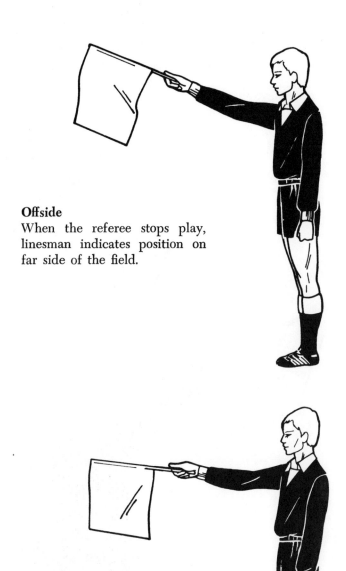

Offside
When the referee stops play, linesman indicates position on far side of the field.

Offside
Position near the center of the field.

Offside
Position on near side of the field.

Throw-in

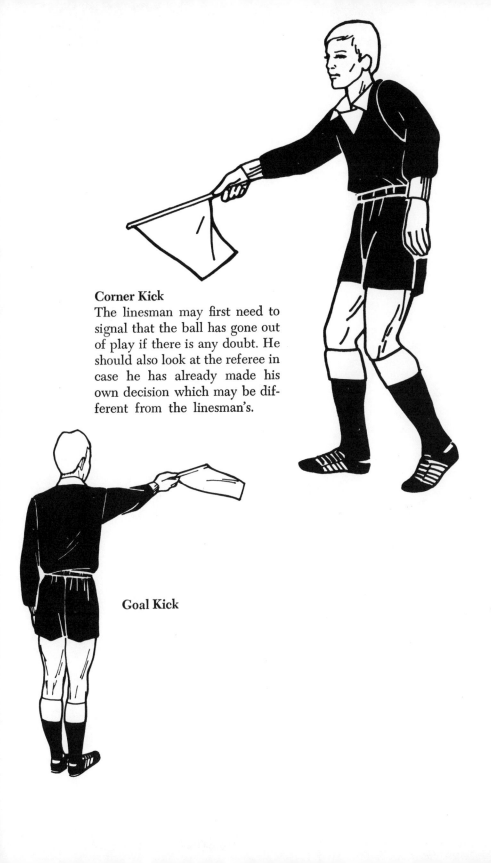

Corner Kick

The linesman may first need to signal that the ball has gone out of play if there is any doubt. He should also look at the referee in case he has already made his own decision which may be different from the linesman's.

Goal Kick

Bibliography

Allen, John, *Soccer for Americans*, Grosset & Dunlap, 1973.
Allison, Malcolm, *Soccer for Thinkers*, Pelham Books (London), 1967.
Bebbington, Jim, *Football in Color*, Blandford (London), 1976.
Brasch, R., *How Did Sports Begin*, David McKay, 1970.
Cottrell, John A., *A Century of Great Soccer Drama*, Hart-Davis (London), 1970.
Eastham, George, *Soccer Science*, Pelham Books (London), 1966.
Fabian, A. H., and Geoffrey Green, *Association Football*, Caxton (London), 1960.
Gardiner, E. Norman, *Athletics of the Ancient World*, Oxford University Press, 1930.
Gardner, Paul, *The Simplest Game*, Little, Brown, 1976.
Gibson, Alfred, and William Pickford, *Association Football and the Men Who Made It*, Caxton (London), 1905.
Golesworthy, Maurice, *The Encyclopedia of Association Football*, Robert Hale (London), 1970.
Granville, Brian, *Soccer Panorama*, Eyre and Spottiswoode (London), 1969.
Harris, H. A., *Sport in Greece and Rome*, Cornell University Press, 1972.
Hopcraft, Arthur, *The Football Man*, Penguin (London), 1971.
Hughes, Charles, *Tactics and Teamwork*, EP Publishing (London), 1975.
Jeffery, Gordon, *European International Football*, Nicholas Kaye (London), 1963.
Kane, Basil, *How to Play Soccer*, Grosset & Dunlap, 1975.
Kane, Basil, *Soccer for American Spectators*, A. S. Barnes, 1970.
Lodziak, Conrad, *Understanding Soccer Tactics*, Faber and Faber (London), 1966.
Mason, Nicholas, *Football*, Temple Smith (London), 1974.
Meisl, Willy, *Soccer Revolution*, Phoenix House (London), 1955.
Mencke, Frank, *Encyclopedia of Sports*, A. S. Barnes, 1969.
Moynihan, John, *Soccer*, Thomas Y. Crowell, 1974.
Rote, Kyle, Jr., *Beyond the Goal*, Word Books, 1975.
Sharpe, Ivan, *Forty Years in Football*, Hutchinson (London), 1952.
Signy, Dennis, *A Pictorial History of Soccer*, Spring House (London), 1968.
Strutt, Joseph, *The Sports and Pastimes of the People of England*, Methuen (London), 1903 edition.
Tyler, Martin, *The Story of Football*, Marshall Cavendish (London), 1967.
Umniger, Walter, *Superman, Heroes and Gods*, McGraw-Hill, 1963.
Wheeler, Kenneth, *Soccer—the English Way*, Cassell (London), 1967.
Young, Percy, *History of British Football*, Stanley Paul (London), 1968.

Index

Abbadie, Julio, 61
Aberdeen (Scotland), 91–92
Accrington (England), 25
Ademir, 41, 59
African Cup, 221
Ajax (Holland), 46–47
Albert, Flórián, 71
Alberto, Carlos, 80, 111, 142, 144
Albertosi, E., 74
Ali, Muhammad, 232
Amarildo, 72
American Amateur Football Association, 30
American-born players: development of skills, 183–86; need to raise level of skills, 184; numbers playing in the NASL, 185
American Football Association, 29–30, 31
American Soccer League (ASL), 33, 50, 181–84; winners, 208
American Youth Soccer Organization (AYSO), 180
Andrade, José, 51
Andrade, Victor, 60, 61
Andreolo, 55
Apostolidis, Kirk, 98
Archibald, Warren, 121
Argentina: champion clubs, 221–22; national team, 36, 50, 51, 55, 74, 75, 76, 82, 85
Arsenal (England), 33, 36
Arsène, Auguste, 105
Aston Villa (England), 25
Atlanta Chiefs, 95, 96, 97, 103
Auld Andy, 50, 51
Austria: champion clubs, 222; national team, 53–54, 61, 62–63

Bahr, Casey, 102
Ball, Alan, 76, 78, 174
Baltimore Bays, 96, 98
Baltimore Comets, 103
Bandov, Boris, 186
Bangu (Brazil), 90, 91
Banks, Gordon, 45, 71, 78–79, 137
Barnett, Geoff, 108, 140

Barraskill, Joe, 87
Barto, Barry, 102
Battles, Barney, 34
Bayern Munich, 46–47, 147
Beckenbauer, Franz, 46–47, 75–79, 82, 111–12, 116, 117, 131, 144, 147, 185
Belgium: champion clubs, 222; national team, 50
Bellini, Luiz, 74
Benfica (Portugal), 91
Ben Millar (St. Louis), 35
Bentley, Roy, 58
Bernabeu, Santiago, 43
Bernabeu Stadium (Madrid), 43
Best, Clyde, 105, 121, 159
Best, George, 43, 108, 112, 120, 142–43, 150–51, 155, 159, 185
Best, John, 117–18
Bethlehem Steel, 30–31, 33, 35
Bick, Sam, 186
Blackburn Rovers (England), 25, 27
Blackpool (England), 37
Blair, Tom, 34
Blanchflower, Danny, 67, 91,
Bloomer, Steve, 27
Bolton Wanderers (England), 25
Bonetti, Peter, 79, 106, 116
Boninsegna, Roberto, 79–80
Borges, R., 61
Borghi, Frank, 58
Boston Minuteman, 107
Botafogo (Brazil), 34
Bozsik, Josef, 61, 66
Bradley, Gordon, 157
Brazil: champion clubs, 222–23; national team, 36, 41, 43–44, 46, 50, 55, 59–61, 63, 66–72, 78–80, 85, 167
Breitner, Paul, 46, 82
Brown, Bill, 91
Brown, James, 50
Buchan, Charles, 33
Budai, L., 64, 66
Bulgarelli, Giacomo, 73
Burnich, T., 79
Burnley (England), 25
Busby, Matt, 43

293

Butler, Davey, 157
Byrne, Roger, 43, 66

Cagliari (Italy), 90, 92
Cahill, Thomas, 24–25, 186
Calcio, 18
California Sunshine, 181
Cambal, R., 54
Campbell, James, 30
Camsell, George, 161
Catenaccio, see Tactics
Cawston, Mervyn, 135, 137
Centenary Stadium (Montevideo), 51
Centenary Stadium (Rome), 54
Cea, Pedro, 51
Cerro (Uruguay), 90
Chapman, Herbert, 33
Charles, John, 67–68
Charlton, Bobby, 43, 71, 75–76, 78–79, 174
Chedgzoy, Sam, 34
Chelsea (England), 27, 40
Chicago Mustangs, 95
Chicago Sting, 105, 108–9
Chico, 41
Child, Paul, 100, 104, 121, 159
Chile: champion clubs, 223; national team, 59, 71
Chinaglia, Giorgio, 108, 111, 121, 123, 143, 157, 159
Chursky, Tony, 111
Clarke, Neil, 30
Clemence, Ray, 111
Clements, David, 119
Clemson, 180
Cleveland Cobras, 181
Cleveland Stokers, 95
Clodoaldo, 80, 82
Cobbold, W. N., 26
Cohen, George, 171
Cohen, Neil, 118, 144, 186
Colaussi, Gino, 56
College soccer, 179–84
Columbia, 24, 29
Columbia Broadcasting System (CBS), 90, 92
Combi, Giampiero, 54
Confederación Norte-Centroamericana y del Caribe de Futbol (CONCACAF) Championship: winners, 221
Concordia, 181
Connecticut Bicentennials, 105
Connecticut Yankees, 181
Connors, Jimmy, 232
Cooke, Charlie, 112, 119

Cooke, Jack Kent, 87–89
Cooper, Kenny, 116, 135, 140
Cooper, Terry, 79
Copa Interamericana (Inter-American Cup): winners, 221
Copping, Wilf, 36–38
Corinthians (England), 26, 30
Cornell, 29
Cosmos, 99, 105, 107, 109–11, 116, 134, 147
Cousy, Bob, 181
Cox, Bill, 88–90
Cremaschi, T., 59
Croatans (Chicago), 181
Croatia, 181
Crompton, Bob, 27
Cromwell, Oliver, 17
Cruyff, Johan, 46, 81–83, 154, 158, 185
Cuba: national team, 56
Cullis, Stan, 38
Czibor, Zoltan, 63–64
Czechoslovakia: champion clubs, 223; national team, 36, 54, 71–72, 80

Dallas Tornado, 98–99, 102, 107, 111, 142–43, 179
Dalmatinac, 181
David, Steven, 112, 122
Davis, Ron, 151
Davis, Rick, 186
Dean, Dixie, 37, 161
Defenders, 131, 143–47
Delaunay, Henri, 50
Del Sol, Luis, 43
Denver Dynamos, 103
Derby County (England), 25, 27
D'Errico, Dave, 186
Deyna, Kazimierz, 82
Didi, 43–44, 61, 66, 69–70, 140, 167
Dillon, Michael, 100
Di Stéfano, Alfredo, 43, 71, 129
Donelli, Buff, 34, 54
Douglas, Jimmy, 50–51
Dribbling, 155
DuChateau, Eugene, 135, 186
Dundee, United, 91, 179
Dunleavy, Chris, 102

Eagles (Chicago), 181
Eckel, H., 64
Eddy, Keith, 117
Edwards, Duncan, 43, 66, 151
Eintracht Frankfurt, 43
Elizabeth (New Jersey), 181
Ellis, Arthur, 63

Ellis, William Webb, 19, 23
Emmerich, Lothar, 76
England: champion clubs, 224; Football
  Association formed, 17; Football
  Association Cup tournament organized,
  25; Football Association joins FIFA,
  28; Football League formed, 25–26;
  national team, 36, 38, 40, 42, 55, 57,
  61, 66, 74–76, 78, 80, 144, 160, 171,
  174
England, Mike, 106, 116–17, 144, 146
English, Sam, 137
English Football Club (Denmark), 28
English Football Club of Dresden, 28
Episkyros, 15–16
Estudiantes (Argentina), 47
European Cup, 43–44; winners, 218
European Cup Winners Cup, 47; winners
  218–19
European Football Championship:
  winners, 220
European Footballer of the Year:
  winners, 229–30
Eusebio, 75, 95, 106, 109, 121, 140, 157
Everton (England), 25

Fall River, 31, 50
Fédération Internationale de Football
  Association (FIFA): founding of, 28;
  International Board, 28–29, 32;
  organization of, 212; members of, 212–
  215
Felix, 78
Fernández, Pepe, 97, 122
Ferrari, Giovanni, 53–54
Ferreira, Ivair, 109
Feyenoord (Holland), 47
Field dimensions, 18–19, 21–23
Finney, Tom, 40, 42, 57–58, 66
Firmani, Eddie, 105
Flater, Mike, 153
Florie, Tom, 50, 53
Ford, James, 30
Fort Lauderdale Strikers, 111–12
Forwards, 133, 154, 159
Foulke, Bill ("Fatty"), 27
Foulkes, Bill, 43, 118, 138, 150–51
Franklin, Neil, 40, 57
Fraydl, Gerry, 91
France: national team, 68
Friaca, 60
Fry, C. B., 26
Fryatt, Jim, 102
Futcher, Ron, 108
Gaetjens, Joe, 58–59

Gallagher, Hughie, 37
Garbett, Terry, 157
Gardiner, E. Norman, 16
Gadocha, Robert, 82
Garrincha, 66–67, 69, 71–72, 74
Gavrič, Gabbo, 119, 150
Gelei, S., 131
Genoa Cricket and Football Club (Italy),
  28
Gento, Francisco, 43
German-American Football Association
  (GAFA), 181
German-Hungarians (New York), 181
Germany: national team (prior to 1945),
  36, 38, 39, 55; West Germany champion
  clubs, 226; West Germany national
  team, 62–64, 67–68, 75–76, 81–83, 85,
  171, 174
Gerson, 46, 79–80, 82
Ghiggia, Alcides, 60
Giles, Professor, 16
Gilzean, Alan, 138
Glasgow Celtic, 47
Glasgow Rangers, 91
Glentoran (Ireland), 92
Goalkeeper, 131, 135–41; anticipation,
  135–36; deflecting, 136–37; forming a
  wall, 140; four-step rule, 139; kicking,
  138–39; narrowing the angle, 136;
  punching, 136; throwing, 138
Gonsalves, Billy, 34, 50, 53
Goodwin, Freddie, 95, 108, 150
Grabowski, Jurgen, 78–79
Greater Los Angeles Soccer League
  (GLASL), 181
Greek-Americans (San Francisco), 181
Griffiths, Arfon, 106
Griffiths, Clive, 145
Grnja, Ivan, 121
Grosics, Gyula, 63
Guaita, G., 53

Hakoah (Austria), 35
Hall, Willie, 38
Haller, Helmut, 75–76
Hampden Park Stadium (Glasgow), 43
Hamrin, Kurt, 68–69
Hapgood, Eddie, 36, 38
Harpastum, 15–16
Harper, Bill, 34
Harvard, 23–25, 29, 180
Haverford, 29
Havlicek, John, 232
Haynes, Johnny, 64
Heading, 145–46, 157–58

Held, Siggi, 75–76
Herberger, Sepp, 55–56
Herman, Robert, 88
Herrera, Helenio, 44
Hiberians (Scotland), 91
Hidegkuti, Nandor, 42, 63–64, 66
Hill, Gordon, 106, 120
Hinton, Alan, 140
Hoeness, Uli, 46, 82
Hofheinz, Roy, 87
Hohberg, Juan, 63
Holand, see Netherlands
Holzenbein, Bernd, 83
Hope, Bobby, 148
Horton Randy, 99–100
Howieson, Jimmy, 34
Huddersfield (England), 33, 48
Hudspeth, Frank, 32
Humphrey, Carl, 155
Hungary: champion clubs, 224; national
    team, 36, 41–42, 56, 61–64, 66, 71, 167
Hunt, Lamarr, 87, 95
Hunt, Steve, 111
Hurst, Geoff, 43, 75, 121, 154, 157

Iarusci, Robert, 109, 119
Inter-American Cup, see Copa
    Interamericana
Intercollegiate Association Football
    League, 29
Intercollegiate Football Association, 24, 30
Inter-Giuliana, 181
International Board, see FIFA
International Soccer League (ISL), 88
Italy: champion clubs, 224–25; national
    team, 36–38, 40, 52–53, 55, 61, 71, 73,
    79–80, 85
Ivanow, Mike, 135

Jackson, Alex, 34, 37
Jackson, John, 135
Jackson, Wattie, 34
Jair, 41, 59
Jairzinho, 46, 79–80
James, Alex, 33, 37, 129
Jeffrey, Bill, 39
Jennings, Pat, 111, 138–39
Joerg, Jimmy, 135
Johnson, Harry, 42
Jokerst, Dave, 135
Jongbloed, Jan, 83
Jonquet, Robert, 68
Julian, Julius, 53, 54
Julinho, 61

Jules Rimet Trophy: retired, 80; stolen,
    74; see also World Cup

Kansas City, Spurs, 96–97, 99
Kelly, Jimmy (Chicago), 120, 151
Kelly, Jimmy (Portland), 121
Kemari, 18
Kennaway, Joe, 137
Kewley, Kevin, 148
Kickers (Chicago), 181
Kicking, 156
Kocsis, Sandor, 42, 63–64
Kopa, Raymond, 43
Kostič, Bora, 91
Kowalik, John, 108, 121–22, 159
Kroll, Rudd, 82
Kubala, Ladislao, 91, 115
Kutis (St. Louis), 39

Laseroms, Theo, 91
Lato, Gregor, 82
Lawton, Tommy, 38, 232
Leidholm, Nils, 68
Leonidas, 55–56
Lewis, Edgar, 33
Ley, George, 118, 146
Liberators Cup, 47; winners, 220
Libero, 142, 171
Linesmen, 129
Lions (Chicago), 181
Lopez, Miguel, 150
Los Angeles Aztecs, 103, 143, 150–51
Los Angeles, Kickers, 181
Los Angeles Lakers, 92
Los Angeles Maccabees, 181
Los Angeles Skyhawks, 181
Lukacevic, Ivan, 109

Maca, Joe, 58
McBride, Pat, 106, 120
McCracken, Bill, 32
McGill University, 24
McGregor, William, 25
McIlvenny, Eddie, 58
McNab, Alex, 34
McNab, Bob, 119
McNutt, Bill, 96
McPartland, Peter, 95
Maier, Sepp, 46, 83, 135
Manchester City (England), 95
Manchester United (England), 91;
    Munich air crash, 43, 47
Manning, Dr. Randolph, 30
Mannion, Wilf, 40, 58
Man-to-man defense, 142–43

Maracana Stadium (Rio de Janeiro), 41, 59
Maroons, 181
Marotte, Luis, 119
Marsh, Rodney, 108, 119, 151–52
Mason, John, 186
Martin, Eric, 116
Martin, Ted, 95
Maschio, Humberto, 71
Masopust, Josef, 71
Maspoli, Roque, 59
Matéos, Enrique, 95
Matthews, Stanley, 36–37, 40, 42, 57–58,
    129, 155–56, 232
Maurinho, 61
Mausser, Arnold, 116, 186
Mazzola, Sandrino, 74
Meazza, Giuseppe, 53–54
Meredith, Billy, 27
Merrick, Alan, 108
Merrick, Gil, 62
Metidieri, Carlos, 98, 99, 122
Mexico: national team, 50, 62, 71
Miami Toros, 100, 104
Midfielders 132–33, 148–53
Miflín, Ramón, 119, 151–52
Milan AC (Italy), 47
Millar, Robert, 30
Millen, Richard, 88
Miller, Al, 102, 150, 180
Minnesota Kicks, 107–9, 143–44, 153
Mitič, Ilija, 95–97, 119, 140, 157
Monterrey (Mexico), 98
Monti, Luisito, 52
Montreal Olympics, 99, 103
Moore, Bobby, 45, 76, 108
Morán, P., 60
Moreira, Zeze, 61
Morlock, H., 64
Mortensen, Stan, 42, 57–58
Morton, Alex, 37
Motaung, Kaizer, 97, 122
Mullen, Jimmy, 58
Müller, Gerhard, 46, 78–79, 82, 158, 185
Mullery, Alan, 78
Mussolini, Benito, 52–54
Myernick, Glenn, 186

National Amateur Cup, 31; winners, 209–
    210
National Association for Intercollegiate
    Athletics (NAIA): winners, 211
National Collegiate Athletic Association
    (NCAA), 179–80; winners, 210–11
National Open Challenge Cup, 31;
    winners, 208–9

National Professional Soccer League
    (NPSL), see NASL
National Soccer League of Chicago
    (NSL), 181
Navarro, Rubén, 91, 120
Neeskens, Johan, 46, 82–83
Nejedly, P., 54
Netherlands: champion clubs, 224;
    national team, 40, 46, 81–83, 85, 160,
    171
Newark All-Stars, 35
New Bedford, 34
Newcastle United, 32
New England Oceaneers, 181
New Jersey Americans, 181
Newman, Ron, 112
New York Apollo, 181
New York Cosmos, see Cosmos
New York Generals, 95
New York Hungaria, 181
Nilsen, J., 53
North American Soccer League (NASL):
    blue-line concept introduced, 102;
    bonus points introduced, 47, 92;
    financial losses, 92, 95; history of, 86–
    114; league reduced to five clubs, 96–
    97; list of players, 187–200; merger of
    USA with NPSL, 93; office moves back
    to New York, 99; review of 1967
    season, 90–94; review of 1968 season,
    95–97; review of 1969 season, 97–98;
    review of 1970 season, 98–99; review
    of 1971 season 99–100; review of 1972
    season, 100–101; review of 1973 season,
    101–3; review of 1974 season, 103–5;
    review of 1975 season, 105–7; review
    of 1976 season, 107–110; review of
    1977 season, 111–13; shootout
    introduced, 112; statistics and records
    of, 205–7; team information, 201–5;
    television coverage of, 92; tie breaker
    introduced, 103–4
Northern Ireland: national team, 40, 67
North Korea: national team, 73–74
Norway: national team, 55
Notts County (England), 25
Nover, Peter, 146

Oakland Clippers, 95
Offside, see Tactics
Old Etonians, 26
Olivieri, 55
Olympic soccer: winners, 217–18
Oneida Football Club, 23

O'Neil, George, 102
O.N.T. Club (Newark), 31
Ord, Tommy, 111
Orlando, 74
Orsi, Raimondo, 53–54
Overlapping, 146

Pak Doo Ik, 73
Paraguay: national team, 50
Pariani, S., 59
Passing, 149–50
Patenaude, Bert, 50
Pecher, Steve, 117, 146, 185, 186
Pegg, David, 43
Pelé, 11, 43–44, 46, 66–69, 71, 74, 79–
    80, 82, 95, 98, 105–6, 108, 111, 116,
    119, 121, 123, 137, 140, 143, 155–58,
    232
Penalty kick, 140–41
Peñarol (Uruguay), 47
Pennsylvania, 29
Peru: national team, 80; riot, 11
Peters, Martin, 76, 78, 174
Philadelphia Atoms, 101, 107
Phillips, Lincoln, 116
Pilgrims (England), 29–30
Piola, Silva, 55–56
Planicka, Frantisek, 54
Pluskal, Svatopluk, 71
Poland: champion clubs, 225; national
    team, 46, 81–82
Pollihan, Jim, 117, 186
Portland Timbers, 105, 107
Portugal: champion clubs, 225; national
    team, 74–75
Pozzo, Vittorio, 52, 56
Preston North End (England), 25, 27, 160
Princeton, 23–25
Prins, Co, 92
Provan, Andy, 102
Puc, T., 54
Puskás, Ferenc, 42–43, 64, 71, 95

Queens Park (Scotland), 160

Racing Club (Argentina), 47
Rahn, Helmut, 64
Ramsay, Alf, 42, 58, 74–75, 78–79, 132,
    174
Rattín, Antonio, 75
Raynor, George, 67–68
Real Madrid (Spain), 43, 47, 91
Reb, Johnny, 82
Referees, 129
Rensenbrink, Rob, 82

Rensing, Gary, 106
Reyes, Salvador, 91, 115
Rial, Hector, 43
Rigby, Bob, 102, 116, 138, 186
Rimet, Jules, 50
Riva, Luigi, 79–80
Rivelino, 46, 79–80, 140
Rivera, Gianni, 71, 73, 79
Rocca, Francesco, 146
Rochester Lancers, 98, 109
Rose, Pete, 232
Roth, Werner, 117, 185
Rous, Stanley, 89
Roy, Willy, 122
Rugby, game of, 19
Rugby College, 19
Rules of soccer: Cambridge rules, 20;
    complete text of rules, 242–76;
    dimensions of field, 18–19, 21–23;
    Football Association's first set of rules,
    21–23; summary of rules, 127–29;
    Thring's 10 rules, 21
Rumania Football Federation, 50;
    national team, 80
Rutgers, 24–25
Ryan, Francis ("Hun"), 34

Sacramento Spirits, 181
St. Louis Simpkins, 39
St. Louis Stars, 95–96, 98, 105–6
San Antonio Thunder, 105, 157
Sánchez, Leonel, 71
San Diego Toros, 95
San Francisco Athletic Club, 181
San Francisco Soccer League (SFSL),
    181
San Francisco Scots, 181
San Jose Earthquakes, 103, 105, 107, 111
Santamaria, José, 43
Santisteban, Juan, 91
Santos (Brazil), 47, 98
Santos, Djalma, 61, 68, 74
Santos, Nilton, 61, 68, 70
Savoldi, Giuseppe, 154
Schaefer, Hans, 64
Schiaffino, Juan, 41, 60–61, 63
Schiavio, Angelo, 54
Schnellinger, Karl-Heinz, 79
Schoen, Helmut, 75–78
Schroiff, Villem, 72
Schwab, Charles, 30
Schwaben (Chicago), 181
Schwarzenbeck, George, 46
Scotland: champion clubs, 225; national
    team, 27, 37, 160

Scott, Elisha, 37
Screening, 154
Scullion, Stewart, 105, 120
Seattle Kingdome, 108, 157
Seattle Sounders, 105, 107, 111, 150–51, 157
Sebes, Gustav, 64
Seeler, Uwe, 66, 76, 78–79
Seerey, Mike, 106
Sekularac, Dragon, 91
Semiprofessional soccer, 180–81
Sesta, V., 53
Sewell, John, 150
Sheffield United (England), 27
Short, Peter, 153
Shoulder charging, 145
Siega, Jorge, 121
Silvester, Peter, 104, 121
Simões, Antonio, 106, 119
Sindelar, Mathias, 53
Sivori, Omar, 71
Skills of soccer: dribbling, 155; goal-keeper skills, 131, 135–41; heading, 145–46, 157–58; kicking, 156; screening, 154; shoulder charging, 145; tackling, 144–45; throw-in, 152; trapping, 149
Sköglund, "Nacka," 68–69
Skotarek, Alex, 117, 185–86
Smethurst, Derek, 105, 121, 123
Smistik, B., 53
Smith, Bobby, 102, 116, 119, 186
Smith, G. O., 26
Smith, J., 161
Smith, Tommy, 118, 145
Soccer: contrast of national styles, 133–134; field dimensions, 18–19, 21–23; history of, 15–85; origin of name, 26; professionalism introduced into, 26–27; promotion and relegation system of, 48; rules of, 127–29, 242–76; skills of, 131, 135–41; 144–46, 149, 152, 154–58; team positions, 130–34; terminology (glossary), 237–40
Soccer Bowl: 1975, 111; 1976, 108–9, 144; 1977, 111
Sons of Italy (San Francisco), 181
Soule, 18
South American Player of the Year: winners, 230
South Bay United, 181
South Korea: national team, 62
Souza, John, 58–59
Spain: champion clubs, 225–26; national team, 54, 58–59, 71

Spraggon, Frank, 108
Sparta (Czechoslovakia), 36, 91
Spartan Stadium (San Jose), 105
Standen, Jim, 116
Stark, Archie, 34
Stepney, Alex, 138
Stiles, Nobby, 75–76, 144
Stojanovič, Mirko, 116, 122
Stoke City, 25, 91
Strikers, 154–56
Stubbes, Phillips, 15, 17
Strutt, Joseph, 15, 18
Sühnholz, Wolfgang, 106, 109, 119, 151
Sweden: champion clubs, 226; national team, 44, 56, 59, 67–69, 82
Sweeper, 142, 171
Switzerland: national team, 40, 62, 76
Szarmach, Andrzej, 82
Szengeller, R., 56
Szymaniak, Horst, 67, 91, 115

Tackling, 144–45
Tacony Club (Philadelphia), 30
Tactics: attack in width, 155–56; catenaccio, 40–44, 171; development of, 160–74; 4–4–2 formation, 171; 4–3–3 formation, 44, 167–71; 4–2–4 formation, 44, 167; offside trap, 32, 161; Scottish influence on, 27, 160; space, 154–55; total soccer, 46, 82, 173; 2–3–5 formation, 161
Tampa Bay Rowdies, 105, 107, 109, 111, 134
Taylor, Tommy, 43, 66
Team positions, 130–34
Terminology (Glossary), 237–40
Thompson, Johnny, 137
Thring, J. C., 20, 23, 129
Throw-in, 152
Tilkowski, Hans, 76
Torino Italy): Superga air disaster, 40
Toronto Metros, 9, 108–9, 144
Tostão, 79–80, 82
Total Soccer, see Tactics
Toye, Clive, 111
Tozzi, Humberto, 63
Tracy, Ralph, 50–51
Trapping, 149
Trost, Al, 106, 120, 183, 186
Tsu chu, 16
Turek, F., 64
Turkey: national team, 62
Turner, Roy, 145, 149

UEFA Cup, 47; winners, 219–20

Ullevi Stadium (Göteborg), 67
USSR: champion clubs, 227; national team, 67–68, 71, 76
United Soccer Association (USA), *see* NASL
United States Football Association (USFA), *see* USSF
United States: national team, 41, 50, 57–58, 62, 85; team records, 227–29
United States Soccer Federation (USSF): founding of, 30; joined FIFA, 30; organized challenge cup and amateur cup, 31; recognized NASL, 87–90
United States Soccer Football Association (USSFA), *see* USSF
University of San Francisco, 180
Uruguay: champion clubs, 226; national team, 35, 41, 50–51, 55, 59–61, 63, 71, 76

Vancouver Whitecaps, 103
Van Hanegem, Wim, 82
Vanninger, Denny, 106, 159, 186
Varela, Obdulio, 60–61
Vavá, 66, 68, 70, 72, 95, 115
Varzim (Portugal), 98
Vee, Julie, 120, 186
Verrou, *see* Tactics
Vidal, Reverend R. W., 26
Vidinič, Blagoje, 91
Viollet, Dennis, 43, 91, 115
Vogts, Bertie, 83

Wagner, H., 63
Wales: national team, 67–68
Walsh, Dick, 26
Walter, A. M., 26
Walter, Fritz, 64, 67
Walter, P. M., 26
Wanderers (England), 26
Washington Darts, 98, 100
Washington Diplomats, 103, 153
Washington Whips, 92
Webb, John, 118
Weber, Wolfgang, 76
Webster, Ron, 108, 143

Wembley Stadium (London), 41
West, Alan, 108, 120, 153
West Bromwich Albion (England), 25
West Ham (England), 91
Willey, Alan, 108
Wilson, Ramon, 76
Wingers, 155–56
Wit, Dennis, 186
Withe, Peter, 106
Wolverhampton Wanderers (England), 25, 90, 92
Woods, Frank, 87, 89
Woodward, Vivian, 26, 29
Woosnam, Phil, 91, 95, 111, 113, 179
World Cup, 35–36, 41, 43–46, 85; review of 1930 tournament, 48–52; review of 1934 tournament, 52–55; review of 1938 tournament, 55–57; review of 1950 tournament, 57–61; review of 1954 tournament, 61–66; review of 1958 tournament, 66–70; review of 1962 tournament, 70–73; review of 1966 tournament, 73–78; review of 1970 tournament, 78–81; review of 1974 tournament, 81–84; winning teams' lineups, 216–17
World Club Championship, 47–48; winners, 221
Wreford-Brown, Charles, 26
Wright, Billy, 40, 42, 58, 67

Yale, 23–24
Yugoslavia; champion clubs, 227; national team, 63, 71, 82
Yugoslavia-Americans (Los Angeles), 181
Youth soccer, 180; advice to young players, 232–36

Zagalo, 66, 70
Zamora, Ricardo, 54
Zemaria, 91
Zischek, R., 53
Zito, 66, 69, 72
Zizinho, 41, 59
Zoff, Dino, 135
Zone defense, 142–43